Branding a store

Publisher's note
Every possible effort has been made to ensure that the information contained in this book is accurate at the time of going to press, and the publishers and authors cannot accept responsibility for any errors or omissions, however caused. No responsibility for loss or damage occasioned to any person acting, or refraining from action, as a result of the material in this publication can be accepted by the editor, the publisher or any of the authors.

First published in Great Britain and the United States in 2006 by Kogan Page Limited

120 Pentonville Road
London N1 9JN
United Kingdom
www.kogan-page.co.uk

525 South 4th Street, #241
Philadelphia PA 19147
USA

© 2006, Ko Floor (text)
© 2006, BIS Publishers, Amsterdam

ISBN 0 7494 4832 6

British Library Cataloguing-in-Publication Data
A CIP record for this book is available from the British Library.

Library of Congress Cataloging-in-Publication Data
Floor, Ko.
    Branding a store : how to build successful retail brands in a changing marketplace / Ko Floor.
       p. cm.
    Includes bibliographical references.
    ISBN 0-7494-4832-6
1. House brands--Marketing. 2. Brand name products--Marketing. 3. Retail trade.
I. Title.
HD69.B7F58 2006
658.8'27--dc22
                          2006023022

Translation by Bojoura Floor
Cover design and layout by Studio Ron van Roon, Amsterdam
Typeset by TE Producties, Haarlem
Printed and bound in Singapore

BRANDING A STORE

How to build successful retail
brands in a changing marketplace

Ko Floor

KOGAN
PAGE

London and Philadelphia

CONTENTS

FOREWORD

With its 118 year-old history, Albert Heijn is one of the oldest and biggest brands in the Netherlands. Even though, in the meantime, our organization has developed into a multinational with Ahold as mother, we have always been able to keep our recognition. Customers have an emotional bond with the Albert Heijn brand. They feel involved and sometimes, as we have experienced in difficult times, also feel abandoned by the brand.

Of course the brand has changed over the years: logically so, because when customers are the priority in an organization, you move along with those customers, and preferably stay one step ahead of them. However, the core of the Albert Heijn brand has been sustained all those years. That core, our brand personality, is the DNA of our organization and is characterized by terms like dedicated, optimistic, reliable and inspiring.

Building a brand in retail is not always easy, especially in a forever-changing environment. After all, we all have stores and sell the same products. Albert Heijn not only sells brands, though, it has also become a very well-known brand itself. Making clear choices in the mix of range, price, quality, convenience and inspiration, helps us making the difference in the market. These choices are based on a clear mission and brand values that direct the entire organization. We consequently translate that mission and those brand values into our communication with our customers. As CEO of Albert Heijn I am convinced that retailers who build on their brands will eventually win the battle.

With this book, *Branding a Store*, Ko Floor talks about emotion becoming increasingly important in the battle for the consumer. And that is not that strange at all, because running a store is and will remain a human function. I have a lot of admiration for the role Ko Floor played in establishing the Albert Heijn brand in the 1980s and 1990s. His vision, originality and expertise have contributed to the Albert Heijn brand of today.

Dick Boer
CEO Albert Heijn

Part 1
Retail brands

1. THE STORE AS A BRAND

In the next few years the retail market will change dramatically. The pace
of change is quickening. In order to survive a store will have to become its
own brand. A strong brand can differentiate a store from the competition.
So far retailers have approached the consumer in a predominantly rational
way. The emotional differences between retail brands will however
become more and more important.

Now that stores are becoming strong brands themselves, a battle of the
brands between manufacturers and retailers has started. Both try to
achieve a strong position in the consumer's mind, and increasingly,
manufacturers will find out that retailers will win this battle. After all,
retail brands have the big advantage that they communicate directly
with the consumer.

1.1 The need to differentiate

The retail industry is undergoing many changes and faces enormous
challenges. The competition is huge. New retail formats are emerging.
Discounting is becoming more popular and price wars are going on
every day. Shopping behaviour is changing rapidly. Value-driven
consumers have more shopping options then ever before, and they are
also much better informed about all options. Retailers are losing share
to markets like leisure, travel and health. Some retail markets seem
saturated. Consumer lifestyles and spending patterns are changing.
Staying ahead of these changes is crucial for success.

People buy what they want, not what they need. So they want retail brands that satisfy wants, more than needs. Consumers who used to wonder what they should buy will in the future often wonder whether they should buy something at all. They already have almost everything they could ask for, at least in the prosperous western world. Buying is about a product and sometimes also about store abundance. And if something is needed after all, there are many alternatives to choose from, both online and offline. A retail company will have to do its very best to be favoured by consumers, and this is getting more and more difficult. Consumers have less time to shop and often do not like to shop any more. Retail companies will have to do more than just meet the consumer's expectations, they will have to exceed those expectations. They should go beyond satisfaction, and stores should be easier and more fun to shop in.

In some sectors sales do not grow and overcapacity occurs. Price competition and pressure on margins are the results. New technologies are emerging and they call for big investments. Consumers want more for less from retailers. They want it cheaper, faster and better. They expect more from the shopping experience, and are looking for shops that can make their hurried and hectic lives a bit easier or more pleasant. Customer loyalty is decreasing, and store loyalty only exists because of a lack of a better alternative. The consumer chooses the store that has the best proposition in the short term. At the same time retailers are also pressured in other ways. They have to increase their sales and at the same time lower their costs, but wages and rent continue to rise. In addition, competition comes not only from domestic retailers, but also from foreign retail companies. The consolidation and globalization of the retail industry continues. Many current, well-known retail companies will have to close their doors forever.

Changes in consumer lifestyles will have a considerable impact on the lifecycle of store formats. The lifecycle of store formats is shorter than before, because the competition rapidly copies successful innovations. And newcomers challenge the traditional way retailing has always been done. In a few years some sectors will change completely. Big successful retail companies like Wal-Mart, Ikea, H&M, Home Depot, Amazon and Starbucks have only existed for a few decades. Existing retail formats will therefore have to be adjusted on a regular basis. Retail companies must rise to the challenge of change and innovation, and in some cases the store format will have to be changed drastically. Retail companies that do not adjust their store format and strategy in time are losing ground rapidly. After all, the battle for the consumer will only get tougher, and keeping the store ahead of the competition will be difficult. To stay ahead, a store needs to differentiate itself.

Retail companies that want to survive among other retailers will have to make sure their store is more than just a collection of products. They have to stand out from the competition and have to become a brand themselves. Branding the store is becoming crucial for success, because retail differentiation cannot be achieved without branding. The retail environment and the retail brand should add extra, differentiating value to the merchandise. Creating a strong retail brand will be one of the most important means to secure survival. Branding the store will be the challenge for the future. By creating a strong brand, the relationship with the consumer will be strengthened. It will become a relationship that is based not only on rational but also on emotional motives. Stores will have to become living advertising pillars, which clearly communicate what the retail brand stands for. But not only that, the stores will also have to prove the brand promise. After all, the store performance will determine the consumer's brand perception.

Consumers are no longer only looking for a certain product, but also looking for a store experience. They want to be more emotionally involved when they are shopping. Shopping used to be about buying something, but in the future shopping will be more about doing something. Shopping is now competing with other leisure activities, and consumers will have to be persuaded to spend their free time on shopping. The winners in retail will either be the brands with the lowest prices or the brands that really differentiate themselves by offering the consumer a unique competitive advantage. The retailer will have to build an emotional connection with the consumer; a connection that will only be realized when the proposition of the retail brand is really unique and relevant. Customers should not just be satisfied with the retail brand; they should be delighted. Their expectations will have to be exceeded every time.

In principle, a retailer can choose from three competitive strategies to help tackle all these challenges and to improve its market position:

- increasing sales;
- cutting costs;
- improving gross margin by increasing differentiation.

Together these, three competitive strategies determine the profitability of a retail brand.

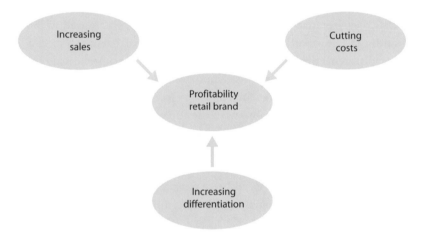

Figure 1.1 Three competitive strategies

1.1.1 INCREASING SALES

First of all, a retail company can improve its market position by increasing sales. It can stretch the brand name by starting to sell more product categories under the same brand. Therefore, many retail companies experiment with enlarging their range: sometimes successfully, but just as often unsuccessfully. Also by autonomous growth, developing new formats, takeovers, mergers, domestic or foreign expansion, or strategic alliances with other retail companies, a retailer can obtain economies of scale and achieve better buying conditions. Lower costs and a higher profit will be the result. That expansion does not only have to take place through existing or new stores. Extra online profit can be achieved without the need to open any new stores. When this online profit is achieved by using the existing stores, as at Tesco, it can lead to attractive synergies.

A retail company can grow by exploiting multiple store formats and brands. For example, Carrefour operates five different store formats and a number of brands in different types of retail distribution. The right store format should be chosen, depending on the local market situation.

- The Carrefour hypermarkets offer a wide range of food and non-food products at very attractive prices. Their shelves stock an average of 70,000 items. Floor areas of hypermarkets vary from 5,000 sq m to over 20,000 sq m, and their catchment areas are very large.
- Supermarkets with brand names like Champion GS, Norte GB and Marinopoulos offer a wide selection of mostly food products at competitive prices, in outlets with floor areas of 1,000 to 2,000 sq m.
- Hard discounters such as Dia, Ed and Minipreco stock 800 food products at the lowest possible prices, in small stores (from 200 to 800 sq m). Half of the products are sold under the Dia brand name.
- Convenience stores include the Shopi, Marché Plus, 8 å Huit and Di per Di chains of stores.
- Cash-and-carry and food service outlets are designed to meet the needs of restaurant and food industry professionals.

The strategy of Carrefour consists of building group market share in each market it does business in, by expanding the store format best suited to that local market. It does this by taking advantage of the way the formats and brands complement one another.

Many retail companies increase their profits by a quick expansion abroad. Benetton, with stores in more than 100 countries, and McDonald's, with restaurants in about 120 countries, are examples of retail brands that are almost as international as manufacturer brands like Coca-Cola, Sony and Chanel. Not only for these manufacturers, but also for retailers, there are various reasons to go abroad:

Further growth
Further growth could be difficult in the originating country. There could be legislative constraints, or the domestic market might be mature or saturated. That is especially the case when the home market

has limited potential. Therefore, the need to go global could be even greater. In general European retail companies are, for this reason, often more global than their American rivals. Retail companies in the United States have an enormous home market. Wal-Mart, by far the biggest retail company in the world, still obtains the biggest proportion of its sales in the United States.

Economies of scale

Retailers go global in order to lower their costs. When a retail company grows, it can profit from economies of scale: not only when purchasing, but for example also with marketing, product development, information technology and physical distribution. The exchange of knowledge between the various countries can also lead to extra synergies and economies of scale.

Spread of risks

A retail company that operates in several countries spreads its risks. A recession never hits every country in the same way, and when a fashion retailer suffers from a bad summer in one country, other countries that have better weather could very well compensate for that loss. For a fashion retailer, it would therefore be smart to exploit stores in countries with various climate conditions.

Profit from advantages in knowledge

Competition abroad can be weaker than in the home country. Or the retailer might have developed such a balanced store format (as a result of the strong competition in the home country), that it is able to challenge the competition in various countries. Mango, the Spanish fashion retailer, mentions the fierce competition of the Spanish textile market and its determination to triumph in it, as the key to its success in other countries.

Exploiting the brand

Sometimes a retail company is already a strong brand in other countries before it even has its own stores there. The retail brand could already be well known through its website, or maybe consumers got acquainted with the stores as tourists. For example, foreigners often visited Tie

Rack stores in tourist centres. The store at Heathrow Airport enjoyed success as a result of this, and therefore Tie Rack concluded that its retail brand had international potential and decided to start up in other countries. Now there are a total of 330 stores in 20 countries.

Countervailing power

In many product categories there is a strong concentration on the manufacturer's side. Manufacturers like Procter & Gamble, Coca-Cola, Sony and Canon have used their brands to build strong positions worldwide. To prevent these manufacturers solely determining all the conditions, retailers will have to make sure they have countervailing power. Growth by internationalization is an important means for that. In the future, global manufacturers and global retailers will become opposing forces because of that.

There could, therefore, be multiple reasons for a retailer to export its retail brand to other countries. Still, there are fewer international retail brands than international manufacturer brands. The most important reason for this is that exploiting an international brand is, in general, more complicated for a retailer than it is for a manufacturer. Every day thousands of decisions have to be made within a retail company. Even the best global retailers sometimes fail because of their lack of understanding of the local market. When Wal-Mart opened stores in Indonesia in the late 1990s, it built American-style stores with bright lights, wide aisles, neatly stacked goods and clear signage. Its competitors had dark lighting, messy merchandise, dirty wooden floors and uncertain prices. Indonesians flocked to the competition. To consumers who were just a few years removed from street markets, the Wal-Mart stores gave the appearance of being upscale, even though they were clearly not. The point is that despite the best of intentions, Wal-Mart misread local consumers (Kalish, 2004).

Retail is detail. A store format is a combination of a lot of elements. The range alone comprises hundreds, and sometimes even hundreds of thousands, of products. It is therefore very difficult to choose all the elements of the marketing mix in such a way that the store format can succeed in a large number of countries. Sometimes you are dealing with very specific local issues, as for example Mango and Zara found out. The designs and sizes that did well in Spain and other southern European countries had to be adjusted for northern European countries, because women in northern Europe are on average bigger than in the Mediterranean.

Internationalization is more difficult for a retailer than for a manufacturer. Manufacturers therefore operate more internationally than retailers do. Companies like Shell, IBM and Siemens operate in 100 to 200 countries. However only a limited number of retail companies have developed into real international brands. McDonald's and Benetton are still exceptions. Even very internationally successful retail companies like the German company Metro (which obtains almost half its sales outside Germany) is with its 2,200 stores 'only' represented in 30 countries. But in spite of all the issues, internationalization will continue in retail, because the advantages of internationalization can be huge. Therefore the growth of global retail brands has been enormous, particularly in the last 10 years. Some retail brands are very successful at this.

Most of the successful international retail companies seem to fall into one of three distinct models:

- replicators;
- performance managers;
- reinventors (Catoni et al, 2002).

Replicators
Long-standing international retail companies such as Benetton, as well as more recent examples like clothing retailer Zara and the US coffee specialist Starbucks, are replicators. Typically, such retailers develop a simple format and business system, identify the markets where they will thrive, then export themselves almost unchanged. Such a company can coordinate its home and overseas businesses under one centralized global or regional management structure. Given the simple format and organization of the replicators, they can capture synergies easily and expand overseas quickly. Replicators can accommodate local variations in consumer demand by tweaking their formats, but only within the bounds imposed by their standard systems. For example, Zara adjusted the sizes of its clothing and McDonald's offers a McRye burger in

Finland, a Teriyaki burger in Japan, a CroqueMcDo in France and a Kiwiburger in New Zealand.

Performance managers

Companies such as Ahold and Kingfisher expanded internationally by acquiring a portfolio of existing retail businesses and developing them as almost completely distinct entities. These retail companies operate a number of store formats and retail brands. They have largely decentralized structures, and run acquired businesses by using local management teams (often those that had previously run the acquisitions) and giving them considerable operational authority. When the price of acquisitions is right, such factors can make performance managers the fastest-growing category of retailers. But the bigger they get, the harder it is for them to realize any synergies at all, since their organizational complexity also increases at a fast rate. Ahold is therefore, after the financial problems of the last few years and the arrival of a new CEO, looking for more standardization and synergy. Fewer store formats, fewer retail brands, fewer countries and more synergy is now the starting point for the revitalization of the company.

Reinventors

Carrefour, Tesco and other reinventors own one or more store formats, which they adapt to the needs of each local market, meanwhile building on standardized behind-the-scenes or back-end processes and systems. Tesco's formula is to develop a world-class hypermarket format with a common layout, common operations and common systems, overlaid with local marketing, local services, local staff and local management. Reinventors create a largely new offer to suit the taste of each new overseas market. While local store managers adapt layouts and ranges to cater to local consumer preferences, higher-level managers try to exploit international scale advantages in back-end processes. Tesco for example uses the same systems for processes such as inventory management, the approval of properties, and merchandising in all of the markets where it sells food and household goods.

The Italian clothing brand Diesel follows the reinventor model in its international expansion. The brand, founded in 1978, goes a long way when adapting to the local market. Its strong growth started in the mid-

1990s, and because of its efforts, jeans have become more of a fashion item. New designs and styles are constantly put on the market. To be able to continually surprise the consumer with new jeans, even top-selling styles are quickly taken out of the collection by Diesel. Innovation and variation is the device. These quick changes in range have contributed to making Diesel one of the leading fashion brands. However Renzo Rosso, founder of Diesel, still wants at all costs to prevent Diesel from becoming a mainstream brand. Diesel wants to be a global brand, without coming across as a multinational. After all, individuality is an important aspect of the Diesel brand personality. Therefore every local store is designed differently, and the range can also be quite different. By doing this, Renzo Rosso is trying to prevent Diesel taking the same road as Levi's did: it became a mainstream brand in the last couple of years and therefore lost a big part of its attraction.

Rules for internationalization

Nowadays the Gap, Footlocker and lots of other American retail companies have stores in Europe. Tesco and Carrefour have among other things entered the Asian market, and the Dutch company Ahold and the Belgian Delhaize have a large number of supermarkets in the United States. So although the internationalization process is moving slower for retailers than for manufacturers, retailing is also becoming truly global. However, not every retailer is successful when expanding internationally. In order to be successful a retailer needs to comply with some rules which are applicable to replicators as well as to performance managers and reinventors.

Strong in its home market

Growing abroad is expensive. In order to expand internationally, a strong position in the home country is an absolute must, because the home country has to generate the cash for the international expansion.

Clustering

A clustered approach, in which a retail company first builds up a good market position in one country before it goes to another country, is usually preferred. After all, the chance of economies of scale will then be greater.

Local range

It is almost impossible to exploit one store format that is exactly the same in every country. This also applies to pure replicators. Almost always the range will have to be adjusted to the local market. In the Chinese Makro about 80 per cent of the range is made up of local products. In practice, about 20 per cent of the total range of many international store formats consists of local products and brands.

Synergy

Some parts of the store format do not have to be adjusted when internationalization takes place. Through synergy, cost advantages can be obtained. Performance managers can also obtain this synergy, because the principles of an attractive store design and visual merchandising can often be applied in every country without any changes. Carrefour hypermarkets for example look practically the same in every country.

Local management

All retail business is local. Knowledge of the local market is essential for a retail company. Therefore, most Wal-Mart store managers are natives of the countries where they operate. The headquarters can employ local management, but the company can also choose more independent management. Franchising is an example of this.

Consistency

When the store format is adjusted too much to the local market, the format and the retail brand will become diluted. Economies of scale will then no longer exist. There will be no more synergy and no consistent retail brand. Performance managers especially have to pay a lot of attention to this aspect, with their portfolio of formats and brands.

Start-up

When market conditions in another country are different from those in the home country, it would be a wise decision to take over an existing company. This will make for an easier start. Wal-Mart and Tesco both entered the extremely competitive Japanese retail market by acquisitions. The choice then has to be made whether to continue with the acquired local retail brand or to replace it with the global brand. This largely depends on the strength of the local retail brand. Sometimes, the acquisition of a local retail company is only useful in order to own a number of stores at once and to immediately have a certain market presence.

Research
Thorough research into the possibilities and specific needs of a country is essential. Much internationalization takes place more or less 'by accident', without any thorough research. Big losses will often be the inevitable result. Even after extensive research it can often take years before stores abroad bring in the desired results. The Dutch department store Hema, for example, found this out when it opened up stores in nearby Belgium. It was only after years that the first successes were achieved.

Like-for-like sales
Sales growth is important for every retail brand, but the best indicator of strength of a retail brand is not the growth of total sales. Growth can be achieved by opening up new stores or by taking over other companies. That is important in order to achieve economies of scale. However, such growth does not say much about the strength of the retail brand. A better indicator is the growth of the like-for-like sales of the existing stores. When this organic growth is small, there might be a serious problem. After all, lack of growth in existing stores means that the retail brand is less attractive to consumers. Buying sales through acquisitions or opening stores abroad only hides the real problem. In order to realize an increase in the like-for-like sales, the retail concept will need to be refreshed, revitalized or even reinvented.

McDonald's is a retail brand that grew rapidly for years. Mainly because of an aggressive expansion programme, McDonald's is now the world's leading restaurant brand. The company operates and franchises more than 30,000 McDonald's restaurants in about 120 countries across five continents. On a typical day, McDonald's serves nearly 50 million customers. Slowly, however, the McDonald's brand lost part of its attraction. More competition arrived and consumers became more critical towards fast food. Results were under pressure. McDonald's therefore announced a new strategy in 2003, reflecting a fundamental approach to growing the business. Previously, McDonald's emphasized adding new restaurants. Today, its emphasis is on building sales at existing restaurants. The short-term goals are to fortify the foundation of the business by returning to the operational excellence and leadership marketing for which McDonald's was once famous. The key is to revitalize the brand and become more relevant to a broader range of people. The first priority is now to improve restaurant operations and create marketing that resonates with people around the world. McDonald's improved the taste of its core menu and introduced a number of new, healthy products. In addition, the management is differentiating McDonald's by creating a more relevant restaurant environment. This includes reimaging some of its restaurants to create a more welcoming, contemporary ambience, as well as testing new ideas, such as providing wireless internet access in the restaurants. McDonald's announced that many of these actions are starting to pay off. Customers are beginning to notice the difference, and McDonald's has recently experienced significant improvements in sales generated at its existing restaurants in the United States.

1.1.2 CUTTING COSTS

The second strategy to strengthen a brand's market position is to cut costs and improve the productivity of existing stores. A retailer that does not have its costs at a competitive level will lose the battle with the competition. Retail companies are therefore working with efficient consumer response (ECR), just-in-time logistics and other efficiency measures. When it is difficult to create a significant distinction from other retail brands, price competition will be the only thing left. Sometimes no money is made at all, particularly on well-known manufacturer brands. In the short term, this can sometimes be successful. In the long term however, choosing price competition as the only weapon of positioning will only make sense if a store is indeed perceived to be the cheapest by the consumer. Such a retail brand needs to have not only the lowest prices, but also the lowest costs. Operational excellence and operational skills will have to be combined with strong buying power. Only then can a retailer be a price leader as well as a cost leader.

Price competition is everywhere, and has a big influence not only on margins, but also on the buying behaviour of consumers. In the

United States, 90 per cent of all consumers think that clothing offered at the regular price is too expensive. More than half prefer to wait for the sales to begin. The regular prices are no longer credible, because the consumer knows from experience that prices will drop soon, and will therefore postpone buying or try to negotiate the price with the salespeople.

Maybe the most obvious example of a retail brand that has chosen low prices and low costs as a competitive strategy is Aldi. This German discounter opened its first supermarket in 1962. Ever since the beginning, the founders, the Albrecht brothers, have tried to keep the costs as low as possible in every possible way. Instead of being situated in expensive shopping centres, the stores are located on the edge of a city or town, or in another inexpensive location. In order to keep logistical costs and stock as low as possible, Aldi only sells products with a high turnover. Aldi buys worldwide and sets up long-term contracts with suppliers. As a result of this, these suppliers are able to use their production capacity more evenly.

The Aldi range includes no more than 600 products. A traditional, not too large supermarket will have a minimum of about 10,000 products. Aldi does not have loyalty programmes. The products are still in their bulk boxes, so no wages have to be paid for pricing individual products, building displays and unpacking the boxes. No more money than necessary is spent on the interior of the stores. The Aldi stores do not have phones and until recently the stores did not have scanning tills. The employees at the tills needed to know all the prices by heart.

The thriftiness of the Aldi founders is sometimes taken to the extreme (Meijssen, 2003). It is known, for example, that when Theo Albrecht enters a room, he will first turn off the lights to make sure the lighting is strictly necessary. The store manager who received a scolding from the big boss is also legendary. 'Can a person write with four pens at the same time?' Theo Albrecht asked the surprised store manager. 'No, sir', the man stammered. 'So then why did you recently order four pens?' were the reproachful words of the Aldi CEO. This thriftiness has served the Albrecht brothers very well. They are now classed as some of the richest people in the world.

High operational efficiency and especially perfect logistics are definite conditions for successful price competitiveness. Excellent efficiency and logistics can also result in competitive advantage. Because of their very effective logistics, fashion chains like Zara, H&M and Mango can more easily respond to fashion trends than for example C&A or Marks & Spencer. There are only a few weeks between the initial design and the delivery of the garments to the stores. Consequently they can offer a much more up-to-date range. In addition, these retailers do not have to put as much on sale to get rid of less successful items. Because of their short lead times, they are very flexible in reacting to changes in demand.

In the past few years, retail companies tended to emphasize the first two competitive strategies: increasing sales and cutting costs. In order to keep costs as low as possible, all frills were taken out of the store format. As a result, differentiation with other retail brands disappeared as well. More and more stores started to look the same. Imitation instead of innovation became standard. When there are no or hardly any differences between two stores, there will also be not much brand loyalty expressed by the consumer. There is no reason for the consumer to prefer one store to the other. Most likely, the consumer will choose the closest or the cheapest one.

1.1.3 INCREASING DIFFERENTIATION

Obviously, increasing sales and cutting costs are important factors for success. Over a short period of time, a retailer can be very successful with that. In the long term, however, more is needed. At a certain point they have to stop cutting costs. And an increase in sales that is not based on a differentiating store format, but perhaps only achieved through heavy price reductions, will not contribute to the profitability of the retail brand. In order to be successful in the long run, a store will have to really differentiate itself from the competition. Differentiation will make the retail brand less vulnerable, and moreover, provide a higher gross margin. The store will have to become a brand, and this retail brand will have to be better, quicker or cheaper than the competition. Competition, however, does not only come from retail brands in the same sector. It comes from all angles.

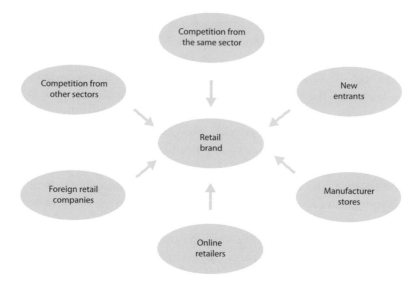

Figure 1.2 Competition from all angles

Of course, the most direct competition a retail brand gets is from other retail companies in the same sector., but a retail brand is also attacked from other angles. Every time new entrants appear on the market they change the rules of the game, and can therefore quickly acquire a large market share. Retail brands like Wal-Mart, Ikea, Zara and Carrefour are examples of this. In a very short time they have given the market a totally different look. Because of ongoing globalization, retail brands also have to deal with foreign parties more often. Most of the times, supported by a strong position in their home market, these foreign retailers can become very strong competitors. After all, they can afford to be satisfied with modest or even negative profitability. In addition, because of the channel blurring, pretty much all retailers compete with all the others. In order to survive all this competition, a store should stand out from the crowd. It has to break through the clutter. In order to be successful, the store should be branded. The brand is the future in retail.

A store will have to be more than a collection of products without a distinct identity. Just distributing products and doing everything the same as the competition will lead to a dead end. A store will have to build up a strong position in consumers' minds by becoming a brand with strong and unique meanings and associations. Branding should be one of the most important business issues for every retail company. It is the brand itself that determines whether the store succeeds or fails. A strong brand can differentiate the store from the competition. Therefore, retailers will have to not only build stores, but build brands as well. By becoming a strong brand itself and by profiling itself with respect to its competitors, a retailer can achieve store preference and store loyalty.

Retail brands must promise the consumer both functional and emotional benefits. The functional, rational differences between stores are getting smaller, however. Based on functional differences there is often no reason for a consumer to prefer one store to another. The emotional differences are becoming more important, and consumers will increasingly determine their store of choice based on the expressive or impressive emotional values that the brand adds to the store format. This means a big change for the retailer. So far, most retail companies have tried to approach the consumer in a very rational way, concentrating mainly on the functional benefits of range and pricing, and paying no or hardly any attention to the emotional aspects of shopping. Nevertheless this will change, because people do not just visit stores, they meet retail brands. These brands exist in their minds. They are association networks, and these associations can be very different from one retail brand to the other, even when the merchandise and prices are the same.

The third strategy for survival is therefore creating a larger distinction from the competition. The consumer can choose from an enormous number of stores. By creating a true, strong brand out of a store format, a retailer can create store loyalty. For consumers a brand is a promise they can trust, and trust creates loyalty. It could be said that the brand is the contract between the consumer and a retail brand. Therefore, a brand can be worth gold for a retail company. The real power of a strong retail brand is that it builds or strengthens the relationship with the customer and adds meaning to the store. Richard Handover, chairman of the British stationery, books and magazines retailer WHSmith, recently formulated it as follows:

At the heart of the WHSmith Group lies the WHSmith brand. All our businesses are either major players or market leaders in their field. But the real opportunity for long-term growth lies in our ability to develop and build upon the enormous strengths of the brand.

In the long term, a retail brand has the potential to generate more sales than the bricks-and-mortar assets of the company. A strong brand helps to create a competitive edge with respect to other retail companies, and it will be less vulnerable than the competition. Especially now that the functional, rational differences between stores are getting smaller, the emotional added value of a brand can create the desired distinction. For example, the range and prices of the Douglas and Sephora perfumeries hardly differ from each other. Both perfumeries sell pretty much the same cosmetic brands, and the manufacturers mostly dictate all prices. Still the French Sephora, because of its distinctive brand personality and its modern store design and visual merchandising, is in the mind of the consumer a totally different perfumery brand than the more traditional German Douglas.

A store is made behind the drawing desk, but a retail brand is made in the mind and the heart of the consumer. The way a consumer thinks about a retail brand can strongly differ from the way in which the retailer wants to position its brand in the market. There can be a big gap between the desired brand identity and the brand perception or image. The brand identity mentions which associations the retail brand wants to evoke via all consumer touch-points: what the retail brand stands for. The brand perception or brand image points out how the consumer experiences the retail brand. As convincing as the advertising of a retail brand may be, the consumer can have a totally different image of a brand. This image is the result of dozens or even hundreds of touch-points between the brand and the consumer, and each touch-point leaves a stronger impression than the advertising message. After all, consumers trust their own experiences more than advertising. The performance in the store has a bigger influence on the brand image than the advertising has.

Retail brands that have always had strong functional appeal will have to pay more attention to the emotional side of shopping. Marks & Spencer (M&S) is an example of this. Over 50 per cent of the UK adult population shop at M&S. In many product categories the company has a very high market share. It sells one in five of the cherries sold in the UK, and one in every four turkeys are bought from M&S each Christmas. The M&S stores sell a third of all purchases of women's underwear in the UK, and the estimate is that one in three men in the UK own an M&S suit. All products are sold under its private brands.

Some years ago, in spite of this strong position, sales and profit were under pressure. M&S apparel lacked appeal because of its poor fashion content and uninteresting design. Moreover, the price/quality ratio deteriorated and bad publicity had damaged the strength of the brand. M&S is now trying to regain consumer confidence by largely focusing on reestablishing the traditional strengths of the business. Its business essence is making aspirational quality accessible to all. Traditionally, this has been associated with the technical and functional performance of the products. In the near future however, M&S wants to create greater emotional value for its customers. It wants its customers to feel about the brand as they might feel about a close friend. The long-term trust is still there from its heritage, but M&S wants to add greater warmth and more fun to the store format. It wants to help its customers secure the quality of life that they aspire to. It will still be largely about product, but M&S also wants to connect, for example, with the pleasure of an al fresco evening relaxing with friends. It wants to provide the inspiration and solutions, from garden furniture to food, wine and even the clothes.

With all the pressures in life, M&S wants to help its customers look and feel fantastic. In a recent lingerie campaign, it still offered great products, but it also connected with the moods of women: sometimes flirty, sometimes sporty, and sometimes comfy. It connected with women's emotions. M&S hopes to regain its customers' confidence by adding warmth and fun to the trust it currently enjoys, by helping customers live their own lifestyle, and by ensuring that it matches its retail formats and formulas to women's different moods and purchase occasions. And importantly, it will continue to target its core audience, the slightly older woman.

The emotional differences between retail brands are usually bigger than the functional, rational differences. Some functional attributes, like for example low prices, are taken more or less for granted by consumers. They do not, or barely, create any differentiation. By creating emotional differences a store format will be quicker to succeed in creating a certain monopoly position. In the mind and heart of a consumer it will in some way take up a special place. Therefore, for a retail company as well as for a manufacturer it is of high importance to have a strong brand. To be able to survive the strong competition, it is necessary to have a strong mind position. By establishing a brand with strong and unique associations, a retail company can build up a strong emotional connection with consumers and acquire a competitive advantage. Retailers that use their stores not only to sell products, but also for building their brands, are worth a lot. The market value of companies like Wal-Mart, Carrefour, Tesco and Home Depot far exceeds the value of their tangible assets.

Multiple strategies

In practice, retail companies often choose a mixture of the three competitive strategies: increasing sales, cutting costs and increasing differentiation. Creating differentiation does not take away the need to keep a close eye on costs. A company that does not control its costs will never be successful, no matter how much the differentiation from the competition. Another basic condition for success is to obtain a certain growth in sales. With a strong brand, however, it will be easier to obtain the required sales increase, and it will also be easier to gain a higher margin and therefore become less dependent on lower costs.

Wal-Mart is a retail brand that follows all three competitive strategies. This world's biggest retailer is barely 40 years old. In this short period of time Wal-Mart has grown rapidly. In 1963 the first store was opened in Rogers, Arkansas. Nowadays Wal-Mart has more than 5,200 stores and employs more than 1.6 million people, not only in the United States, but also for example in Mexico, the UK and Germany. Every week Wal-Mart welcomes more than 140 million customers into its stores. Because of the large sales volumes in food and general merchandise, Wal-Mart can negotiate tough conditions with its suppliers and also obtain many other economies of scale.

In addition, Wal-Mart is known for its striving for maximum efficiency. It exchanges sales information with manufacturers. In close coordination with manufacturers, Wal-Mart succeeded in vigorously streamlining its logistics. And through its merchandise mix, client approach and very low prices, Wal-Mart also differentiates itself from its competitors. The supercenters offer the customer a huge range of food and general merchandise. In spite of the emphasis on low prices, every Wal-Mart store always has someone at the entrance to welcome customers and to help them if necessary. Wal-Mart is now one of the strongest brands in the world.

A mixture of the three competitive strategies can also be found at the British Dixons Group, the leading European specialist retailer of consumer electronics, with operations in 12 countries. Its future strategy is based on:

- enlarging its trading space;
- expansion into selected European markets;
- improving its operating efficiency;
- developing its specialist electrical retail proposition;
- exploiting its portfolio of retail brands.

The first two strategies focus on increasing sales by enlarging the trading space of existing stores, opening up new stores, and also expanding into other European markets where the group identifies profitable opportunities. Improving its operating efficiency should lead to lower costs. The Dixons Group wants to be the lowest-cost operator in cost ratio terms in each of its markets. The last two strategies concern building strong brands. The Dixons Group trades via a range of different retail brands, each with its own market approach. Besides Dixons, Currys and PC World are also among its famous brands. Currys is the UK's largest electrical retailer. PC World is Britain's largest specialist chain of computer superstores.

1.2 Manufacturers versus retailers

Branding in retail has its roots in the small, uninviting, overcrowded grocery shops of British industrial cities like Newcastle, Glasgow, Liverpool and London (Holzhauer, 1992). In Glasgow for example Thomas Lipton, known for his good tea, opened his own store. The products in the store were not prepacked, but were mostly sold out of big bags, barrels, pitchers or cases. Shopkeepers not only sold products that they had bought from other traders or artisans, but together with their often very young employees, they also produced all kinds of their own products: from jam to cookies, to toys or even ham and sausages. The products were put in bags or wrapped in paper, and sometimes the name of the shop was mentioned on these. Little by little grocers started to prepack their products. That made things easier when the store was busy; it also gave shopkeepers the chance to differentiate themselves from the competition through their own unique packaging. Soon afterwards, manufacturers adopted this idea, and around 1850 they started to prepackage groceries.

During the industrial revolution factories were built and continually bigger volumes were produced. Because of this mass production stocks increased, and production and consumption were no longer equal. In order to solve this problem, the manufacturer needed the retailer. Redistributing the manufacturer's mass production became a continually larger task for retail; hence the retailer became less of a producer and more of a trader. Retailers became the link between manufacturers and consumers. However, to continue to be in touch with consumers, manufacturers branded their packaging and introduced fixed retail prices. Without the involvement of retailers, they tried to create consumer loyalty, and the retailer became more and more a kind of warehouse for the manufacturer. Retailers were not thinking yet in store formats and strategic marketing concepts. Manufacturers did not take the needs and wants of the many small retailers into account. It was the manufacturer who decided what was happening, and retailers accepted that, because they just did not have the power and the knowledge to change anything.

The dominance that manufacturers used to have can still be found in the range of some stores. Products that from a consumer's point of view do not have much to do with each other are sold together in one store because they used to come all from the same manufacturer. Electronic stores like the French Darty, the German Media Markt and the American Best Buy are still examples of that. They sell televisions, DVD players and sound equipment as well as refrigerators, washing machines and microwaves. The only thing these product categories have in common is that the products all have a plug, and they all used to come from Philips and other electronics suppliers. However, for the consumer, these are products that represent completely different states of mind. Washing machines, refrigerators and other household appliances are mostly bought when the old one breaks down. On the contrary, televisions, DVD players and sound equipment are often bought because something new appears on the market, which gives a better picture or sound, or has a more beautiful design. Buying a washing machine is functional, whereas buying a television is more emotional and recreational. That both types of products are sold in one store can only be explained by the previous dominance of the manufacturer.

1.2.1 CHANGES IN THE RELATIONSHIP

The relationship between retailer and manufacturer has changed rapidly in the last few years. The power has increasingly shifted from the manufacturer to the retailer. Retailers no longer just pass things on for the manufacturer, but now have their own brand strategy, and manufacturers are now becoming mere suppliers to the retailers. The most important reasons for this power shift are discussed below.

Consolidation

Manufacturers are strongly consolidated. In many product categories, the three biggest manufacturers control more than half the market. Nevertheless, even the biggest manufacturers often only represent just a few percentage points of a retail company's sales. In contrast, it often happens that one retail company is good for a quarter or even half of the total sales of a manufacturer. For example, the three biggest drugstores in the United States together have a market share of almost 50 per cent. Because of their strong buying power, retail companies can make demands on their suppliers.

Lead in information

With the data from RFID (radio-frequency identification) and checkouts, retailers now have much more information than they used to have. The retailer now has more complete and current market information than the manufacturer has. In the past, manufacturers more or less considered the consumer to be their possession. After all, they had the most knowledge about consumers and approached the market without involving the retailer. In most sectors however, the positions are now reversed. Nowadays it is the retailer that 'owns' the consumer. Compared with a manufacturer, a retailer can now experiment quicker and more easily to find out which marketing activities will work best.

Product abundance

Manufacturers offer more products than retailers can put in their stores. For example in the food industry in the United States, more than 10,000 new products are introduced every year. At the most one in ten becomes a success, because, among other things, they are usually not really innovations but just variations on existing products. Moreover, many products and brands are mutually exchangeable. A retailer can play manufacturers off against each other. The manufacturer with the best proposition for both consumer as well as retailer gets a position on the shelf.

Fragmentation of the media

On a daily basis the consumer receives thousands of advertising messages. Countless brands are screaming for attention. Only a small part of all communication is more or less perceived consciously. Because of the enormous fragmentation of media, it is getting more difficult for a manufacturer to approach the consumer through traditional mass media. Mass communication is broadcasting. Narrowcasting is possible via (digital) in-store communications, and the head office can adapt the advertising message in real time to the needs of every individual store or department.

Professionalism

Just like manufacturers, retailers started to apply new marketing techniques and develop professional store formats. And just like products, stores became brands. In many cases these retail brands are now stronger than manufacturer brands. Most buying decisions are made in the store, and retailers learned to react to this with their store design, visual merchandising and employees, changing their store into a real selling machine. What this selling machine sells is determined by the retailer. Nowadays the manufacturer only has a small influence on that.

Vertical integration

Especially in the fashion industry there is a strong vertical integration. Retail companies like Zara and Mango own their own factories, not only to obtain a higher margin, but also to be able to quickly react to demand. This vertical integration enhances the power of the retail company. A retailer that owns its own factories does not need the manufacturer any more. But there could also be a completely different reason for a retailer to own its own factories. If a manufacturer still has a dominant position in a certain product category and there is a chance that the retailer will become completely dependent on it, then it would be beneficial for the retailer to have its own production capacity.

Private brands

Because of strong consolidation in retail, the share of private brands will also increase in many sectors. With private brands the retailer is in direct competition with manufacturer brands, and more often than not the retailer will be the winner. After all, with its market approach the retailer has a number of advantages over a manufacturer. The most important one is that the retailer has full control over all activities that take place in the store with regard to the private brand. It can decide how to bring the private brand to the consumer's attention. A manufacturer would have to rely on the cooperation of the retailer.

Local marketing

A retailer is closer to the consumer and can more easily adapt its proposition to the needs of the local markets. This is more difficult for a manufacturer. At most, a manufacturer can adjust its proposition for each country or region. A further refinement in the market approach is only possible if the manufacturer takes on the retail function itself. A Dell computer is a good example of that. Because of direct contact with customers, the computers can be offered completely tailor-made.

Communications budgets

In order to support their brand, big retail companies have communication budgets of tens of millions of euros. With that they exceed most manufacturer brands. In every country retail brands are among the biggest advertisers. With these huge budgets retailers are on their way, like manufacturer brands, to building up strong positions in the consumer's minds. In addition, retailers have the big advantage of having direct contact with their customers. As a result the effectiveness of their communications budget is much better. After all, in a store the retailer can provide follow-up to the out-of-store communication. The special offer the consumer saw on television or in the newspaper at home can be seen again on display in the store.

Therefore, retail companies are no longer focusing only on distributing products from the manufacturer to the consumer. In the past few decades they have developed into market players that definitely have to be taken into account. An increasing number of retail companies now have the same brand power as well-known manufacturer brands. The consumer's mind is therefore no longer the domain of the manufacturer. Moreover, the Dutch Hema, the American Gap, the Swedish Ikea and the Spanish Zara are examples of retail brands that prove that even without the help of manufacturer brands, they can become brands themselves.

1.2.2 BATTLE OF THE BRANDS

Now that retail companies have become strong brands themselves, there will more often be battles of the brands between manufacturers and retailers. The interests of manufacturers and retailers are partially parallel, because manufacturers need stores for the distribution of their products and retailers need products in their stores. But there will always be important conflicts of interest between retailers and manufacturers:

Perspective

A retailer's store format and range are the two starting points, and then it will decide which role manufacturer brands will play. In principle, it will not matter to the retailer with which manufacturer it can realize its objectives. In contrast the manufacturer's starting point is its brand, and then it will wonder how its brand could contribute to realizing the retailer's brand objectives. If this were to lead to a favourable brand shift for the manufacturer, it would be happy with that. But when sales increase for one particular manufacturer brand only at the cost of another manufacturer brand, the retailer will not consider that a success. After all, the retailer is most interested in a total product category sales increase.

New product

When competing with other manufacturers, a manufacturer will have to introduce new products to the market on a regular basis. But it is impossible for retailers to include all new products in their range Shelf space is too limited for that, so they will only choose products that they think will have a high chance of success. Because this is very hard to predict, retailers are often stuck with unsuccessful products. Therefore, retailers and manufacturers often agree on a right of return. That way the risk of new products is completely shouldered by the manufacturer.

Price

The manufacturer strives for a consumer price that fits the positioning of its brand. In addition, it would like all stores to sell the brand at (about) the same price. After all, big differences in price will have a negative influence on the quality appeal of the brand. But a retailer often uses the price to differentiate itself from the competition. Well-known brands in particular are used for promotions during price wars. In order to make the margin on these brands a little more attractive, a retailer will ask its suppliers for better buying terms.

Communication

In its marketing communication the manufacturer tries, in the long run, to work on building its brands. In general, thematic communication is used, in which only one brand gets all the attention. A retailer puts more emphasis on short-term promotional communications. Price is almost always the key element. Moreover, the manufacturer brand is only part of the retailer's advertising. In the retailer's brochure or advertisement, the manufacturer will have to compete with other manufacturer brands, just like in the store. Its carefully built-up brand image can be damaged as a result.

Exclusiveness

When a retailer runs a promotion together with a manufacturer, it wants it to be exclusive. Running a promotion that is also being carried out by other retail companies will not create a competitive advantage. On the contrary, a manufacturer would be more interested in running a promotion through multiple retail companies. After all, for it that is the best way to obtain attention and increase sales as much as possible.

Shelf position

The location in the store and the shelf position both have a big influence on sales. Every manufacturer wants the best location and the best shelf position for its brands. However, a retailer will only choose those manufacturer brands that are best for its brand, sales or profit to fill these prime positions, and in many cases these will be its private brands rather than manufacturer brands. The private brand will get an eye-level shelf position and extra visibility through the help of displays. A location on one of the bottom shelves will be left for the manufacturer brands.

In future years there will be a continuous power shift from manufacturers to retailers. Retailers will change their stores into strong brands, and concentration in retail will continue. Retail brands will use their private brands as weapons even more in competitive battles. And there will be more manufacturer brands than there is space for on the retailer's shelves. Because of that, retail will have even more power, and this will result in an increase in the profitability of retail brands. At the moment, that profitability is still far behind that of the strong manufacturer brands (Corstjens et al, 2004). While retailers have delivered superior sales growth (11.2 per cent net sales growth versus 3.9 per cent), manufacturers' profit margins have been consistently higher: 5.5 per cent versus 0.9 per cent. Retailers have become more powerful, but manufacturers are still much more profitable.

The enormous price competition in retail just does not allow for any high profitability at the moment. The extra margin retail acquires from the manufacturer is (almost) completely transferred to the consumer. Functional differences in convenience and store experience between retail brands are often too small to create a competitive advantage. The differences between manufacturer brands are usually larger. Moreover, a manufacturer can, unlike to a retailer, use a brand portfolio, through which multiple price segments are covered and maximum proceeds are obtained via price differentiation. For a retail brand that is much harder to do. After all, most retail companies only work with one brand.

Within that one brand it is hard to apply price differentiation. But as retailers start to succeed more in turning their stores into strong brands, profitability in retail will rise to the same level as that of manufacturer brands.

1.2.3 SHELF POSITION VERSUS MIND POSITION

Because retail in the past few decades has developed itself into a market player that has to be taken seriously, every manufacturer is forced to commit not only to consumer marketing but also to trade marketing. Consumer marketing alone will not be enough any more. Through consumer marketing the manufacturer tries to build up a strong position in the consumer's mind. Via trade marketing it tries to obtain a good shelf position from the retailer. This is not only about shelf positioning in a quantitative way: qualitative aspects are also an important part of it. When a manufacturer brand is located at eye-level on the shelf it will sell better than when it is located on the bottom shelves, and the location in the store will influence the ultimate sales as well.

Manufacturers will have to completely integrate their consumer marketing and trade marketing in order to confront consumers with the same message everywhere. Together, the position in the consumer's mind and the shelf position at the retailer will have to give the manufacturer the desired market position. These mind positions and shelf positions strongly influence each other. Brand preference that is a result of a strong mind position will influence the shelf position a retailer might give to the manufacturer brand. The stronger the mind position, the better the shelf position will be. The retailer that does not honour the brand preference of consumers runs the risk of missing out on sales. Similarly, the shelf position can also influence the mind position. When the retailer supports a manufacturer by giving it a good shelf position, the position that brand has in the consumer's mind might become stronger. Consumers often make a final brand choice in the store. If they are confronted with a manufacturer brand with an optimal shelf position, this will influence the positioning of that brand in their minds, and therefore their buying behaviour.

The relationship between shelf position, mind position and market position is illustrated in Figure 1.3 (Floor, 1996: 40):

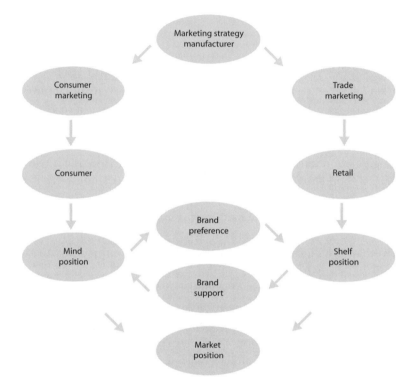

Figure 1.3 Relationship between shelf, mind and market position

Every manufacturer will have to find the right balance between market activities that are aimed at building a mind position, and activities that are trying to realize the desired shelf position. The available marketing budget will have to be divided between consumer marketing and trade marketing. In the past, most money was spent on consumer marketing. Via a strong position in the consumer's mind, a shelf position was extorted from retailers. Therefore the manufacturer also had a certain indirect control over the shelf position. After all, the retailer could not afford to disappoint the consumer. Now that the power of the retailer has become much stronger, the situation has changed. The retailer has regained control over the shelf position, and is not going to give it back to the manufacturer. The manufacturer now needs a very good argument to change that.

Under the influence of the power shift from manufacturers to retailers, a shift also took place in the allocation of the manufacturer's marketing budget. Trade spend is taking an increasing share of marketing spend, so much so that trade promotions now account for over 50 per cent of the marketing and promotional budget for manufacturers, compared with only 22 per cent for advertising media (Accenture, 2001, 2003).

The choice of how to split the marketing budget into consumer marketing and trade marketing can differ from manufacturer to manufacturer. There are however some factors that have a great influence on this split. Manufacturers will have to spend a large part of their marketing budget on trade marketing for the following types of product.

Homogeneous products
With homogeneous products, it is difficult for manufacturers to get consumers to prefer their brand. In this kind of situation the manufacturer strongly depends on the willingness of the retailer to bring the brand to the consumer's attention. Because it does not really matter to consumers which brand they buy, it is the retailer that decides which brand to include in its range.

Impulse products
To obtain sales, this type of product depends largely on location and presentation in the store. An impulse product that is in the wrong location or is not presented in the correct way will hardly generate any sales. In order to obtain a prime location and good presentation, the cooperation of the retailer is needed.

Small brands
Brands with a small marketing budget have a hard time building up brand preference in consumers' minds to a point where the retailer cannot do without that brand. Most of the time it is more effective for small brands to enter into cooperation with a retailer in order to get the consumer's attention. In general, a smaller advertising budget

will then be sufficient, and once sales have reached a certain volume, the manufacturer can start with consumer marketing to help build consumer loyalty. For manufacturer brands that operate in small markets with more limited marketing budgets, it would also be beneficial to spend relatively more money on trade marketing.

Complex products

When it comes to complex products, the consumer will be strongly led by the salesperson's advice when choosing a brand. Therefore it is of utmost importance that with this type of product retail employees prefer to sell that specific brand. The buying conditions then play an important role.

Strong concentration

There is strong concentration in almost all retail sectors, and many retailers are much bigger than well-known suppliers. In countries like the Netherlands, Finland, Sweden and Switzerland for example, the top three retail companies cover about 80–90 per cent of the food market. In these situations it is inevitable that manufacturers will use a large part of their marketing budget in an attempt to do business with these retailers.

Selective distribution

When a manufacturer prefers selective distribution for its brand, it will have to make sure that the small number of stores that sell the brand pay a lot of attention to it. In exchange for the selective distribution, the retailer will have to support the brand as much as possible.

Consumers who are difficult to reach

Sometimes consumers with very specific characteristics are difficult to reach with traditional mass media. The manufacturer then depends strongly on the cooperation of the retailer. In the store, the manufacturer can communicate with this target group at the moment of purchase. There is no better timing.

Manufacturers can no longer afford to focus only on strengthening the mind position. Prime shelf positioning no longer goes without saying.

Manufacturers now have to compete not only with other manufacturers to obtain limited shelf space, but also with the retailer's private brands. Obviously, these last brands will have the retailer's preference. Even the biggest manufacturers now have to exert themselves to acquire the retailer's support. Shelf positions are just as difficult to capture as mind positions are. The mind of the consumer and the shelf of the retailer can only hold a limited number of brands. Adding one brand means dropping another brand. The consumer cannot remember everything, and the retailer cannot put everything in the store. The store is not elastic.

Despite the importance of trade marketing, the position the manufacturer has in the consumer's mind also continues to be of utmost importance. A strong mind position offers the manufacturer the best protection against the power of the retailer. A strong brand gives the manufacturer a countervailing power when negotiating with the retailer. If the mind position is weak, the manufacturer depends entirely on the willingness of the retailer to still give the manufacturer brand the necessary support. In practice, this willingness will have to be bought by the manufacturer with guaranteed margins and all kinds of allowances. This is something that can only be prevented if the manufacturer is able to differentiate itself from its competitors in other parts of its trade marketing. For example, a manufacturer can develop a unique presentation technique or rise above its rivals in logistics.

Retail companies will increasingly develop into brands, which have an equally strong mind position as the manufacturer brands have themselves. Because of that, positions in the consumer's minds will no longer only be the domain of the manufacturer. Retail companies will also build up mind positions with their consumer marketing. The battle between the retailer and the manufacturer for the goodwill of the consumer is no longer only focused on the mind position of the manufacturer brand versus the shelf position of the retailer. In future, retail brands and manufacturer brands will also battle for the strongest position in the consumer's mind. More and more manufacturers will then come to the conclusion that they are bound to lose to the retailers. The manufacturers that produce private brands for Ikea, the Gap and many other retailers have already come to this conclusion. They limit themselves to delivering the products demanded in the cheapest possible way. They do not focus on consumer marketing, as these activities have completely been taken over by the retail brands.

The strength of a manufacturer brand versus that of a retail brand can be measured by the effort the consumer will make to buy the manufacturer brand. When a favourite manufacturer brand is not available, the consumer will decide between switching stores and switching product brands. Consumers are loyal to a manufacturer brand when they are prepared to go to another store for it. In this case, the loyalty to the manufacturer brand is stronger than the loyalty to the retail brand. However, if the consumer decides to buy another brand while in the store, the retail brand is stronger. In order to determine the loyalty towards retailer and manufacturer, an experiment was done in the Netherlands a few years ago. Five well-known manufacturer brands were taken off the shelves of eight supermarkets and consumers' reactions were checked. The outcome of this experiment is shown in Table 1.1 (Verbeke, 1993).

Product	Switch store %	Switch brand %	Defer purchase %	Total %
Soft drink	47	33	19	100
Bakery product	64	12	22	100
Coffee creamer	62	20	17	100
Rice	50	28	22	100
Washing powder	30	22	46	100
Total	56	25	19	100

Table 1.1 Consumer behaviour when confronted with a brand out of stock

On average, half the customers chose a different brand when their favourite brand was not available. With these customers loyalty for the manufacturer brand was not so strong that they would go to another store for it. In this case, the retail brand took over part of the function of the manufacturer brand. The customer had enough trust in the retail brand to be satisfied with another brand that the retailer had selected. Of course, this trust also depended on the strength of the other manufacturer brand. In about a quarter of the cases customers went to another store to see if it had their favourite manufacturer brand. This resulted in a direct loss in sales for the retailer that did not have stock available. This is a loss in sales that, of course, only got bigger when the customer also bought other products at that other store.

The success of a manufacturer brand therefore does not only depend on the preference and the loyalty of the consumer. The support the manufacturer receives from the retailer can be an equally important and sometimes even more important factor. If a manufacturer brand does not get the retailer's maximum support at the point of sale, it will never be able to fully profit from the sympathy of the consumer. Because of a strong mind position, the manufacturer brand extorts, as it were, a shelf position from the retailer. But when the retailer does not provide this wholeheartedly, for example when the margin is too low, a retailer will focus a lot less on this product in its advertising and visual merchandising. Therefore the strength of a manufacturer brand also depends on the support it receives from retail. This support can only be achieved through good trade marketing.

Based on the position in the consumer's mind and the shelf position at retail, the actual power of a manufacturer brand can be determined, as shown in Figure 1.4.

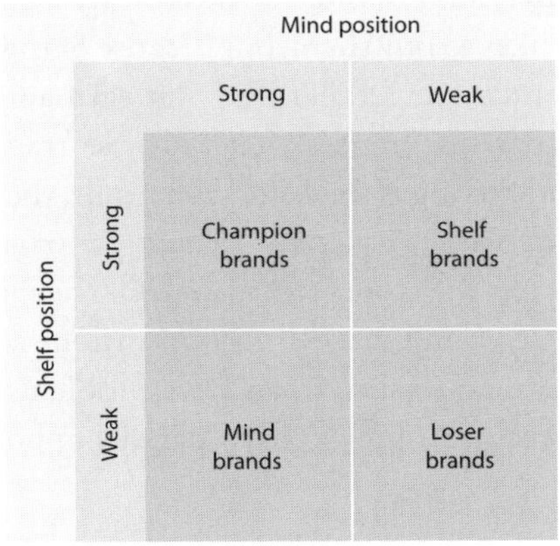

	Mind position	
	Strong	Weak
Shelf position — Strong	Champion brands	Shelf brands
Shelf position — Weak	Mind brands	Loser brands

Figure 1.4 Power of manufacturer brands

Champion brands

Brands in this category are worth gold to a manufacturer. They are the strongest possible brands. Champion brands, like for example the Apple iPod, have a large share of loyal customers and have also build up a lot of goodwill in retail. The consumer likes to buy them and the retailer likes to sell them. Lately, more and more private brands have been falling into this category. In the past, private brands generated large sales because again and again they were brought to the consumer's attention both in the store and in advertising. Consumers bought them because they were obviously cheaper than the manufacturer brands. One could, however, not speak of a strong position in the consumer's mind, and in particular the quality of the private brands often left much to be desired. Now that the quality has improved a lot and companies like Albert Heijn, Boots and the Gap are trying to give their private brands an emotional added value, more private brands are starting to achieve stronger mind positions. Because of this, the threat to manufacturers is becoming bigger.

Mind brands

Some manufacturer brands have a strong position in consumers' minds, but despite that, they do not succeed in getting support from retailers. Often, well-known manufacturer brands in the food sector fall into this category. The consumer likes to buy them, but because of the many price promotions on these brands, the retailer does not earn a lot of money on them. This mainly concerns brands that only use traditional pull marketing. Their trade marketing is weak and as a result, they do not get optimum attention in the store. Perhaps the profit contribution is too low or the brand does not fit the store format well. Or the manufacturer simply did not succeed in creating successful cooperations with its retail partners. For example, a manufacturer can have problems with retail because it does not succeed in stopping cheap parallel imports.

Shelf brands

To become successful, a manufacturer brand should have good distribution. Some manufacturer brands get a lot of support from retail, despite the fact that the consumer does not or hardly ever requests the brand. In this product category, brands are not that important.

Many fresh products in the supermarket fall into this category. The manufacturer mostly relies on its push marketing: for example, it has excellent logistics or a unique product presentation. Because it helps the retailer exploit the store, this type of brand is bound to obtain a lot of support from retail. That is why, despite a weak position in the consumer's mind, these brands can still work on increasing their sales.

Loser brands

Manufacturer brands in this category have little chance of survival. In the short term only a very low price for the retailer and the consumer could result in a small success. However, this does not offer a lot of hope in the long term. After a while, the retailer will drop the brand and use the available shelf space for another brand, and the consumer will not be sad about it.

1.3 Strength of a retail brand

So store formats are developing more into retail brands. However, not all retail brands are equally strong. The strength of a retail brand can be measured, as with a product, by two criteria (Franzen and van den Berg, 2002: 501–4).

Mind position

A strong retail brand has a strong position in the mind of the consumer. It has a high top-of-mind awareness and is trusted by the consumer. When hearing the brand name, the consumer will derive positive associations. The retail brand is relevant to the consumer because it has important functional as well as emotional benefits. It clearly differentiates itself from the competition, in the eyes of the consumer.

Influence on shopping behaviour

The choice for a store is partly determined by convenience and habit. When it concerns a strong retail brand, however, the consumer is led not only by these pragmatic considerations but also by an emotional bond with the brand. A strong retail brand has many loyal customers and a high share of wallet. The consumer does not go, or hardly ever goes, to competitor retail brands. The relationship between the retail brand and the consumer goes further than just buying a number of products. The consumer feels connected with the story behind the store. There is an emotional store loyalty.

1.3.1 BRAND VALUE

The strength of a retail brand can also be expressed in monetary terms. The value of a strong retail brand often makes up a certain percentage of the total balance sheet of that company. In practice, various calculation methods are used to determine this brand equity. Interbrand, a company that specializes in brand valuation, values brands the same way financial analysts value other company assets. It values brands based on how much these brands are likely to earn in the future. Then the projected profits are discounted to a present value, based on the likelihood that those earnings will actually materialize. The first step is figuring out what percentage of a company's revenue can be credited to the brand. Based on reports from analysts at JP Morgan Chase, Citigroup and Morgan Stanley, Interbrand projects five years of earnings and sales for the brand. It then deducts operating costs, taxes and a charge for the capital employed to arrive at the intangible earnings. The company strips out intangibles such as patents and customer convenience to assess what portion of those earnings is due to the brand. Finally, the brand's strength is assessed to determine the risk profile of the earnings forecast. This risk profile generates a discount rate, which is applied to brand earnings to get a net present value. To calculate the brand's risk profile, Interbrand looks at seven factors.

Market leadership

A retail brand that is obviously the market leader will in general have better financial results than retail brands with smaller market shares. After all, it can realize economies of scale in numerous fields.

Stability

A retail brand that has had a steady, loyal customer base for a while will most probably generate a fixed income flow in the future. It has become the absolute authority in its sector. The customer goes to the store almost automatically.

Kind of market

A retail brand is worth more when it operates in a growing market. The same goes for retail brands in markets with little price competition. In the future, retail brands are likely to continue to enjoy good sales and margins in these markets.

International potential

A retail brand that has stores in multiple countries is often of more value than a retail brand that only operates regionally or nationally. With an international brand, risks can be spread and moreover, economies of scale can be obtained.

Trend of sales

The trend of sales of a retail brand in the long run is a strong indication of the brand's health. In particular the development of the like-for-like sales shows if the brand is still considered to be relevant by the consumer.

Brand support

A retail brand that has been supported for years by heavy and consistent marketing communications will have built up a strong consumer franchise. Because of that consumer franchise it will be less vulnerable to attacks by the competition in the future.

Legal protection

The way in which the brand name and the store format enjoy legal protection will of course also influence the value of a retail brand. A retail brand that can be easily copied gives no guarantee for future income.

To qualify for the top 100 list, each brand must have a value greater than US$1 billion, derive about a third of its earnings outside its home country, and have publicly available marketing and financial data. One or more of those criteria eliminate heavyweight retail brands such as Carrefour and Wal-Mart. Some of the retail brands that are part of the top 100 list of most valuable global brands are McDonald's, the Gap, Ikea, Avon, KFC, Pizza Hut, Amazon, Zara and Tiffany & Co. Of these,

McDonald's is the only retail brand in the top 10, with a brand value of more than US$26 billion.

1.4 Advantages of strong retail brands

A strong retail brand has advantages for both the consumer and the retailer. A strong brand, in combination with a good location, good employees and perfect operational excellence, is the most important asset for a retailer. But a strong retail brand also has a number of advantages for the consumer.

1.4.1 ADVANTAGES FOR THE CONSUMER

To the consumer a strong retail brand has both functional and emotional benefits.

Convenience

In many countries there is overcapacity, and stock ranges are also getting bigger every year. Supermarkets in the Netherlands stock around 15,000 products. A supermarket in the United States, though, will have more than 40,000 different products on its shelves. The consumer does not have the knowledge or the time to compare all the alternatives. However, a strong retail brand can make life much easier. It offers the consumer trust and reassures customers that they will get what they are looking for. Choosing between the different stores then becomes easier. A couple of years ago, the list of most trusted brands was exclusively led by big, well-known manufacturer brands like Coca-Cola and Nike. Nowadays, retail brands also communicate trust. The perceived risk is less when buying at a well-known retail brand. It will be easier for the consumer to make decisions, because the brand is a kind of landmark. It gives the consumer something to hold on to when choosing between the enormous numbers of stores.

Self-expression

A consumer does not only shop at a specific retail brand for reasons of function or convenience. Emotional reasons also have an important influence on choosing which store to go to. Emotional benefits can, among other things, concern what the brand says about its customers. The stores that consumers shop in contribute to determining their identity. Being a customer of a certain retail brand can be a symbol of communication to others about what someone considers to be important in life. Brands form a kind of social language; shopping at a specific store is a statement about the customer. Buying at The Body Shop means that someone cares about the environment, and choosing to shop in an Apple store creates the statement that the person is an individual.

Good feeling

Retail brands can have an expressive function, but can also have an impressive function. This function is about how they make people feel. Being a customer of a certain retail brand can provide an uplifting emotional experience. Buying at The Body Shop can be a statement to others, but it can also give consumers the feeling that they are doing something good for humanity, animals and the environment.

1.4.2 ADVANTAGES FOR THE RETAILER

A retailer that succeeds in changing a store into a strong brand will offer a number of advantages to the consumer, but a strong brand identity can also offer a number of advantages to the retailer itself.

Higher price

A strong retail brand diminishes the price sensitivity of consumers. Because there is an emotional bond between the retailer and its customers, they will not immediately go to a competitor if there is a price promotion. A strong retail brand can afford to ask more for its private brand than a retailer that does not have that brand power. Sometimes it can even ask a higher price than for well-known manufacturer brands.

Higher profitability

Strong retail brands show better financial results than weaker brands. Strong brands result in strong profits, because consumers make more frequent visits, fill larger than average shopping baskets, or pay price premiums at the stores of brands they perceive to be strong (Court et al, 1999: 100). A strong position in the mind of the consumer leads to a high market share. Research shows that, with manufacturer brands, high market share generally results in a high return on investment. There is no reason to assume that this will be different in retail. As the market position of a retail brand is stronger, profitability will be higher. Manufacturer brands in the UK food industry have a relationship between market share and net profit margin that is summarized in Table 1.2 (Chernatony and McDonald, 2003: 44).

Market share (in descending order)	Net profit margin %
Brand number 1	17.9
Brand number 2	2.8
Brand number 3	− 0.9
Brand number 4	− 5.9

Table 1.2 Relationship between market share and net profit margin

It is apparent that the market leader obtains a much higher profit margin than brands with a smaller market share.

Barriers against competitors

A strong retail brand takes, as it were, a monopoly position in the consumer's mind. The customer experiences a clear differentiation from other stores, and it is difficult for competitors to attack such a brand. Over a short or medium period of time, that brand cannot be copied. Especially when the retail brand has a strong emotional bond with the consumer, imitation by others will be difficult. The brand will then be a strong defence against other retail companies.

Higher customer loyalty

A strong retail brand builds up a loyal customer base. In the process, success comes not only from actual behaviour but also more importantly from the emotional connection the customer has with a retail brand. A high retention rate does not always automatically mean a high level of loyalty, though. Maybe there is no other store (yet) in the area, or the store visit usually takes place out of habit instead of being based on a conscious decision. The loyalty is then more passive than active.

Lower marketing costs

Because of the loyal customer base, the retail brand does not have to attract new customers every time. As a percentage of sales, but also mainly because of economies of scale, a lower communication budget would be sufficient. Moreover, a clear focus from a strong brand results in more efficiency, because every employee in the organization knows what is expected of him or her.

Franchising possibilities

In order for a retailer to open its own stores, high investments are necessary. Through franchising, however, a strong retail brand can also grow rapidly. This method enables expansion to take place at lower capital cost. Independent entrepreneurs are often very willing to work under the umbrella of a strong brand. After all, they know that a strong retail brand guarantees high sales. For its part, the retail brand can benefit from the local power of independent entrepreneurs and quickly build up market share and brand equity.

Brand extensions are easier

A strong retail brand can more easily launch new activities on the market. The brand is an excellent ambassador when a retail company wants to enter a new market. A brand transfer is much easier than it is for a weak brand. For example, Tesco and Sainsbury's can therefore be quite successful in selling financial services. Their consumer franchise as a supermarket is a leverage for new products and services.

Better deals with suppliers

Manufacturers and other suppliers like to do business with a leading retailer. A strong retail brand is offered the best locations by project developers, and manufacturers are prepared to grant that retail brand higher margins and, for example, give it exclusive rights to sell new products for a certain period of time. After all, they know they cannot survive without the retail brand.

Talented employees

Employees can make or break a retail brand. It is therefore of the utmost importance to hire and keep good employees. A strong retail brand will succeed in that more easily than a weaker brand. As with consumers, employees are more likely to want to be part of a strong, successful brand than a brand that is struggling. The cost of recruiting talented employees will therefore be lower for a strong brand, and by attracting the best people, the retail brand can only become stronger.

1.4.3 DIFFERENCES BETWEEN RETAILER AND MANUFACTURER

Not every product is a strong brand, and not every retail brand is a strong brand either. In order to build up a strong brand, more is needed than just a nice brand name. Especially now that there are increasingly more brands and an overkill of communication, a brand really has to try hard to attract attention over all the clutter. The approach of a store will then be different from that of a product. After all, a retailer and a manufacturer are different in a couple of important ways.

Range of goods

Most manufacturers have a limited range. Coca-Cola, for example, has an range that only includes a handful of brands and products. Even Unilever, the world's biggest manufacturer of food and detergents, has an range of not more than about 400 brands. A retail brand, on the contrary, has a much larger range. Even a food discounter with a very small stock offers around 600 to 800 different products. And in a department store, the range easily includes hundreds of thousands of products and brands.

Communication

A retailer has more functional and emotional possibilities through which to communicate the brand than a manufacturer. In addition, these possibilities are more powerful. A retail brand is more multi-sensory than a manufacturer brand. A retailer communicates with the entire store: not only through the choice of merchandise, but with the complete store experience, including the store design, visual merchandising, employees, services and all other store activities. Each store visit is a three-dimensional, multi-sensory brand experience. Compared with this, the possibilities for a manufacturer are limited. To communicate about a product, a manufacturer depends mostly on mass media, and the power of the mass media is less than that of a store. In a store, the retailer is in direct contact with customers.

Control

A retailer controls all its marketing tools. It can determine its range, prices, the location of the store, and decide which products to promote. In contrast a manufacturer depends heavily on the cooperation of the retailer for its marketing strategy. It is the retailer that determines which brands it includes in its range and at what prices it will sell them. And, of course, the retailer also chooses the location in the store where it will display the manufacturer brand, and the way in which it will do that. Only in one respect does the retailer have less control than the manufacturer. A retail brand is mostly created in the store. The experience the consumer has in the store will mostly determine his or her perception of the brand. The retailer then strongly depends on employee performance, and this performance cannot completely be controlled. A manufacturer has much less trouble with this, because the performance of a product can be determined in the factory.

Planning horizon

In order to build up a brand, money, time and patience are needed, but retailers always have the tendency to focus mainly on the short term. The reason for this is probably that they are confronted with consumer reactions every day. When sales are a little bit disappointing, they will consider taking measures to adjust tactics or strategy. Manufacturers, on the other hand, are further away from the consumer. In addition, an adjustment to a product typically takes a lot of time, and therefore manufacturers are mainly more focused on the longer term. A long-term perspective is, in principle, necessary to build up a strong brand.

Local adjustments

A manufacturer is not able to adjust its product to meet local needs; the entire market area gets the same product. A retailer, on the other hand, can adjust its store format to local market conditions when necessary. If the consumer or a competitor demands action, range, prices and service levels can be adjusted accordingly. With these local adjustments, a retail company can strengthen its relationship with its customers.

1.4.4 MONO-BRAND STORES

Clearly there are differences between manufacturers and retailers, but these differences are getting smaller. Retailers are more focused on the production process, and manufacturers sell directly to the consumer through internet or even mono-brand stores they open themselves. Because of the internet, it has become relatively easy for manufacturers to communicate directly with and sell to consumers. Nespresso, the coffee manufacturer, sells its coffee almost entirely through its own website and a few of its own stores. Dell too sells its computers only through the internet. Boss, Levi's, Apple, Nike, Swatch and a number of other manufacturers have opened a large number of their own stores, and L'Oréal recently bought The Body Shop. Retailers become manufacturers when they set up their own production facilities and start selling their private brands via other channels. Starbucks, for example, sells its coffee not only in its own outlets, but also through supermarkets, and even makes special blends for the department store Nordstrom and for United Airlines.

Mono-brand stores often have the primary objective of enlarging the visibility of the manufacturer brand and supporting its brand values. These brand values can be communicated directly to the consumer via the store. The brand experience can therefore be exploited better in a store of its own. Coca-Cola for example is opening Red Lounges where teenagers can relax in comfort, hang out with their friends, socialize and enjoy being entertained with exclusive music, movies and games. Manufacturers' own stores can also add value to the manufacturer brand by exposing the full width of its range. Sports stores, for example, often only stock 5-10 per cent of the entire Nike range. The only way to introduce the entire range to the consumer is by opening an own-brand store. In an own-brand store a brand does not have to fight with other brands to get attention.

The different reasons a manufacturer might have for opening up a mono-brand store can also lead to different types of store in this category.

Flagship stores

The most important reason to open up a flagship store is to make the brand visible and alive. A flagship store is a physical manifestation of the brand identity. In a store of its own, a manufacturer can determine the surroundings of the brand itself. A flagship store is a three-dimensional advertisement for the manufacturer brand, because the consumer walks through the brand, as it were. The store itself is the brand experience.

The flagship store can also be used to develop and support a market. In a flagship store the entire range can be shown, there is direct contact with the target group, and changes in consumer behaviour can be noted straightaway. Flagship stores like Nike Town, the Apple Store in New York, the Ferrari and Armani stores in Milan, the Sony Style store in Berlin and the Volkswagen Autostadt in the German city of Wolfsburg serve mostly as giant advertisements for their brand. The primary objective of this type of store is not to make a profit. In principle, sales and profit are subordinated to communicating the brand identity. Sometimes the interior design of flagship stores is so expensive that they will never make a profit. However, when expenditure needs to be reduced, flagship stores often become the first victims. For that reason, Warner Bros, Coca-Cola and Viacom closed the doors of their flagship stores a few years ago.

Whether people are long-time Mac users or just getting started, the Apple Store is the best place to learn about the Mac. The stores are filled with Apple products, including the entire iPod family, as well as a variety of digital cameras, camcorders, software and accessories. Everything is on display, so customers can test-drive the Mac and experience it for themselves. They can also talk to one of the many Mac specialists who are there to demonstrate products and answer questions. The Apple Stores in New York and London offer over 300 unique educational events every month, covering every aspect of the Mac. Apple even has wireless internet access throughout the store, so customers can 'get connected' from anywhere.

For a flagship store, the aim is usually to find an expensive location, where lots of consumers pass by, so that as many people as possible will be confronted with the brand. After all, the flagship store is a kind of billboard for the brand. Global giant Nestlé for example, opened an immaculate gourmet Nespresso boutique on the most expensive street in Amsterdam, which sells espresso machines and coffees in a space designed as the purest of brand experiences (Retail Week, 2003: 44).

Nespresso's aim is to reposition the brand as an expert at the top of its market. The staff is knowledgeable and enthusiastic and, as Coffee Trainers, they extol the superior taste and quality of the product.

At M&M World in Las Vegas consumers can enjoy everything that the M&M brand has to offer on three floors. They can choose between dozens of colours of M&M candy, but it is not just about candy. There are also T-shirts, mugs, pillows and many other branded products available. Moreover, customers can visit a 3D movie theatre. Together, all of this makes M&M World a really fun place for consumers. To M&M, this store is a wonderful tool to bring the brand alive, and for the consumer it is a wonderful experience during a vacation in Las Vegas.

Now that tobacco advertising is very restricted or even totally forbidden in many countries, a flagship store of its own is one of the very few possible channels through which a tobacco manufacturer can still communicate. For example, in Amsterdam Camel has its own store in one of the busiest areas of town. For a while Lucky Strike also had a store there. In this way many consumers are still confronted with the brand, despite the advertising ban.

Chain stores

A flagship store is mainly a marketing communication tool; a chain of stores is primarily a distribution tool. Under pressure from economic circumstances, the focus of mono-brand stores has been more on the distribution function in the last couple of years. The primary objective is to realize sales and profit. Manufacturers have become retailers in their own right, or have started up franchise operations, in which they combine their marketing knowledge with the retail expertise of franchisers.

The most important reason to set up chain stores is usually that the manufacturer wants to be less dependent on retailers. Because the range in retail outlets keeps getting bigger, individual manufacturer brands have less shelf space. In addition, in the eyes of the manufacturer, a retailer might not pay enough attention to a brand. In the manufacturer's own stores, a brand can be presented in an environment that has been especially designed to communicate its specific brand identity. For that reason Mont Blanc for example, opened its own stores.

A manufacturer like Apple could even be said to be forced to open its own stores. Consumer electronics stores do not, or barely, include Apple computers in their range. Apple's market share is too small to justify stock-holding. Especially when retail sets high demands, manufacturers feel the necessity to look for alternative distribution channels. With their own chain stores, manufacturers can form a counterbalance against retailers that start selling more private brands. However, when exploiting chain stores, a manufacturer soon realizes that running stores is a different profession than running a factory. In addition, a manufacturer can risk its existing distribution and sales relationships when it opens up its own stores. Retailers to which it sells can see the manufacturer's own store as a direct and unwanted threat. Therefore, sales to these retailers become endangered.

Shop-in-the-shops
By giving a shop-in-a-shop concession its own identity, a manufacturer brand can differentiate itself from other brands that are also offered in the store. However, not all stores allow manufacturers to completely design a shop-in-a-shop for themselves. In their cooperation with manufacturers, retailers are searching for the right balance between manufacturer brands and their own retail brand. When a manufacturer draws too much attention to its products, it does not go unnoticed by the retail brand that this will be at the expense of its own brand appeal.

Factory outlets
Manufacturers open up factory outlet stores to get rid of their old or damaged stock. By selling remainders like these in their own stores, they prevent all kinds of cheap shipments, for example parallel imports, appearing on the market uncontrolled. Moreover, these factory outlets strongly attract customers. In many countries shopping centres are being built that pretty much consist only these types of store.

No matter what the retail activities of a manufacturer are, it is certain that in the future manufacturers will sell directly to consumer more: through their own stores, but also via catalogues and websites. However, if a manufacturer only chooses to sell through its own stores, a problem could arise, because the range of these stores could be too specialized to appeal or seem relevant to many consumers. Consumers can only do part of their shopping in manufacturer stores like these. For other products and brands they will have to go elsewhere to multi-brand stores. However when a manufacturer sells its products through its website or catalogue, the limited range on offer will not be a problem most of the time. After all, consumers do not have to go to the store any more: they can order what they need from different companies, from home.

2. BUILDING A BRAND IDENTITY

Every strong brand identity is built on three pillars: a clear, differentiating positioning, a distinct personality and consistent communications. The brand positioning is the mix of functional, tangible attributes that the retail brand has to offer to the consumer (the 'what'). The brand personality describes the characteristics of the retail brand (the 'who') and is strongly emotional. The brand communication informs the consumer through its own look and feel (the 'how') of the positioning and the personality. But the way everything is communicated also has an influence on the brand identity. Together the positioning, the personality and the communication form the retail brand circle. Only if all these three aspects form a consistent and integrated whole can we talk about a strong brand.

2.1 Brand positioning

In order to differentiate a brand from the competition and to create consumer loyalty, a strong brand identity is needed. To build up such a brand identity, a retailer needs more than just a striking advertising campaign. It is not only about what the retailer says, but mainly also about what it does. A strong brand identity has both functional and emotional characteristics, and consists of three connecting instruments:

- a clear, differentiating brand positioning;
- a distinct brand personality;
- consistent brand communications.

These three instruments for building up a brand identity can be found in the retail brand circle. These same instruments are also the basis for a manufacturer brand identity. Their implementation by a retailer, however, strongly differs from that of a manufacturer. The biggest difference is that a retail company can use its stores to build the brand. Because of that, the contact with the consumer is more direct and more intense than it is for a manufacturer. Via a store, the retailer can determine right away what the consumer's desires and needs are, and in its market approach, the retailer can benefit from the store to a maximum.

At the same time, the retailer is also most vulnerable in its stores. After all, every touch-point in the store is a moment of truth for the consumer. This makes retail branding more difficult than product branding. The brand performance and the brand promise will have to be the same. When the performance does not stand up to the promise, the retail brand will directly be affected. So in regard to positioning, a retail brand is very vulnerable. A retail brand is judged by its performance, and everything that takes place in the store can influence the brand identity. A small mistake or failing by the store can affect the entire brand identity. A manufacturer has less direct and less intense contact with its customers, but is also less vulnerable. After all, it has, in principle, complete control over the quality of the product. Therefore the chance that there will be a difference between what its advertising says and what it does is much smaller.

The three rings of the retail brand circle rotate, as it were, around each other. With a certain brand positioning, some brand personalities fit better than others, and the brand positioning mix and the brand personality also call for a specific type of brand communication. Consistency is of the utmost importance: not only in timing, but also between all touch-points of the retail brand.

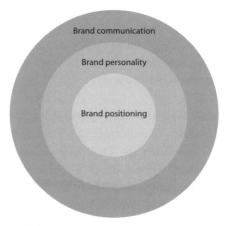

Figure 2.1 The retail brand circle

The inner ring of the retail brand circle consists of the brand positioning. In its positioning, the retailer determines which position it wants the retail brand to have in the consumer's mind in relation to competitor brands. In retailing, positioning is mainly about functional, tangible attributes and the brand performance that goes with those: more so than for manufacturer brands. In a store, the consumer can, as it were, walk through the brand, and more easily than with a manufacturer brand, a consumer can form a positive image about the store's brand proposition before the actual buying takes place. Therefore, the positioning of a retail brand is mainly about the concrete offer (the 'what'): the attributes that can be observed with the senses form the core of every retail brand. This positioning does not have to be unique, but the retail brand will always have to achieve better than the competition. Without strong, functional attributes, a retail brand cannot obtain a mind position and will struggle to be successful. Only stores with a strong positioning will do very well.

The positioning will have to find its counterpart in a matching performance. It is therefore important to have a clear focus in the positioning. There is no store that can be everything for everyone. In order to have a clear positioning, a retailer will have to choose which target group it wants to focus on, and with what attributes it wants to differentiate itself primarily from the competition. Positioning is the basic promise a retailer makes to a target group, and that promise has to be relevant to the target group. The functional, tangible attributes of the positioning will therefore have to match consumers' values, and will have to be translated into consumer benefits. These benefits can be both functional and emotional, and because of them, the consumer's life will become cheaper, easier or more pleasant.

Buying at an outlet of a certain retail brand can also give consumers a good feeling. Buying at a discounter, for example, can give consumers the feeling that they are smart buyers. In the positioning of the retail brand, the retailer may choose to communicate the functional attributes, but the functional or emotional benefits can also be emphasized. Many stores try to position themselves through their range, prices or the convenience they offer the consumer. Consumers' lives can however also be made easier or more pleasant through the store experience if it offers them not only functional but also emotional benefits.

2.2 Brand personality

There are various possibilities when positioning a retail company via functional, tangible attributes, and many retailers stop at this point in their brand building process. However, positioning is only the first step in building up a strong brand identity. A retail brand has to be more than a collection of functional attributes. After the desired positioning has been determined, the brand personality will also have to be formulated. This brand personality is always based on emotional, intangible attributes and benefits, which consumers experience and which should match their values.

The positioning is what you get; the personality is what you feel. When there is a strong, differentiating brand personality, an emotional bond can develop between the consumer and the retail brand. A bond that is based on emotional benefits can have considerably more influence on shopping behaviour and choice of store than functional attributes can. The brand personality can give the brand identity an extra dimension.

The brand personality is the middle ring of the retail brand circle. It is the context in which the brand positioning takes place. The brand personality describes the human characteristics of the store, and the values that the store stands for (the 'who'). It gives the brand a face. That face is of the utmost importance, because consumers base their choice of store not only on a differentiating, functional positioning, but also on a likeable personality; a personality that fits with their (desired) self-image.

It is becoming harder for retail brands to position themselves on range, price, convenience or store experience. The consumer often does not experience many differences between retail brands when looking at functional, tangible positioning. And when there are differences, they will quickly be copied, especially when they are successful. Just as for soft drinks, coffee and other commodities, it is becoming more important for retail brands to profile themselves on an emotional level via their own brand personality. Retail brands that have exactly the same positioning can still have a different brand personality. In the eyes of consumers they will then be different brands. Just as with positioning, the retail company will also have to choose a clear focus for the brand personality. And with the brand personality it will also be impossible to please everyone.

A very distinctive brand personality can further strengthen the positioning, because an emotional bond will develop between the brand and the consumer. Holiday Inn Express for example, hopes to differentiate itself by providing customers with the emotional benefit of feeling like 'a smarter business traveller', and attempts to convey a brand personality that is 'fun', even a bit 'wacky'. For the road warrior whose expense limit has been cut, an opportunity to be 'smarter' and 'fun', not just cheaper, is attractive. Further up the price scale, Westin Hotels & Resorts is trying to differentiate itself from Hilton, Marriott and Sheraton by claiming to offer 'serenity and efficiency'. Among high-end customers, the Four Seasons seeks to distinguish itself by providing what it calls an 'escape from the ordinary' and a personality of 'calm sophistication' (Aufriter et al, 2003).

2.3 Brand communications

The outer ring of the retail brand circle is the brand communication. When the desired brand positioning and brand personality are set, both will have to be communicated. Often, differences between the desired and the perceived positioning and personality will have to be redirected. The consumer has to recognize the promises that are made in the brand positioning, in the content of the brand communications. And the look and feel of the communications will have to reflect the brand personality. But each communication itself also contributes to the total brand identity, because the way in which the retail brand communicates says a lot about that brand. Therefore, it is of the utmost importance that the advertising and direct marketing communications, the store design, the visual merchandising and the employees, all communicate the same consistent message.

Brand communications will have to make the positioning and the brand personality visible both inside and outside the store. Some brand personalities are a better fit with a particular positioning than others. So the mix of positioning and brand personality also asks for aligned communications, not only in advertising and other kinds of out-of-store communications, but especially in in-store communications: the store design, the visual merchandising and the employees. These in-store communications can bring the brand to life by conveying its positioning and personality, and can be used as communication tools to make it clear what the brand promise is.

Communication at the point of sale can be very influential over whether a purchase will take place or not. Many buying decisions are not made until the consumer is in the store. In the past, store design and visual merchandising have not been used enough as strategic weapons because retailers assumed that their range and prices already communicated enough about their brand. However, a retailer can no longer survive with good positioning alone. The chance to differentiate is too small, and in addition, consumers demand more of a store than just good merchandise and good prices. For example, consumers also expect the store to offer all kinds of sensory experiences. Stores that react well to this and offer in-store experiences that the consumer can see, hear, feel, taste and smell strengthen their brand and can ask higher prices than their competitors. That is why Starbucks can charge US$3 or more for a cup of coffee.

The brand identity of a retail company always needs to be based on an integrated whole of a positioning, a personality and communications. Then the brand identity will have both functional and emotional attributes and benefits. These benefits should then match the values and the self-image of the target group. (Figure 2.2)

In general, retailers focus too much on the functional aspects of their brands. Almost all attention goes to creating a differentiated positioning, and the strategic importance of a strong emotional relationship with the consumer is not acknowledged enough. The brand identity is more or less an automatic result of the thinking and doing of the retail company. There are a few exceptions, but in general there is no or hardly any conscious focus on it. In brand communication, almost all attention goes to the functional positioning attributes. There are not many retail brands with their own look and feel for their out-of-store and in-store communications. Because of this, retailers mainly have a functional relationship with their customers. In the future, to become stronger as brands, retailers will have to invest much more in the emotional aspects of their brand.

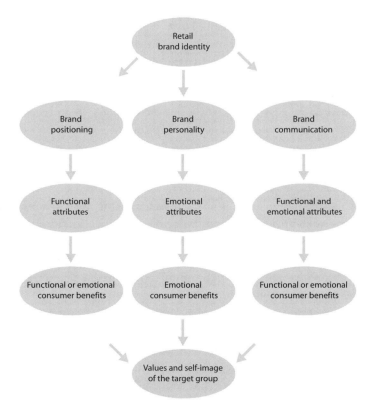

Figure 2.2 Functional and emotional aspects of a retail brand identity

Both brand personality and brand communication can contribute considerably to building a strong retail brand. The brand personality is becoming more important, especially because it is becoming increasingly difficult to create a distinction based on functional positioning attributes. The intangible characteristics of a brand are, after all, much harder to imitate than the tangible positioning attributes. Additionally, through brand communication with its own look and feel, a retail company can stand out in the crowd. The retail brand can become tangible and visible through its store environment, and when consumers feel happy there, they will stay longer. And the longer they will stay, the more they will spend.

Ralph Lauren, for example, has translated the positioning of its Polo/Ralph Lauren and Polo Sport brands successfully in its store designs (Schmitt and Simonson, 1997: 288). The Polo/Ralph Lauren stores have the look, feel and smell of an American country house. They are ornamental/realist, dark and rusty, and full of natural materials. Polo Sport stores in contrast are minimalist and no-frills; bright and clean and full of synthetic materials. The Old Navy clothing stores have a store design that looks like a warehouse. Because of this very basic look, the stores very clearly communicate a message of low prices. And the Virgin stores in England offer a lot of in-store entertainment. To complete the range of options, the stores differentiate themselves from the competitors by offering this entertainment.

Via the store design and the visual merchandising the consumer can, as it were, walk through the brand. Both communication instruments say something not only about the positioning of the retail brand, but also about the brand personality. Only when the brand positioning, brand personality and brand communication match perfectly can a store become a strong brand.

The communication efforts of the Italian clothing group Benetton illustrate the danger of activities that send the wrong message and do not express the brand positioning and brand personality (Joachimsthaler and Aaker, 1999: 13–14). Founded in the 1960s, Benetton began with a coherent identity that conveyed youth, cultural diversity, racial harmony and world peace; and it stayed directed for a long time. Then came the 1984 United Colors of Benetton campaign, which made use of print media, Formula One sponsorship, and intensive in-store communications, including the distribution of one million copies of the customer magazine Colors through more than 5,000 stores worldwide. Initially the campaign was a great success. Sales of Benetton products grew rapidly. Over the years, however, Benetton's art director, the highly creative and talented photographer and artist Olivieri Toscani, developed his own style of advertising, independent of the Benetton brand positioning and personality. He produced images for Benetton's communications campaigns that included a dying AIDS patient, a nun kissing a handsome priest, and a baby's bottom stamped 'HIV positive'. Although very successful at creating publicity and visibility, Toscani's work appeared inconsistent with Benetton's established brand identity, and instead of building the brand and increasing sales, it alienated the target market and Benetton retailers. Benetton became one of the most controversial brands in the world. People did not understand what this kind of advertising had to do with the Benetton clothes. In an official statement Benetton explained itself as follows:

> Benetton believes that it is important for companies to take a stance in the real world instead of using their advertising budget to perpetuate the myth that they can make consumers happy through the mere purchase of their product.

The brand identity describes the brand the way the retailer desires. The brand perception or brand image points out how the target group experiences the brand. The desired brand identity of the retailer and the brand perception of the consumer, therefore, do not have to match. There can be a big difference between what the retailer wants and what the consumer experiences. The brand performance, what the consumer experiences in the store or on the website, often determines the brand perception. Jeff Bezos, CEO of Amazon, once said: 'It has always seemed to me that your brand is formed, primarily, not by what your company says about itself, but by what the company does.' If the brand promise is not proven in the store in any way, the desired brand identity will not be obtained.

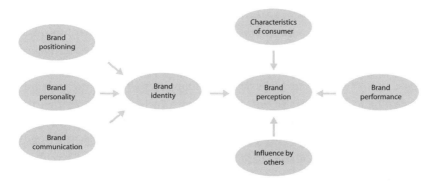

Figure 2.3 Factors that influence the brand perception

Consumers' perception of a retail brand also depend on their own characteristics and interests, and are influenced by others. A consumer, who, for example, has hardly any interest in a certain type of store or has had bad experiences with it in the past, will react differently than someone who has a lot of interest in it and who has had good experiences. The competition and the influence of family, friends and other associates can have a big influence on people's brand perception as well. The perception of a retail brand is brought about in different ways:

A retail company that succeeds in building its own, unique brand identity through the right mix of positioning, personality and communication, and clearly differentiates itself from the competition, has a strong weapon in its hands. The brand identity can influence consumers' buying behaviour. As long as the store experience matches the brand identity, the consumer will come back. The only interference could be other people influencing the consumer's opinion. This could especially be the case with retail brands that have a strong expressive value. With this type of stores, a consumer will take into account the opinions of friends, family and other reference groups.

2.4 Operational excellence

A strong brand can give a retailer a start over the competition. However, that will only be beneficial if the retailer also succeeds in attaining extreme operational excellence in sourcing, warehousing and distribution. Even the strongest retail brands are founded on perfect operational excellence. It is difficult to create a unique positioning and personality, and it is just as difficult to translate this into a day-to-day way of thinking and operating a large organization. A strong retail brand will, however, only exist thanks to operational excellence. Operational excellence provides the tools to keep costs under control and to prove the brand identity. Strong retail brands not only have a differentiating brand identity, but based on their core competences, they are also able to prove the brand promise by displaying operational excellence every day. Good execution determines ultimate success in retail. The instruments of operational excellence are mainly about the following.

Organization
The business culture, the quality of the management, the innovative power and the flexibility of the organization are important factors for the success of a retail brand. And most important are the entrepreneurial spirit and the willingness to react quickly to changes in the market.

Logistics

Smart supply chain management can be an important competitive weapon. By cross-docking and using other logistic systems, Wal-Mart was able to take the lead over its competition. Good logistics can result in lower costs, lower stocks and fewer out-of-stock situations in store. Moreover, quicker reactions to changes in demand are possible, resulting in sales increases, and fewer price reductions will be needed, because there will be less or no outdated stock.

Administrative systems

Good management information systems are indispensable for every retailer. Only then can it monitor brand development. Changes in market position need to be recognized straightaway, and when necessary, the marketing strategy needs to be adjusted quickly. Good administrative systems also enable the retailer to determine the profitability of the various product categories. This information is necessary to obtain good category and space management.

Relationships with suppliers

Finding the right suppliers is essential in developing a differentiating merchandising mix. When a retailer succeeds in finding the best suppliers, exclusive to its own market area, it can very much increase its competitive power. Hema has, for example, built up a very strong position in the underwear segment, because it has an exclusive relationship with an excellent supplier in Israel.

Financing

Financial planning is also an absolutely essential factor for success. The budget has to be sufficient to make the necessary brand investments, and capital is also needed to increase the number of stores.

2.5 Vision, mission and values

Brand positioning, brand personality and brand communications should be founded on a clearly formulated vision, mission and set of corporate values. Only then can a retail brand really be part of the company. The brand identity is then not just 'thought of', but a logical result of the thinking and behaviour of the company. The brand vision shows what part the retail brand wants to play in society, and more specifically, in its sector. It is the outlook on the world and the kind of trade in which the brand operates. The vision is the reason for being. It answers the question of what society would miss if the brand would not exist.

The brand mission voices the assignment the retail brand has formulated for itself, and it is, of course, closely connected to the brand vision on society and the sector. The mission expresses how the brand vision can be accomplished.

The corporate values express what the retail brand considers to be important when conducting business, and how the company wants to deal with consumers, suppliers, employees, shareholders and other stakeholders. These values are, among other things, expressed in the brand personality and the tone and style of the brand communications. Only with a clearly formulated vision, mission and corporate values set can consistency of behaviour and customer experience be obtained.

Brand vision

All successful retail brands have a clear vision. The vision is translated into a differentiating store format. Brand visions that are vague, abstract or uninspiring do not offer guidance to employees in their everyday activities. A vision needs to be short and sharp, and as concrete as possible. It needs to match the values and ambition of the retail brand. At the same time, the vision needs to offer room to react to drastic changes in market relationships. When these criteria are met, the vision can be the driving spirit behind the company's strategy. The vision will then be the starting point for formulating a unique brand identity.

Brand mission

The vision of the retail brand is mainly focused on the outside world. The brand mission on the contrary has an internal focus. It is the concrete assignment the retail company imposes on itself. The brand mission directs all the retailer's strategic choices. It states what (within a certain period of time) needs to be achieved. Therefore, all the company's efforts have a clear focus. The mission is a source of inspiration because all objectives are clear. These objectives can be both qualitative as well as quantitative, but a good mission always inspires employees to pursue common goals.

Here are some examples of the mission statements of well-known retail brands.

Sainsbury's supermarkets

Our mission is to serve customers the best quality and choice to meet their everyday shopping needs. To deliver our mission, and restore profitable growth we are focusing on our four bubbles:

• Outstanding quality and choice in food and then importantly, in other general merchandise products and customer services that make the weekly shop more convenient.

• Delivering great service, serving customers consistently well in all our contacts with them, but especially at checkpoints and in shop floor availability.

• Having competitive costs, implementing our transformation programme to create an efficient business, so we can pass the benefits of lower costs onto our customers in competitive prices.

• Doing all of this 'faster, simpler, together', working as a team to meet the needs of customers and our stores which serve the customer.

Aveda

Our mission at Aveda is to care for the world we live in, from the products we make to the ways in which we give back to society. At Aveda, we strive to set an example for environmental leadership and responsibility, not just in the world of beauty, but around the world.

Starbucks

Establish Starbucks as the premier purveyor of the finest coffee in the world while maintaining our uncompromising principles while we grow. The following six guiding principles will help us measure the appropriateness of our decisions:

• Provide a great work environment and treat each other with respect and dignity.

• Embrace diversity as an essential component in the way we do business.

- Apply the highest standards of excellence to the purchasing, roasting and fresh delivery of our coffee.
- Develop enthusiastically satisfied customers all of the time.
- Contribute positively to our communities and our environment.
- Recognize that profitability is essential to our future success.

Marks & Spencer

To make aspirational quality accessible to all.

Barnes & Noble

At Barnes & Noble, we take our mission seriously to create an inviting experience in our stores:

- For our customers: We work hard to ensure that we offer our customers a special experience each time they connect with Barnes & Noble, whether it is in one of our stores or online. We are committed to providing our customers with a friendly, comfortable environment, helpful and knowledgeable booksellers and the widest selection at the best prices.
- For our authors: We are committed to providing our authors with the best environment in which to showcase their works, and to creating forums in which they can exchange ideas and opinions with the people who matter most: their readers.
- For our booksellers: We strive to create and maintain a fair, professional and diverse work environment in which our people can flourish and grow. Our stores and offices are friendly, supportive places that run our shared love of books and our respect for others.
- For our shareholders: Our management team is an experienced group of executives and professionals who are committed to a strategy of growing our company in ways that build the most value for our shareholders over time.
- For our communities: We consider our communities to be friends and family. They give so much to us. We are committed to giving back to them, through community events, educational activities and programs that put books in the hands of disadvantaged children.

The mission statements of Marks & Spencer and Aveda are short and sharp. Those of Sainsbury's, Starbucks and Barnes & Noble are more extensive. For internal use, they will have to be translated into a number of short, sharp references. Only then will the mission start to mean something to the employees.

Corporate values

The brand personality will have to be consistent with the corporate values. These corporate values are not invented; they are in the genes of the retail company. The corporate values are the essence of the company and they do not change every year. Corporate values are permanent, unchangeable basic principles for everything the retail company thinks and does. They are the basic rules for all company's employees, and drive all decisions. They define the company's business culture, therefore they form the basis of the brand personality, which the retail brand then communicates to the outside world. Corporate values are directives for what is right and wrong. No concessions are made to these basic principles. When the financial situation might not be that positive at a specific time, the corporate values will still stand. Everyone within the company knows that and behaves in that way. Because the corporate values are really part of the core of the retail

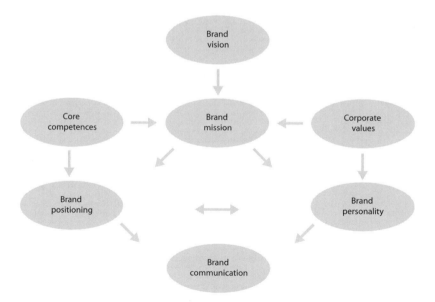

Figure 2.4 Relationship between brand vision, mission, values and branding

brand, there will never be many. Marks & Spencer has, for example, five corporate values: quality, value, service, innovation and trust. All Marks & Spencer's activities are tested against these principles.

The corporate values and the core competences of the company are the framework within which the brand mission is formulated. They are the starting points and rules of the game that need to be taken into account in all choices that are made. The core competences mainly direct the positioning of the retail brand. What the retail brand promises to do better, faster or cheaper than the competition has to match the core competences. The corporate values define the brand personality. The way, in which the retail brand wants to deal with its customers has to correspond with the way in which people within the company deal with each other.

The chosen positioning and personality are expressed to the target group through the brand communications. The way in which the target group reacts to the brand identity will be expressed in the financial results of the retail company.

Part 2
Retail brand positioning

3. POSITIONING THE STORE

A differentiating functional positioning is the foundation for a successful retail brand. If this foundation is not correct, the retail brand will not survive the battle with the competition. A perfect brand personality and brand communications can never compensate for weak positioning. The number of stores a consumer can choose from is too great for there to be any room for error. There are many alternatives to every retail brand. When formulating a differentiating brand positioning, the retailer considers four attributes: range, price, convenience and store experience. The retail brand strives to be better, faster or cheaper regarding all these attributes than the competition. Based on the focus in positioning, a distinction can be made between range brands, price brands, convenience brands and experience brands. Until recently a retailer could afford to focus on only one attribute, and therefore did not pay too much attention to the others. That is not possible any more. Consumers want it all, and they do not want to pay too much money for it either. In the current competitive battle a retailer has to focus on all four positioning attributes.

Every retail brand will have to find its own suitable mix of range, price, convenience and store experience. Within that mix priorities will have to be set. After all, it is impossible to excel in all attributes. Depending on the extent to which a retail brand achieves better than the competition, a distinction can be made between differentiating, supporting, competitive and qualifying attributes.

3.1 Shopping modes

The multi-dimensional consumer buys in different ways. Store choice and buying behaviour depend on the type of product, the time of purchase, the available budget and lots of other factors. For each purchase, the consumer decides where and what to buy. Sometimes that is a well-considered decision, but it can also be an impulse or a routine purchase. It is of utmost importance to a retail company to understand this behaviour and identify the shopping behaviour it primarily wants to target. For a retail brand to formulate its target group and brand identity, it now must consider buying behaviour amongst its most important criteria, along with the traditional criteria like income and age. After all, the same consumer can have different buying behaviour at different moments. For example, he or she might go to the supermarket and almost thoughtlessly fill up the fridge one time, and then the next time do an extensive shop because he or she wants to prepare a special meal that night.

Based on the criteria consumers use when shopping, four different kinds of shopping behaviour can be identified (Retailforward, 2003).

Speedy, low-cost replenishment shopping

This is mainly about routine purchasing of daily necessities. The customer involvement is low for these types of products. They need to be bought easily, quickly and cheaply. Strong manufacturer and retail brands can help make this choice easier. Important criteria for choosing a store, besides the retail brand and low prices, are proximity, parking and shopping convenience, and increasingly, fixed low prices as well. Not having to search through all the promotions from various retail companies saves a lot of time and effort.

One-stop shopping will increasingly define convenience for these efficiency-minded shoppers, who seek to meet more of their everyday household and personal needs on the same shopping trip. The frequency of shopping for these products will decrease and e-commerce will likely be a factor in this as well. Retail brands that focus on this type of shopping behaviour focus on building low-cost, highly efficient delivery mechanisms.

Solution-driven shopping

In this case the consumer is consciously looking for products, services, information and support to solve a problem or to reach a certain goal. Shopping is no longer about individual products, but more about a holistic approach to meeting life's needs. Retail brands that focus on this kind of shopping will have to make sure that their range of stock offers the consumer a complete one-stop solution, because everything consumers need, they will want to buy under one roof. This will necessitate new approaches to marketing and merchandising, in order to package products and services together to provide seamless solutions.

Through building up a good relationship with customers, the retailer can find out what they are involved in and what their desires and needs are. Examples of retail brands that focus on this type of shopping behaviour are, among others, do-it-yourself stores like Gamma and Praxis in the Netherlands, Homebase in England, Hornbach in Germany and Home Depot and Lowe's in the United States. These do-it-yourself stores not only have an enormous range, but also provide advice, installation services and tool hire, as well as truck rental to get purchases home.

Self-expression shopping

This shopping mode reflects the shopper's individuality or provides external validation of a fashion preference or lifestyle perspective. This way of shopping is ego-intensive, emotional and cognitive. It is more about wishes and desires than about necessities. Because the desire for self-expression is very strong, choice criteria like distance and price can become completely irrelevant. On the contrary, a clear focus on a sharply defined lifestyle is essential, and the range has to be a confirmation of this individual lifestyle. But range is not the only important factor for retail brands in this segment; brand personality is as well. This personality has to match the values of the target group. Consumers want to identify with the retail brand they buy from.

The American Abercrombie & Fitch stores, for example, are a real reflection of life at American colleges. The range, the visual merchandising, the salespeople and the catalogues all fit exactly with this lifestyle. The clothes are specifically what young people of that age want to wear. The visual merchandising consists of many pictures with sex appeal. There is hardly any difference between the models in the catalogue and the employees in the store. The employees are the same age and are dressed the same way as the target group. And every season the catalogue gets a lot of publicity, because it always includes a lot of pictures that, in the eyes of prudish Americans, go too far.

Sense of discovery shopping

This type of shopping behaviour has a strongly impulsive nature. In the last few years, consumers have started to shop more purposefully. They want to spend their time and money more efficiently and are not prepared to waste their leisure time on stores that are not worth it. But they are also sensation-seekers who like to be inspired by a unique range or an experiential shopping environment. Sometimes it is simply the thrill of the hunt: finding something one would not normally buy, but that has to be bought, perhaps because of the price.

Consumers that show this kind of behaviour are particularly after pleasant shopping experiences. The shopping experience is almost as important as the merchandise. These consumers are open to innovative ranges of goods and like their senses to be stimulated by everything they discover in the store. Department stores like De Bijenkorf in the Netherlands, Selfridges in the UK and Galeries Lafayette in France are examples of retail brands that focus on this type of shopping behaviour.

Responding to the multi-dimensional consumer mindset will mean harnessing all of the aspects of the retail mix in different ways, to create multiple formats each with a distinctive shopping appeal. The most successful retail brands will carefully engineer a particular shopping proposition. Then they will communicate their positioning in the market by explicitly presenting consumers with a coherent series of visual and experiential clues, emitted by the physical environment, the range strategy, employees, processes, customer communications and other managed touch-points.

3.2 Positioning attributes

When formulating their brand positioning, most retail brands look at the competition and then try to create stronger market position for themselves by doing things better. However, determining the strategy in this way means there is often not enough distinction between the various retail brands. They all try to differentiate themselves through the same positioning attributes. But this achieves no difference in the eyes of the consumer, unless one retail brand is doing considerably better than the others. A retail brand would do better to differentiate itself by offering the consumer unique benefits.

To create a strong retail brand sometimes you need to avoid the beaten track. Home Depot for example has revolutionized the do-it-yourself market in North America. It has created a new market of 'do-it-yourselfers' out of ordinary home owners (Kim and Mauborgne, 1999: 83–86). Home Depot got its original insight into how to revolutionize and expand its market by looking at the existing industries serving home improvement needs. It saw that people had two choices: they could hire contractors, or they could buy tools and materials from a hardware store and do the work themselves. Professional contractors only have one decisive advantage: they have specialized know-how that the home owners lack. So executives at Home Depot made it their mission to bolster the competence and confidence of customers whose expertise in home repair was limited. The company now recruits sales assistants with significant trade experience, often former carpenters or painters. These assistants are trained to walk customers through any project: installing kitchen cabinets, for example, or building a deck. In addition, Home Depot sponsors in-store clinics that teach customers such skills as electrical wiring, carpentry and plumbing.

The flipside is that people choose hardware stores over professional contractors to save money. Most people can do without the features that add cost to the typical hardware store. So Home Depot has eliminated those costly features, employing a self-service warehouse format that lowers overheads and maintenance costs, generates economies of scale in purchasing and minimizes stock-outs. Essentially, Home Depot offers the expertise of professional home contractors at markedly lower prices than hardware stores. By delivering the decisive advantages of the substitute industries, and eliminating or reducing negative factors that held customers back. Home Depot has transformed enormous latent demand for home improvement into real demand.

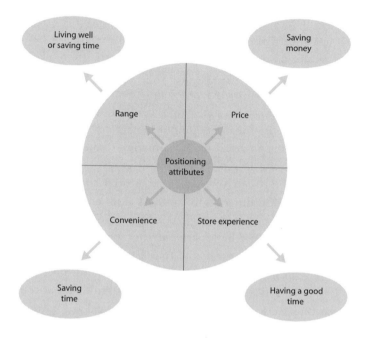

Figure 3.1 Retail positioning attributes and consumer benefits

All consumers have functional and emotional needs when shopping. They want to find the products they are looking for quickly, easily and cost-effectively, but all the while preferably in a pleasant environment. Or perhaps consumers want to buy at a particular store because it contributes to their own identity. All these needs play a role when choosing a store. Depending on the type of consumer, the nature of the product, the shopping mode, the moment, the location and many other factors, either the functional or the emotional need will take the lead. In its positioning, the retail brand has to connect functional attributes not only to functional benefits, but also to emotional ones. The positioning attributes of range, price, convenience and store experience will only be relevant to consumers when they offer them a functional or emotional benefit. The consumer's life will have to become cheaper, easier or more pleasant because of it. Especially in communications, the positioning attributes always have to be translated into specific benefits for the consumer. Only then will there be a relevant connection with the needs of the target group. As the retail market becomes more saturated, the emotional benefits will become more important. Creating a distinction is easier with emotional benefits than with functional benefits.

In retail a distinction can be made between range brands, price brands, convenience brands and experience brands by focusing on different positioning attributes. Brands that have no clear focus and are a little bit of everything to everyone miss clarity in their positioning, and therefore do not give their customers a clear offering.

Range brands

Attractive merchandise is the foundation of every retail brand, but retail brands that want to position themselves as range brands will have to go further. They will have to offer a range of stock that is clearly better than the competition. Category killers like Home Depot, Bed Bath & Beyond, and speciality stores like Foot Locker and Swatch, have such distinctive ranges. Because of the size or the specialization of their range, these retail brands offer the consumer a unique proposition. It is a proposition that Home Depot and Bed Bath & Beyond support by low prices as well. Customers know they will not find a better range anywhere else, especially not at those prices.

Retail brands fulfil not only functional, but also emotional, needs with their range of goods. When consumers save time because they can buy everything they need in one store, then this fulfils the functional need to shop quickly and easily. But the range can also fulfil an emotional benefit of better living for example. Consumers can buy certain products that locate themselves in relation to others, therefore expressing their own identity.

Price brands

Because of economic development, consumers have become more price conscious as well. A good price is at the very least a minimum requirement for every retail brand (with the exception of true up-market stores), just as is a good range of stock. Without the right price a retail brand will not survive, no matter how good the other positioning attributes are. A retail brand that does not offer fair prices just does not qualify in the competitive battle. But retail brands that want to position themselves as price brands have to do more than just offer low prices. After all, every retailer that wants to be successful offers low prices, therefore in the eyes of the consumer there has to be a noticeable price difference from other stores.

Just like the range, price can also offer both functional and emotional benefits. A consumer with not a lot of money to spend will visit a low-price store to make ends meet. On the contrary consumers with a higher income will shop there to give themselves and others the feeling of being a smart shopper. Low-income people need low prices, whereas rich people love low prices.

Convenience brands

Consumers have less time to shop. That is why they are sometimes prepared to pay a little more for daily necessities if it makes life easier. Turning shopping into an easy experience can therefore also be the foundation for a successful positioning. Examples of retail brands that differentiate themselves mainly by the convenience they offer are mail order companies, online retailers, neighbourhood stores and shops at gas stations, but also McDonald's with its easy access, drive-in and quick service. Saving time is a functional need. Convenience can however also be based on excellent service. Easy and pleasant shopping in a store with perfect service provides that emotional benefit.

Experience brands

Although range, price and convenience all offer both functional as well as emotional benefits, the emphasis in the positioning is usually on the functional benefit. The consumer can be pretty objective in determining what the store offers in the way of range, price and convenience, but determining the offer when a retail brand has positioned itself primarily on its store experience is more difficult. Judging the store experience is more subjective, because the customer personally experiences all functional and/or emotional attributes of the retail brand.

A visit to Starbucks does not just mean buying a cup of coffee; it is a total coffee experience. A positioning on experience is therefore the most emotional of the four positioning possibilities. Disney stores and Nike Towns are stores that combine merchandise and store experience. Not only is the particular product important, but so is the emotional shopping environment in which the merchandise is offered. The experience of shopping becomes an entity in itself. Shopping as a way to spend leisure time is then compared with other ways of spending leisure time. That is why Ikea states that it competes more with amusement parks than with other home improvement stores. Ikea's president Anders Dahlvig feels that his stores should be a sort of Disneyland.

The UK department store Selfridges has the objective of creating excitement in its customers, delighting them with an unrivalled shopping experience. Through massive investment across all its stores, Selfridges want to remain at the forefront of shopping entertainment. Every aspect within each store encapsulates the spirit of modern society. As it aims to keep reinventing the meaning of 'leisure time', it becomes necessary to stay absolutely focused on individual customer needs. From its fashion departments to its food halls, Selfridges is a place for everyone. It is a place to relax, a place to be energized and also a place to shop. The result is an invigorating, inspiring and addictive bond to the retail encounter it offers. Selfridges is the definitive shopping destination, demonstrating that shopping is about entertainment, inspiration and fun.

The chosen positioning attribute directly influences the required operational excellence. Depending on the chosen positioning, there will have to be a corresponding emphasis in operations. Range brands make higher demands on the purchasing and logistic processes. With these types of retail brands, purchasing is key. After all, having the right products is the foundation of the positioning. However, logistics are of utmost importance as well. The purchased products will have to be in the store on time. Out-of-stock situations are especially fatal for range brands. As for price brands, the operations emphasis will mainly be on costs, as low prices are only possible if costs are low as well. With convenience brands the employees and logistics are the most important operational factors. Both determine the convenience the retail brand can offer the consumer. And finally experience brands will focus mainly on store atmosphere in their operations.

3.2.1 MIX OF ATTRIBUTES

There has to be a clear focus on one attribute in the positioning. A retail brand cannot excel in all attributes. It cannot be all things to all people. That is unaffordable, plus consumers will not know what the retail brand really stands for. They must be able to directly associate the retail brand with one attribute, otherwise the image will be way too diffuse. Focusing on one attribute, however, does not mean the retailer can ignore the other positioning attributes. In retail it is no longer either/or: consumers are too demanding for that and the competition is too strong.

Their enormous range of stock is the power behind Amazon. Amazon's objective is to have the earth's biggest selection. Amazon wants to build a place where people can find and discover anything they want to buy online. It does this using its own range, but also through links to third-party sellers. Initially the range consisted only of books, but nowadays it also offers, among other things, music, video games and software, electronics, toys, tools, housewares, magazines, office products, apparel, accessories, gourmet food, jewellery, personal care products and musical instruments.

The large range, however, is not the only pillar on which Amazon's positioning strategy is built. Convenience and low prices also contribute a lot to its success. The starting point for a convenience proposition is with the customer, then you work backwards. So working from the idea of customer convenience, Amazon enables its consumers to research books online using its website, pick up their orders at a branch of Borders, Circuit City or Office Depot, or choose an accelerated delivery service.

Of course a lot of attention is paid to the accessibility and simplicity of the site. Amazon states, 'If you have to contact us, it is not convenient.' The price proposition is determined by, among other things, offering exclusive products like diamond rings at low prices, but also by free shipping and agreements with third parties. By relentlessly expanding its range and convenience while at the same time lowering prices, Amazon scores strong ratings in customer satisfaction research.

Focusing on one attribute does not mean no attention is paid to the other positioning attributes. Every retail positioning is always a mix of range, price, convenience and store experience. Consumers want it all, and want it now. They want more for less: more choice of stock, more convenience and more experience for lower prices, less risk, less time and less effort. In the current competitive battle, a retail brand just cannot afford to forget one of these four attributes. After all, the consumer's store loyalty ends when another retail brand appears with a better proposition. Even a retail brand that scores extremely well on one attribute will be forced to work on the other positioning attributes as well.

The extent to which a retail company succeeds in choosing the right mix of the four interrelated positioning attributes, and translating these into benefits for the consumer, determines its success. Not all attributes can be equally important, and not all attributes have equally relevant benefits for the target group. But the battle for the consumer is huge. Nowadays offering a fair price is simply the cost of entry for every retail brand. Consumers are much more aware of prices than they used to be, and are no longer prepared to pay too much. But the fiercer the price competition and the lower the margins, the more important it will be to pay attention to other positioning attributes. A fantastic range of stock, a very accessible store or a surprising store experience can make the retail brand less dependent on price. Therefore retail brands that in the past may have primarily positioned themselves on price might no longer do so. Real customer loyalty is almost never attained through low prices alone. More is needed than that. With respect to the other positioning attributes too, a price brand will have to meet certain minimum requirements. The success of Aldi for example is not only based on low prices, especially in Germany. Convenience, through its presence on every street corner, plays an important role as well. Half of all German consumers have an Aldi within a kilometre of them.

A retail brand has to determine how to position itself in relation to its competition on range, price, convenience and store experience. And it is the way in which these four positioning attributes are combined that makes a retail brand unique. This unique mix, the consumer benefits it offers, plus strong operational excellence together form the foundation of a successful retail brand. Within this mix of attributes, clear decisions have to be made between important and less important attributes. In this field a distinction can be made between four levels of importance. (Note: in their excellent book *The Myth of Excellence* (2001), Fred Crawford and Ryan Mathews are the first to make a distinction between three levels of positioning attributes: dominate, differentiate and operate at par. We prefer to talk about four levels, because we believe it is also possible for a retailer to score a little lower than the competition, but still be acceptable to the consumer. In addition, we use other vocabulary in order to point out that, with a strong retail brand, the supporting attribute is clearly in line with the most important differentiating attribute.)

Differentiating attribute

A retail brand can only be successful if, in the eyes of the consumer, it rises far above the competition in one positioning attribute. The retailer has to determine which positioning attribute will be its differentiating one. Then that will be the attribute focused on in the marketing strategy. In the first instance, the consumer has to associate this attribute with the retail brand, as it is the foundation for the positioning. The differentiating attribute directs the entire organization and business culture. It is an important and relevant attribute to the target group, which can tip the scales when it comes to store choice. A high score on this attribute turns a store into a destination store. Consumers are prepared to drive a couple of kilometres extra just to visit it. After all, they know that no other retail brand performs as well on this attribute.

Supporting attribute

To really be able to achieve a strong competitive position, other attributes have to complete the differentiating attribute. The supporting attribute then becomes the most important complementary one. The supporting attribute gives the consumer an extra reason to choose that retail brand. The retail brand implements this attribute better than the competition does. However a supporting attribute on its own is not strong enough as a foundation for positioning. The difference from the competition is too small for that, in the eyes of the target group. Nevertheless, a supporting attribute can and must strengthen the chosen positioning. It should also naturally follow the differentiating attribute as much as possible. For example, the price positioning of

Wal-Mart is completed by its strong range. And the positioning of Zara, which is primarily based on a very up-to-date, fashionable range of merchandise, is completed by very low prices.

Competitive attribute

With the competitive attribute, a retail brand positions itself in relation to its competition. Often a retail brand will only score about the same as other stores for this attribute. However, a competitive attribute is still more or less a minimum requirement to be successful. A retail brand that scores high on price, for example, will be able to afford to pay less attention to the store experience. The consumer will accept that low prices compensate for possible inconvenience in the store. Even better, a basic store experience actually contributes to the perception of low prices.

Qualifying attribute

In some cases the retail brand can afford to achieve less than the competition. That will particularly be fine if the attribute is less relevant to the target group or the low score is more than compensated for by the score on other attributes. The retail brand need only make sure that, with regard to this attribute, certain minimum requirements are met. If the retail brand does not succeed in that, consumers will not visit the store. What those minimum requirements are depends particularly on the way in which the attribute is offered by other retail brands. The other retail brands act as references to the consumer, to which the retail brand in question is compared.

The differentiating attribute is most important for the positioning of the retail brand. After all, this attribute differentiates the retail brand the most from the competition. The supporting attribute can strengthen the positioning even further. The competitive and qualifying attributes are not unimportant, but they do not contribute, or barely contribute, to the positioning. They are rather minimum requirements. The relative importance of the various attributes to the positioning can be illustrated as in Figure 3.2.

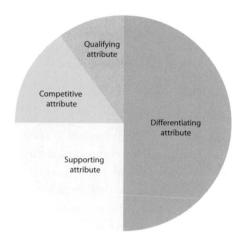

Figure 3.2 Importance of attributes for the positioning

The four different levels at which the positioning attributes can be implemented form, as it were, a sliding scale in the consumer's mind: from acceptable in comparison to the competition to much better than the competition.

Implementation of positioning attributes	Positioning versus competition
Differentiating	Much better than competition
Supporting	Somewhat better than competition
Competitive	About as good as competition
Qualifying	Acceptable versus competition

Table 3.1 Implementation of positioning attributes

How the positioning mix is ultimately made up depends, among other things, on the needs and wants of the target group, the core competencies of the retail brand and the positioning of the competition. Not every positioning is possible, and not every possible positioning is equally relevant to the target group. But whatever the positioning is, the ultimate choice has a lot of consequences for the actions and decisions of the retail brand. And only if the entire organization rallies behind the positioning mix will the brand promise be proven. In the future the demands consumers make on the retail brand will only increase. An attribute that is currently qualifying will perhaps become competitive in the future, and an attribute that is currently competitive might have to become supportive.

Table 3.2 shows positioning mix for a number of well-known retail brands.

Retail Brand	Differentiating	Supporting	Competitive	Qualifying
Wal-mart	Price	Range	Convenience	Experience
Zara	Range	Price	Experience	Convenience
Starbucks	Experience	Range	Convenience	Price
Dollar General	Price	Convenience	Range	Experience
Nordstrom	Convenience	Range	Experience	Price
Mcdonald's	Convenience	Price	Experience	Range
Disney Store	Experience	Range	Convenience	Price

Table 3.2 Positioning mix of some retail brands

Wal-Mart and Dollar General both position themselves primarily on price. However, the remainder of the positioning mix is different. At Wal-Mart the enormous range is a clear supporting attribute. Consumers buy at Wal-Mart not only because of the low prices, but also because they can buy everything under one roof. At Dollar General the emphasis, after price, is mainly on convenience. Location and store interior contribute to make everything as easy as possible for the customer, a positioning that is strengthened by the small range of stock.

Starbucks and Disney Store both have store experience as their differentiating attribute. However, this experience is implemented in a different way by the two brands. Starbucks is a real indulgence store, whereas the Disney Store is mainly about the entertainment it creates. The experience both retail brands offer is directly reflected in the range. Starbucks offers a large variety of delicious coffees, and at the Disney Store the range of various well-known character products supports the experience. Because the experience and the range of these two brands are so different from other stores, the price is of less importance.

Nordstrom and McDonald's both position themselves first and foremost on convenience. The implementation of this positioning attribute, however, is again completely different for the two retail brands. Nordstrom differentiates itself from the competition by offering excellent service to make shopping as easy as possible. This perfect service really contributes to making a visit to a Nordstrom department store an experience. The price is then of less importance. McDonald's makes sure it has a restaurant everywhere that people can get hungry. Combined with low prices this enables McDonald's to stand apart from the competition.

3.3 Positioning and shopping modes

Retail brands that want to cater to low-cost replenishment shopping should position themselves as a price or convenience brand. Price brands try to differentiate themselves from the competition with rational arguments. The stores have a sober look and in advertisements their own prices are often compared with those of the competition. As for the range, a distinction can be made between price brands that sell food and other daily necessities, and price brands that sell durable goods. In the first category are, among other things, supermarkets and drugstores, and in the second category are clothing stores, for example. Price brands in the first category cater to speedy low-cost replenishment shopping. But besides price, convenience is also important. After all, this is about routine products that consumers need every day. A consumer who chooses a low-price store to buy these daily products is prepared to make concessions on other attributes in favour of low prices. There are however limits. A certain extent of convenience when shopping will be taken for granted by most consumers: convenience regarding location, parking, width of the aisles and waiting time at the checkout, for example. For price brands that sell durable goods, convenience will be of less importance, because consumers visit this type of store less frequently. The few times that they do so, however, they will be prepared to make more concessions in this area.

Convenience brands also cater to speedy low-cost replenishment shopping. This type of shopping can be made easier for the consumer if the retailer already applies some kind of preselection to the range. If the number of alternatives is limited, it will be easier for the consumer to choose. This will also be the case if the merchandise is presented clearly. But a positioning on convenience does not only make demands on range and visual merchandising: everything that makes purchasing easier for the consumer can be the foundation for a positioning on convenience. Home delivery, installing computers after purchase and offering after-sales service are examples of that. Lots of e-commerce retailers position themselves on convenience as well as price.

Retail brands that implement their convenience positioning by offering an excellent service focus not just on speedy low-cost replenishment shopping, but also on solution-driven shopping. They do everything to meet the customer's needs and wants with their service.

Catering to solution-driven shopping asks for a positioning based on range or convenience. To solve a problem or meet a need, consumers often need a mix of products, services, information and support, and they would prefer to get all this in one store. So the merchandise and visual merchandising together need to solve a problem for the consumer. Products and services that belong together should therefore be presented together. That is why in do-it-yourself stores for example, entire bathrooms and kitchens are presented. Everything the consumer needs to build such a bathroom or kitchen can be found together. Dominance in merchandise is the most important means of differentiation in this type of store.

Retail brands that want to cater to self-expression or discovery shopping will use their range or store experience as their main differentiating attribute. Retail brands that focus mainly on self-expression shopping will have to make sure that their range and store experience are a confirmation of a sharply defined lifestyle. For discovery shopping however it is mainly about constantly surprising the consumer. The range and store experience have to encourage new reactions every time.

So the relevance of different positioning attributes strongly depends on the type of shopping trip. There is a big difference between retail brands that want to cater to low-cost replenishment or discovery shopping, and brands that focus on self-expression or discovery shopping. These last two are much more emotional. They are driven by desires instead of needs. Creating the right store experience then becomes at least as important as offering the right merchandise.

Shopping mode	Responding positioning attribute
Speedy low-cost replenishment shopping	Price or convenience
Solution-driven shopping	Range or convenience
Self-expression shopping	Range or store experience
Sense of discovery shopping	Range or store experience

Table 3.3 Shopping modes and positioning attributes

3.4 Retail positioning requirements

To be able to meet the demands of a particular shopping mode, a retail brand has to make clear choices. Commodities, solutions, speciality goods and experiences have to be offered through various retail formats. Because the positioning of every retail brand is always a mix of important and less important attributes, there are often lots of variations in practice. The chosen positioning however, will always have to meet a couple of requirements.

Specific shopping mode
The positioning of a store should cater to a specific shopping mode. It is almost impossible for a retail brand to cover multiple shopping modes with one store format. Every shopping mode asks for a specifically tailored positioning and store format. Ahold, for example, has four different supermarket formats in the Netherlands: conventional supermarkets, superstores, contemporary convenience stores and a home delivery service. Each store format suits the needs of a specific customer at a certain time and place.

Clear focus
No store can be everything to everybody. Trying to be all things to all people, it will end up being nothing to anyone. Without losing sight of other attributes, each brand has to choose what it wants to be best at. In the mind of the target consumer, the retail brand should be associated with one (specified) attribute, like Aldi with price and Nordstrom with service. Even Wal-Mart, the most successful retailer in the world, does not excel in all four positioning attributes. A retail brand that does not choose a clear target group and positioning attribute will therefore

come across as unclear to consumers as well. It will not achieve a strong mind position and the consumer will not know what the brand is offering.

Link with vision, mission and values
The chosen positioning has to be proven. Consequently the positioning has to match the core competencies of the retail brand. A strong retail brand will have a positioning that originates in the history and/or unique capabilities of that company. Every strong retail brand has a vision, a mission and values that are truly understood and lived by everyone who is working for the brand. Especially in retail it is of the utmost importance that every employee is completely familiar with them. Without a common starting point it will be hard for a store to present itself clearly to the customer.

Distinctive compared with the competition
Differentiation is the key to brand success. A retail brand that does not differentiate itself, or no longer differentiates itself, from other brands will fade away. A decline in differentiation is a clear signal that there is something fundamentally wrong with the brand. A retail brand has to stand for something. In the eyes of the consumer it has to be better, quicker or cheaper than the competition. Without being entirely unique, a brand promise and brand performance can still be superior to the competition. A retail brand needs to make it really difficult for any of the competition to choose a similar positioning. An attempt to compete with Wal-Mart on price probably does not make sense. Kmart tried and failed.

Relevance to target group
Not every consumer group will be of equal interest to a retail brand. Choosing the right target group is therefore of the utmost importance. The positioning should be relevant and inspiring to this target group. They should get the feeling that the retail brand is there especially for them. The answer to the question how upset consumers would be if the store no longer existed is enlightening in this respect. Unfortunately, for many retail brands, the answer is that consumers would not care if the store disappeared.

In order to be relevant, good insight into the needs and wants of the target group is essential. For example, Petco, a leading speciality retailer of premium pet food supplies and services in the United States, understands that its customers are pet lovers, not just pet owners. Their customers view their pets as members of the family and believe they deserve the same level of care and comfort. So Petco invites its customers to shop at their stores with their pets. This makes purchasing the right product easier and a lot more fun.

Some retail companies have multiple target groups. Home Depot includes not only do-it-yourselfers ('home perfectors') in its primary target group, but also small and medium-sized professionals. These professionals have different demands from do-it-yourselfers. To them, among the most important things are a dedicated account manager, flexible ordering and delivery options, a greater depth in certain product categories and a professional shopping environment. To a regular consumer these are less important. Therefore different aspects have to be emphasized in the positioning to appeal to both target groups. However, this is something that does not cause any problems for Home Depot, because the communication channels to both target groups are largely separate.

Keeping the promise
The brand promise needs to be delivered via the store performance. Every positioning depends on the in-store performance. If the positioning is not proven at all touch-points, consumers will disappointedly turn their back on the store and will not come back. After all, there are always other stores. In determining the desired positioning it is therefore of the utmost importance to make sure that the chosen direction can be achieved.

Keeping up with the consumer
The retail industry changes constantly. Retail brands disappear because they are no longer relevant to the consumer or have become completely interchangeable with the competition. Established retail brands must innovate to stay current. Many successful retail brands are real innovators. They can conquer the market by changing the rules of that market.

Just like products, retail formats have a lifecycle. This lifecycle is becoming shorter because consumer behaviour is changing more rapidly. Today's retail innovations become tomorrow's clones. Within a short period of time, striking new retail concepts become well-known everywhere and are then quickly copied. Nowadays a retail format has a lifecycle of about four to five years. To lengthen this lifecycle, the store concept continuously needs to be refreshed, revitalized or reinvented.

Even Wal-Mart adjusts its format again and again. For example, now it is working on cleaning up its stores and adding upscale products like fashionable clothes and organic fruit and vegetables. The positioning needs to keep up with changing consumer behaviour, but remain recognizable over time. B&Q, the number one home improvement retailer in Europe and third largest in the world, positioned itself in the beginning as the affordable and accessible do-it-yourself store. But because of the increasing customer desire to live in a personalized, fashionable environment, the proposition needed to evolve to more: helping people make their homes better. At the same time however, B&Q wanted to retain its core brand values: cost-effective, honest and trustworthy, and innovative.

Recognizable and memorable

A retail brand is not what the retailer says it is. It is what the target group thinks and feels it is. It is their perception of the brand. There can be a big difference between the desired positioning and the brand perception. Perhaps the marketing strategy specifies how exactly the retail brand's positioning differs from that of the competition, but if the positioning is not credible or the target group does not recognize the brand promise and therefore does not realize how the store differs from the competition, a retail brand will have little chance of being successful. The marketing strategy will then be nothing more than a piece of paper.

Consistency

Building up a strong brand takes time. The chosen positioning has to be carried out consistently in all aspects of the business. Without consistency there will not be recognition. All the signals the consumer receives will have to communicate the same brand message. The brand positioning, the brand personality and the brand communications all have to connect seamlessly. And throughout time the brand has to be consistent in what it is. All customer experiences with the brand and all touch-points should reflect the positioning. The promise made in the out-of-store communications should be proven in-store. Consistency and coherency are essential.

When the Gap deviated too much in its range from the clothing it had become known for, it lost a large number of customers. It was not until it returned to its core range that it was able to regain lost territory.

Profitability

A positioning is really only interesting to a retailer if the financial results are also satisfying. The positioning should have market value. The positioning has to be interesting to a target group that has sufficient sales potential. A niche positioning can only be successful if the store covers a large market area. As a retail brand focuses on a smaller market segment in its positioning, the market area has to become bigger. Very specialized stores are therefore only usually found in locations that cover a very large market area.

A retail brand should regularly check if its positioning is still meeting all these requirements. It has to make sure that it consistently overdelivers on its positioning. The flexibility to continually adjust to changing market conditions is indispensable. Some retail brands go to great lengths with this flexibility, especially in Japan and London, where there is a rise of the 'flatpack label' and the 'keyboard brand' (Hancock, 2002: 45).

The notion of the 'flatpack label' is a simple one: a shop or brand that changes with the needs of the market appears and then disappears when appropriate. It works much like a film or theatre production in that a cast of players (designers, sales executives and marketeers) are assembled, a venue is booked and the 'show' or label is 'opened'. When it comes to the end of its run, the production (label) is flatpacked down, and another label opens in the same venue. In Tokyo for example, there was a great store a few years ago called Cleaning, which used laundromat iconography. It was open for about 18 months and then disappeared.

The company that owned the store then opened something else in the same location, but this time with four different labels.

Japanese department stores have a similar pace of change. Seibu, Marui and Parco are flexible spaces, where the layout is changed and swapped around every weekend. The Vacant store also looks a little like a theatre production. Vacant is the original travelling guerrilla retail concept and exhibition store, opening for one month only in an empty space in major cities including New York, London, Tokyo, Shanghai, Paris, Berlin, Stockholm and Los Angeles. The Vacant store showcases an exclusive range of one-off, hard to find and strictly limited edition products, from major brands to emerging designers. Not until right before the opening will the location be announced. This happens via private invitations that are emailed only to members of the Vacant Club. This emphasizes the feeling of exclusivity even more. As soon as too many people discover where the Vacant store is located, the doors are closed and the store is moved to its next location. Vacant is not just a store: it is an experience.

The Commes des Garçons Guerrilla Store in Berlin was the first example of provisional retailing by an established fashion house. The store, which was opened in spring 2004, was planned to close in one year, even if it was making money. Instead of spending millions to build or renovate a building, Comme des Garçons spent just US$2,500 to fix up a former bookshop in the historic Mitte district. Because the company did not plan to stay long in the 700 sq ft space, it did not even bother to remove the name of the previous tenant from the windows. Advertising consisted of 600 posters placed around the city, and word of mouth. Of course, it helped to have a story about the venture appear on the front page of the *New York Times*. This new store, whose monthly rent was US$700, provided Commes des Garçons with an inexpensive solution to channel avant-garde pieces from the catwalk, sell off clothes from past seasons and reduce inventory. As the sheer glut of information clogs up the sensory channels, making traditional news media less effective, the way in which a product is sold can help break through the clutter. All 20 stores the company plans to open within the next year will adopt the same guerrilla strategy, disappearing after only a year (www.bookofjoe.com, 10 March 2004).

3.5 Creating disruption

Disruption began in the early 1990s. The method was initially developed by the advertising agency TBWA\. (Most of this paragraph is a summary of *Beyond Disruption*, 2002, a collaborative book by Jean-Marie Dru and his TBWA business partners.) It was designed to help produce more intrusive advertising strategies, and to give brands more substance and weight, by making a clean break from the status quo, and creating a 'disruption'.

Disruption soon proved to cover much more than just advertising. It turned out to be relevant for business in general. It gradually evolved into a way of thinking that encouraged companies to create and manage change at all levels in their organizations. The original source of inspiration came from the success stories of retail and other businesses that had achieved exponential brand growth in an established, yet stagnant, climate. TBWA\ discovered that all these cases shared certain characteristics. They all overturned convention in some way, by means of product or format innovation, marketing stance and/or advertising. Disruption was thus designed as a means of questioning the established order, of challenging tried-and-true approaches. By challenging the way things are done, by developing new hypotheses and unexpected scenarios, by searching for unprecedented angles of attack, visions can be created that represent a distinctive point of view; visions that have the power to transform markets.

Successful retail brands run the risk of becoming stagnant champions. Retail brands that do not continuously stay in tune with changes in the marketplace run the risk of losing their unique position. Constant innovation is needed, as new retail brands often change the rules in the marketplace. These newcomers reframe, restage and reshape the retail market, by rejecting the obvious. These disruptive ideas are at the core of many success stories. Disruption is based on the premise that fresh ideas can be generated through the systematic challenging of conventional beliefs and patterns of behaviour. As a business practice, disruption pays off when these fresh ideas force audiences to positively reassess a company's offering.

The notion that the customer is always right is probably as old as marketing itself. Today, customers are not only right, they are heroes.

This is conventional wisdom, and it is inherently limiting. To think about why, we might recall Henry Ford's remark, 'If I had asked the public what they wanted, they would have asked for a faster horse.' Today's equivalent might be, 'If I had asked the public how they wanted their coffee, I doubt that they would have requested a double short caramel skim cappuccino.' Heroic business ideas rarely come from letting the customer make all the decisions. Most people cannot tell you what they want, and when they try to do so, they base their decisions on logic, familiarity and past experience. Of course, there can be little argument that businesses need to treat their customers with respect and gain their input. But the real challenge is for the company to generate original ideas, so that it can be seen as a hero in the customer's eyes, rather than the other way around. A retail brand cannot surprise people with something they asked for in the first place. And it is hard to truly delight people by giving them what they expect. Leadership brands are customer-informed, but they are idea-led.

By recognizing and acting upon the following seven disruption triggers, retail champion brands can navigate the ever-changing retail landscape. When confronted with these challenges, champion brands should look to be guided by the ideals of the ingenuity and entrepreneurial thinking upon which their company was originally founded, and the challenger conventions that can help foster successful disruption.

The retail brand is no longer setting the sector values

This is a good indication that the retail brand has crossed the line and is now embracing conventions that inhibit disruption. This was certainly the situation that many traditional furniture stores found themselves facing in the 1980s and 1990s, when Ikea introduced the self-service concept in this market. Within a few years Ikea was setting new sector values. Consumers did not have to wait weeks or even months for their new furniture to arrive, but could take it home immediately.

The retail brand is relying more heavily on deals and promotions

This could mean the retail brand has assimilated centrist sector values, rendering attempts at differentiation internally unpalatable. As a result, today we are seeing an acceleration of commoditization in many not yet mature retail sectors, where deal has replaced differentiation. In many sectors all stores look the same. This type of environment can create opportunities for challenger brands that embrace disruptive conventions. In the United States and numerous other countries, supermarkets compete heavily with each other using all kinds of promotion. Profitability is under pressure. Organic supermarket brand Whole Foods proves the success of a different route: not price but range is its differentiating attribute.

The retail brand feels invincible

Failure to recognize changing marketplace dynamics along with potential new customers will make the retail brand vulnerable. Many department stores have been forced to shut their doors after not having responded sufficiently to changing consumer behaviour and the rise of specialist stores. Facing the challenges head-on will be vital in securing the brand's position within the marketplace. In particular market leaders often find it difficult to respond to a changing environment in a flexible way.

The competitive set changes

This is a signal that conventions have probably changed as well. The fashion retail industry has changed dramatically since the rise of brands like Zara, H&M and Mango. The industry was used to a few collections per season. The 'new kids on the block' however showed the possibility of launching a new collection every two weeks. Many 'old-fashioned' fashion retailers discovered this too late.

The customer base begins to look different

This could include such things like the brand's marketing message being in danger of losing relevance. The success of a retail brand can often be directly attributed to its astute, disruptive decision to market to previously undervalued consumer segments. Seniors represent a growing and affluent consumer segment. Most retail brands however still focus on young consumers. Stores that focus on the undervalued older consumer segment have enormous potential.

The customer base fails to look different

This could signal a failure to capitalize on demographic or societal trends. When entrepreneur Ray Kroc started the US quick-service restaurant business, his success in establishing McDonald's was aided by the growing mobility of the US population and recognition of baby-boomer buying clout. Overall industry growth in the 1970s and 1980s was fuelled by the seemingly endless supply of 18 to 34-year-olds, the core users of these fast food restaurants. Since the early 1990s, one of the few brands to achieve significant same-store sales growth is entrepreneurial Wendy's, which has recognized the lucrative opportunity beyond the 18-to-34 demographic. By using its mature founder, Dave Thomas, in advertising to appeal to an older demographic, Wendy's has been able to achieve gains in both frequency and size of average spend.

The brand cannot articulate a clear vision for its business

This situation manifests itself in many ways, both internally and externally, and can consequently not only damage the brand's performance, but lead to a malaise that starts from the inside and works its way out. This often results in confusion and alienation among employees, which leads to centrist and counterintuitive behaviour in the absence of any clear direction. Brands without a vision have probably already ignored at least one of the previous disruption triggers as they drift in the marketplace. With luck, there will still be time for them to embrace values and find their vision through disruption.

Disruptive retail companies bring a genuinely new perspective to the way business is conducted, which is often disturbing for competitors. The industry map changes irrevocably and competitors struggle in the newly created framework. Whether the disruption lies at the core of the retail company or occurs after the birth of the organization, these disruptive companies generally hold the same beliefs and goals over the long term, giving both internal and external participants a sense of trust, confidence, pride and continuity. All these disruptive companies are in love with being different, but not necessarily in love with change. Disruptive retail companies are focused on changing how things work, not primarily on changing themselves. Their disruptive approach can come from anywhere, but usually arises from observation of the outside world, not from self-referenced analysis.

Key characteristics of disruptive organizations

Disruptive organizations often have a childlike talent for expressing the vision of the brand in a clear, simple way. When Mark Constantine started Lush, the purveyor of fresh, hand-made cosmetics, he visualized himself not as a supplier of youth fantasies and over-packaged luxury goods, as many cosmetic brands probably see themselves, but as a grocer, a self-appointed cosmetics grocer with a company culture and values more often associated with the food world than with the world of cosmetics. This overall vision of himself and the business he was in was highly disruptive, and guided the total development of the company and the Lush brand. Grocers have a personal relationship with their customers. They sell only fresh, natural products by the pound. This disruptive strategy pervades the attitude and the tone of voice that radiates from the company: no nonsense (a grocer talks about the weather and asks how the kids are doing rather than holding philosophical debates or selling jargon) and a sense of humour; elements dramatically absent from the conventional cosmetics world. By employing the grocer metaphor and references from this other world, Mark Constantine does not just bring a new marketing idea and positioning to his brand, he creates an inspiring yet very explicit message for his staff, and communicates his strategy and vision in just one word. Now, this is fresh.

Second, disruptive organizations thrive on doing, not lecturing. And they do it close to the ground, in action, not simply at the level of vision. All these companies have a combination of passion and pragmatism and a strong emphasis on providing tangible evidence of the company's disruptive approach, offering all constituents proof that something radical is going on. This proof is not provided by the management, but by the frontliners, the sales staff: the most visible people.

An empowering approach was used in the United States by Nordstrom, which recruited staff not on the basis of their sales expertise but on their personal ability to take on responsibilities and run a business within the business. Nordstrom broke many of the conventions ruling the world of department stores, such as that of territory-based jobs, whereby you sell socks or you sell ties, but not both. The overall theme crafted by Nordstrom was that the store should be operated more like a home, in which staff would be hosts. As a host in your own home, you welcome guests (not customers), make them feel comfortable, and try to find out whether they need anything. This metaphor of the host at home conveys the high expectations that Nordstrom has of its sales staff, both tangible and emotional. It also ensures that the company has a guaranteed critical mass of personnel, a prerequisite for the success of such a disruptive programme.

Finally, because disrupters look at things from the outside in, these organizations share a radical view of their place in the bigger world which redefines the nature of their interaction with partners, suppliers and users. Having understood that the new customers will soon be asking for a new type of interface from the organizations they deal with, some businesses have already disrupted the conventions of the customer relationship. With any database marketing activity comes the concern that the organization will know things about customers that they do not want known and cannot fully control. Dell took the concept of co-production and applied it to its customer relationship marketing. Any Dell customer has full access to the total history of his or her interaction with Dell: the time and contact name of the last call to the help desk, the status of a brochure request, and so on. This new form of contract between the organization and its customers is disruptive news for most of the business world, which still operates by a logic wherein they handle the customer and not the other way around.

Some retailers may find it difficult and even risky to challenge these conventions. But those that do and succeed will change the marketplace forever and force others to adapt to their 'new rules'.

4. POSITIONING ON RANGE

The range of stock is the foundation of every retail positioning. For range brands the merchandise is the most important positioning attribute. Depending on the merchandise mix a distinction can be made between:

- merchandise brands, which offer a range that cannot be bought elsewhere;
- selection brands, which differentiate themselves either by an unusually broad range of product categories or by a narrow but very deep offer within one category;
- brand-mix brands, which offer the consumer a unique combination of private and/or manufacturer brands;
- product-mix brands, which in a surprising way combine a number of completely different product categories;
- target-group brands, which stand out from the competition by focusing their entire range on one specific target group;
- speed brands, which are faster than any other retail brands in adjusting their range to consumer behaviour;
- ideology brands, which are mainly led by their social ideology.

For retailers with a large range of private brands it is easier to build up a competitive advantage than it is for those that mainly sell manufacturer brands. With manufacturer brands a retailer finds it hard to differentiate itself from the competition. After all, most manufacturer brands can be bought everywhere. With a private brand however, differentiation is more easily attained and in addition a better margin can be achieved. The often qualitatively inferior private labels of the old days have developed into mature brands over the last few years. In terms of consumer perception, private brands can often now be compared with well-known manufacturer brands.

4.1 Foundation of each positioning

A retail brand without a strong range will never show up on the consumer's shopping list. Successful retail brands always have a clear, recognizable range. Strong brand personality and consistent communications cannot compensate for a weak range. The customer will see through that and will not put up with deficient merchandise. Good merchandise is therefore a basic condition for every successful retail brand. A range brand, however, has to go even further. It has to offer a range that is better than the competition in one or more dimensions. Dominance, product abundance and uniqueness are key words here. The consumer must be surprised by the enormous, unique offer. A retail brand that positions itself on range should give the target group an unparalleled choice for a particular need or want. After all, the promise of a range brand is that the consumer will not find a better range anywhere else.

A good example of a retail brand with strong range dominance is Victoria's Secret. This American retail company has more than 1,000 stores and offers a choice in lingerie that is clearly beyond that of the competition. In addition, Victoria's Secret offers the customer an intimate, romantic and feminine shopping environment that adds an extra dimension to the merchandise offer. Victoria's Secret is now one of the world's most successful speciality stores. Gross margin per square metre is far above that of other speciality stores, and aside from the stores, Victoria's Secret also has a very successful catalogue and internet business. In particular, its store on Herald Square in New York dominates all other lingerie stores with its 2,500 sq m area of different offerings. The brand personality of Victoria's Secret, which can best be illustrated by words like sexy, glamorous, intimate, refined and super-feminine, is reflected in the modern colours of the store design: black, grey and beige. The pink that used to be very characteristic for Victoria's Secret is now hardly used any more.

The most up-to-date and most exciting lingerie can be found on the ground floor. The brand's cosmetics are also presented here. The upper level includes the majority of the range, divided into eight 'rooms'. The most striking aspect of the store however is the visual merchandising. Life-size mannequins are everywhere; there are big video screens, large pictures and a fantastic product presentation. The 'compression area' at the entrance is also striking. When entering the store, after the hectic pace of Herald Square, the consumer can take some time to relax. This compression room is filled only with two enormous showcases, containing a couple of mannequins wearing the sexiest lingerie.

Category management

Not every product category is equally important to range brands. And for retail brands that position themselves through other attributes as well, there will be important and less important product categories within the range. A retail brand can profile itself better with some product categories than with others. Via category management, the role of each category within the range portfolio is determined. Strategy and priorities can then be formulated within each category, depending on the role of the category itself. This category role and matching strategy form the foundation for dividing all resources and budgets.

Within a range portfolio the following category roles can be singled out:

Destination role

Product categories with a destination role are critical to the positioning of the retail brand. They are the categories with which the retail brand wants to clearly differentiate itself from the competition. These categories determine the 'face' of the retail brand. They are the categories the store wants to become known for. Retail brands attract customers with these categories, because their merchandise offerings within these categories are much cheaper, bigger or better than that of the competition. The shoe department in Nordstrom, for example, is two to three times bigger than those of other American department stores. Destination categories are the main reason for visiting the store. That is why these categories receive extra attention in the store and in out-of-store communications.

Routine role

These product categories are part of the consumer's regular purchases. The products are available everywhere and the retail brand can usually only differentiate itself by price. The visual merchandising of these product categories mainly has to be functional, clear and price-aggressive.

Convenience role

To make shopping as easy as possible for the consumer, a retailer may also sell products that represent only a small volume of sales. These products will receive hardly any or no attention in in-store or out-of-store communication. It is true that the gross margin is probably high, but sales will be limited. For these product categories visual merchandising should also be functional and clear.

Impulse role
With these product categories a retailer tries to increase sales and profit per customer. Consumers do not come to the store especially for these products; they have to be tempted to buy them. That is why the visual merchandising is particularly important for these products. The consumer needs to be surprised. Impulse products should therefore always be positioned in high-traffic locations, and visual merchandising should always include displays and other temporary product presentations.

Occasional role
Most retailers do not always sell the same products throughout the year. For example they have seasonal products, and also one-off purchases. A retailer uses these products to keep the store and brand exciting and surprising. Occasional products can help build store traffic and generate cash.

Range matrix
To assemble a range that reflects the chosen positioning, it is not only the category role that is important. The style and price ranges of the merchandise also have a big influence on the positioning of the retail brand. To be sure that the range is also consistent, a matrix can be drawn up and used for each product category. One side of the matrix should represent the price range and the other the style of the merchandise. Assuming, for example, that there are three price ranges and three styles, the range matrix of a particular product category might look as shown in Table 4.1.

Price range	Classic	Romantic	Trendy	Total
Less than € 250	–	5	15	20
€ 250 To € 500	10	10	30	50
More than € 500	5	5	20	30
Total	15	20	65	100

Table 4.1 Range matrix

In this example, the retail brand is positioning itself in the mid-price segment of the market. As for style, the brand is focusing mainly on consumers who have a preference for trendy products. By filling in a matrix of this kind, a retail brand can make sure that its range always has a consistent look. And for every product category the retail brand can divide the range into price ranges and styles. If similar starting points are used for all product categories, they will have a large amount of consistency. Moreover it can be determined how far the retail brand differs from the competition by comparing its range matrix with those of other players in the market.

Various kinds of positioning on range

The choice between range, price, convenience or store experience as the differentiating attribute is the first step in the positioning process. However, such a decision on its own is still too general. A retail brand that chooses its range to be its differentiating attribute will have to further define how to implement this attribute. After all, a retail brand has many different ways in which it can profile itself through its range of goods. The main ones however are price range, variety, quality and speed to market. Based on this, the following range brand types can be distinguished in retail: merchandise brands, selection brands, brand-mix brands, product-mix brands, target-group brands, speed brands and ideology brands.

After choosing one of these possibilities, range brands then have to go one step further. Within each of these categories there are lots of alternative ways to create even more focus. For example, a retail brand that wants to build up a differentiating mind position with the customer through the uniqueness of its merchandise can obtain that by negotiating an exclusive sales deal on a foreign brand, but it can also develop and sell its own private brand, or offer only products from a particular region. So only after further fine-tuning around the chosen positioning attribute is a retail brand truly able to attain differentiation from its competition.

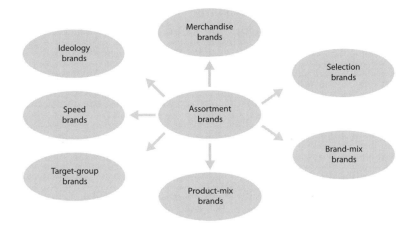

Figure 4.1 Types of range brands

4.2 Merchandise brands

Consumers get tired of products that you can buy everywhere and find in any store in the world. Therefore they will be prepared to pay a little more for a unique product. A retailer who succeeds in offering products that (almost) cannot be bought anywhere else will have a head start over the competition. But with this type of positioning the retailer has to make sure it has as much exclusive merchandise as possible. The uniqueness of the merchandise will mostly be based on a clear recognizable style. In fashion and home-furnishing stores for example, the style might be classic, exclusive, basic or trendy. Fashion retailers such as Ralph Lauren and Levi's mainly offer 'classics' in their stores and so meet a need for authenticity. The Dolce & Gabbana and Prada stores focus especially on the need for status, and therefore only sell exclusive, expensive clothing. Shops like the Gap and Old Navy are more about meeting the need for functionality and durability, and include mainly basic clothing. In contrast, H&M, Zara and Mango focus mainly on the need for variation, and therefore attract customers because of their trendy, constantly changing clothing.

Saks Fifth Avenue, the leading luxury retail brand in the United States, tries to achieve product differentiation through merchandise from unique vendors, selections from emerging suppliers, exclusive products from its core vendors and its private brands. Differentiated products now represent nearly 30 per cent of Saks' revenue; up from just 17 per cent two years ago.

In the cosmetics industry, the British brand Lush is an example of a retail brand that strikingly differentiates itself from the competition though a unique range of hand-made cosmetics. The first store was opened in 1994. Today Lush has around 300 shops throughout the world and also operates a mail order business. Lush makes its cosmetics by hand in Europe, Canada, Australia, South America, Singapore and Japan, in its own production facilities. So every product available in its shops, or sent to customers by mail, is as fresh as it can possibly be, because fresh products work better and contain fewer preservatives. Lush's aim is to have the youngest, freshest products in the history of cosmetics.

The philosophy of Lush is to make effective products out of fresh fruit and vegetables, the finest essential oils and safe synthetics, without animal ingredients. As all the products are hand-made, bath bombs and bars are individually hand-moulded. The soaps are hand-poured into moulds and hand-cut. The fruit is freshly squeezed, and bottles are hand-filled and labelled with the producer's name. Lush uses very few preservatives in its products, and wherever possible it uses clever combinations of ingredients to stabilize the products so they have a natural shelf life. All products are marked with a production date and use-by date. Quite often the products look like large pieces of cheese, apples, bonbons and other fresh products, and are presented in a way that strongly resembles a market. It uses product names like Utterly Nutterly soap, and unpacks and cuts the soaps in the store so they are as fresh as possible. The look and smell of the products, the visual merchandising and the way in which Lush communicates with its customers in-store, make the store experience a supporting attribute which furthermore strengthens the uniqueness of the Lush range.

L'Occitane en Provence is also a cosmetics retail company with a unique range. L'Occitane was founded by Olivier Baussan in the south of France in 1976, selling his own rosemary oil at street markets in Provence. Today it employs some 1,200 people. In addition to mail order sales, there are more than 400 L'Occitane stores in nearly 40 countries. All products and stores reflect the brand's core values of authenticity, simplicity, sensory pleasure and respect for people and the planet. L'Occitane creates natural body, skincare and fragrance products for men, women and the home. All the products are presented in traditional packaging that reflects the true elegance of simplicity.

The philosophy of L'Occitane was stated as follows by the founder, Olivier Baussan:

> The sun smiles on Provence. Its warmth makes the soil generous and the people openhearted. Its bright rays are reflected in the crafts, customs and traditions that have been handed down from generation to generation. The sun, the products of the soil and a love of nature are the essence of my Provence. It is this essence I want to share with the world. It is what inspired me to create L'Occitane.

With its roots in the French region of Provence, L'Occitane shares the colours, scents and traditions of the south of France with the world. Stimulated by local folklore and history, L'Occitane developed products that represent the Provencal land and people. Behind each of L'Occitane's products is 'a true story'. As the company continues to grow, L'Occitane remains committed to its core values of simplicity, sensuality, authenticity and respect. The pleasant lifestyle and abundant soil of Provence remain the inspiration for all L'Occitane's products and stores.

The Dutch retail company Oil & Vinegar creates a strong differential advantage for itself with an assortment of all sorts of splendid culinary gifts from all four corners of the world. At Oil & Vinegar you will find delicious original culinary gifts, such as more than 25 varieties of special olive oils, different types of vinegar, dressings, olives, dried tomatoes and balsamic vinegar. There are various types of pesto, bruschetta, herbs and spices, chutneys and pasta in a wide range of colours, types, sizes and so on. In every Oil & Vinegar store the enjoyment of food takes pride of place. The top-grade range of products provides maximum inspiration for the most magnificent dishes. All senses are stimulated by the delicious presentation of the vast selection of culinary products. Furthermore, many of the products on display can be sampled in the store, which makes choosing between them a very special experience. This store experience is well matched with the differentiating attribute of the range of stock. With a well-chosen gift from Oil & Vinegar you know you have something special. Moreover, you can ask to have your gift individually and expertly wrapped so that it looks distinctly festive, whether it is just for you or a surprise for another culinary enthusiast. Oil & Vinegar now has stores in more than 10 countries all over the world, and new locations are being added on a regular basis.

A final example of a retail brand with a unique range is Crate & Barrel in the United States. It opened its first home and kitchen store in 1962 as a family business, just a husband and wife team named Gordon and Carole Segal, and one sales associate who was enthusiastic about their vision. Having just returned from their honeymoon in Europe where they saw and bought all kinds of unique, functional and affordable designs for their home, the Segals looked around and realized no one in Chicago was selling great designs without charging the equivalent of a mortgage. Not being able to afford much of a mortgage themselves, they decided to lease an abandoned elevator factory in Chicago to showcase the products they were finding all over the world.

No budget for drywall? Nail up crate lumber. Display shelves? Stack the shipping crates and fill the barrels. And so out of necessity was born what immediately became the unique, down to earth Crate & Barrel style. It also made for an offbeat, albeit memorable, store brand name. Today's Crate & Barrel family has grown to over 145 stores and over 7,000 associates nationwide. Passion is the word that probably best captures its fascination and obsession with innovative, high-quality design. While many of the customers are more than familiar with the Crate & Barrel look, what most of them do not know is that the majority of the designs are created exclusively for Crate & Barrel. Its buyers travel the world developing new product ideas with skilled craftspeople and artists. Many prototypes are rejected until every curve of a sofa, every stem on a goblet and every weave on a chair is just how the store's buyers want it. The Segals' passion for products is what started Crate & Barrel, and it will be what moves the company forward.

A retail brand that wants to position itself via its own, unique range will, in the long term, find it difficult to obtain that with only manufacturer brands. After all, other stores also sell most of these brands. To create a real distinction, the retailer will have to launch a private brand, develop its own products and perhaps even take over part of the production process. Vertically integrated fashion retailers design their clothing themselves and also have their own factories to produce it in. That not only enables them to react quickly to demand, it also gives them a merchandising mix that is not available anywhere else. In addition, vertical integration gives a higher profit margin.

4.3 Selection brands

A retail brand can obtain a strong differential positioning by offering the largest selection in one or more specific product categories. It can exceed shoppers' expectations by providing the added value of an exceptional range of stock: either an unusually broad range of product categories, or a narrow but very deep offer within one category. The breadth of the range is the reflection of the extent to which a retail company specializes. Some stores specialize more than others. Depending on the extent of specialization the following store categories can be identified.

Speciality stores

Not only big but also small stores can position themselves by their dominancy in their range. The difference is that small stores will have to limit themselves in the number of categories they sell. Speciality retailers like Victoria's Secret and Tiffany's sell a limited number of categories. Their merchandise range is narrow, but deep. The strong growth of this type of speciality store has had a big influence on present-day retailing. The traditional speciality retailer used to only have one store, but the new speciality retailers on the contrary often open up hundreds of stores within a short period of time. That way they quickly profit from the power of their brand. Lots of specialist stores now belong to the world's biggest retail companies.

Superspecialists

Superspecialists like Tie Rack and Swatch have an even narrower range. Their focus is extremely specialized. They focus on only one product category: ties at Tie Rack and watches at the Swatch stores. By concentrating on one product category, these kinds of retail brands become very strongly associated with that product category in the minds of consumers. However, superspecialists, with their narrow range, need a large market area to obtain their sales. When they are successful, though, these superspecialists often develop into chain or franchise stores faster than speciality stores. After all, only small investments are needed to open a superspecialist store, and they can still obtain economies of scale through small-scale mass distribution. In addition, it becomes more difficult for other retailers to enter the market with a more or less equal concept.

Rice to Riches is a retail company that superspecializes in a blisteringly new dessert phenomenon: rice pudding. The man who brought Rice to Riches to life was vacationing in Italy one summer, and was inspired by the beautiful gelaterias he witnessed in Milan and Florence. Motivated by the range of flavours, and the ultra-inviting design, he set out to recreate that experience back home in New York City. The minute he returned, the little men in his head began to work. He had played a year earlier with the idea of a restaurant that would feature a menu made up entirely of rice-based dishes, and he had a relentless drive to be completely unconventional. He began to manifest his vision of the world's first rice pudding snackateria. For the next three years, this rice pudding architect worked seven days a week toward what he dreamt would some day become a New York landmark. First, there was the high-tech rice pudding test kitchen. It took six months of (never good enough) simmering with a team of expert dessert chefs honing various recipes until they arrived at the sacred ones. Then came another year of intensive design of the store's every detail. Even the bowls and spoons had to be meticulously styled to match the wild vibe of the Rice to Riches concept. It all came together with a fizz and a bang in April 2003, and Rice to Riches has roused the passion of New Yorkers and dessert-adoring people around the world ever since.

Category killers

Category killers like Bed Bath & Beyond, Amazon and Home Depot sell multiple product categories which meet one consumer need. Bed Bath & Beyond sells a large range of home textiles and household products. Amazon has the biggest choice in books and entertainment products, and Home Depot has an enormous range of do-it-yourself and home improvement products. Fulfilling one broad consumer need, these mass merchandisers can offer such an overwhelming range that they become real category killers. Because of their mega-range on the one hand and their low prices on the other, these big-box speciality stores can offer the consumer a very strong proposition. They attract customers from far away with their large stores and specialist positioning. That is why category killers can even become a real threat to Wal-Mart. Home Depot, for example, is so strong in do-it-yourself and home improvement products that Wal-Mart clearly loses out to it in these categories. Over the years, Wal-Mart has decreased its range in these categories and given more attention to others. Other category killers are less successful. Toys'R'Us, which was one of the world's first category killers, has lost the battle with Wal-Mart, and consequently Wal-Mart sells considerably more toys than Toys'R'Us.

General stores

General stores, like department stores and hypermarkets, offer many very different product categories in the same store. Their appeal comes from their enormous breadth of range. This results in one-stop shopping for the customer. In each category the range within general stores is not as deep as at (super)specialists and category killers. That is why general stores need to have a few product categories within their wide range in which they excel, and for which they are a real destination store. When they do not have those, they really become very 'general': a little bit of everything, but nothing really good. They will therefore lose the battle with (super)speciality stores and category killers because of their undifferentiated positioning.

Specialization versus parallelization

With regard to the breadth of range carried, two opposite trends can be observed. On the one side more superspecialists are appearing. In Paris, for example, there is a store that only sells Bordeaux wines. Alongside these superspecialists, category killers are also becoming successful with their specialization. However, on the other side parallelization also continues in retail. That is why the stock ranges of various stores are starting to overlap each other more and more. Supermarkets sell televisions and computers, clothing stores extend their range with cosmetics, bags and shoes, and drugstores do not only sell drugstore products any more, but now also offer glasses, contact lenses and toys. The best-selling products from other sectors are used to generate store traffic. Profit is not made, or hardly ever made, on these sales, but as long as customers are visiting the store and hopefully buying other (high-margin) products, all is well. Apart from that, the danger of this parallelization is that retail brands will become unclear. If there is no focus or consistency in the range, the consumer will not be able to form a notion of the brand positioning.

So in contrast to the strongly specialized stores are the more parallelized stores. Retail brands that are not (super)specialists or category killers and also do not have a recognizable range as a general store have a high chance of being squashed in the middle. However, stores that do succeed in positioning themselves by the breadth or depth of their range will have to make sure that their large range does not result in high stock levels. If inventory turnover is low, the chosen positioning will probably not bring in the desired economic result. Large ranges lead to higher stock levels and higher costs. Moreover, stores that try to differentiate themselves through the size of their range will increasingly face more competition from online retailers. In principle, these retailers can offer an unlimited range. They do not have the physical limitations of a store and they do not even need to have the goods in stock. They order from the supplier only after the customer's order has been received.

Just like manufacturers, retailers try to capitalize on the strength of their brand by extending their range:

• Armani opened a department store in Milan, where besides clothing it sells cosmetics, books, flowers, bonbons and home decoration, for example.
• Hema extended its range with, among other things, glasses, jewellery, insurance and even energy.

- Abercrombie & Fitch launched the Abercrombie store concept for boys and girls aged 7 to 14, with the same kind of casual, classic American styles as are sold in their usual stores.
- At the end of the 1960s, Richard Branson started the Virgin mail order record company. Under the same brand name he has now introduced, among other things, an airline company, a cola drink, cosmetics and financial services into the mix.
- Pottery Barn was founded in New York on the idea that home furnishings should be exceptional in comfort, style and quality. Its in-house designers draw their inspiration from time-honoured models in America and around the world to create unique collections at good value. All of Pottery Barn's products are exclusive to its catalogues, website and stores. A few years ago it launched Pottery Barn Kids, a collection of furnishings for babies and kids which inherited Pottery Barn's comfortable and well-designed aesthetics. The first catalogue contained the following birth announcement: 'As proud new parents, we'd like to announce the arrival of Pottery Barn Kids, a unique catalogue of children's furnishings, bedding and accessories. Forgive us for bragging, but it's a charming chip off the old block.' The positive response from its customers led to the opening of retail stores a year later.

However, not all brand stretches are as successful. Retailers, like manufacturers, will run into the question of just how far can they stretch their brand. If it involves interrelated products, a brand stretch will be easier than with unrelated product categories. The border lies with the question of whether or not the product matches the associations consumers have with the retail brand. The common aspect in all Virgin brand stretches, for example, is the brand personality. The Virgin brand always dissociates itself from big established brands.

Some retail brands are strongly associated with one product category. Brand stretches are then very difficult. The strength of the retail brand lies in the consistency with which all brand stretches are developed. The store format has to stay understandable to the consumer. If the new product categories or services are too far away from the original brand associations, the existing brand name will have hardly any meaning to the new activities. The range extensions can then even harm the original brand identity. The further the stretch goes, the more investment is needed to bridge the credibility gap and to decrease the risk of failure.

So as not to endanger the existing brand identity, some retailers choose to launch their range extensions under an entirely new brand name. The Gap did not do that, though, when it started to sell lingerie, baby clothes and kids' clothes. Instead it chose the brand names Gap Body, Gap Kids and Baby Gap. The most important reason for this strategy was undoubtedly that the Gap intended to continue to focus on the same customers with these new ranges. However the Gap also developed completely new retail brands for other market segments with Old Navy and Banana Republic. The brands the Gap, Old Navy and Banana Republic now offer the company a brand portfolio in the retail world that covers the entire fashion market. Old Navy covers the bottom end of the market, the Gap is positioned in the middle and Banana Republic sells to the top end of the market. Inditex follows the same strategy. The brands Massimo Duti, Zara and Bershka respectively cover the top, middle and bottom segments of the fashion market.

Extending the range without stretching one's own retail brand too much can also be achieved through a cooperation with another retail brand. The toy department at Albertsons supermarkets is run by Toys'R'Us. Starbucks runs coffee shops in SuperTarget, Wal-Mart and Barnes & Noble stores, and sells coffee through supermarkets as well. Supercentres and supermarkets are high-traffic locations. They are very attractive locations to other retailers, and the store-in-a-store concept cost relatively little, so it can be realized quickly. This strategy provides added value to both retail companies.

Brand stretches lead to channel blurring. However channel blurring does not only come about because of retailers. Often consumers are looking for it because buying everything in one store is easy, so the retailers further extend their ranges because they are reacting to a need. Adding new products or services can help consumers save time, not only when it comes to routine purchases, but also with fashion and home decorating. For example, it is so easy for a man when he can buy not only a suit at Armani, but also matching shoes, eau de toilette and a bag for his laptop. The range is then based less on product relationship and more on consumption or purchase relationship. Products that the consumer buys or consumes at the same time are offered in one store.

A good example of channel blurring is La Maison de L'Indochine in Paris. In this store, in the St Germain neighbourhood, people can buy pottery, tea, clothing, art, travel guides and lots of other Asian products. Those who might want to see all of these things in their place of origin can also book a trip to the Far East in this store.

Because of this increasing channel blurring it is becoming increasingly difficult to divide stores according to traditional sectors. The borders between the various sectors are fading, and every retail brand pretty much competes with all other retail brands now. So it is time for a new classification, which originates no longer from the type of range, but from the proposition that is offered to the consumer: a proposition that, besides range, can also be based on price, convenience or store experience. The differentiating positioning attribute now determines the sector a retail brand belongs to.

Usually there is a relationship between the breadth and depth of the range of stock. As the range becomes narrower, it will in general become deeper. The depth represents how much choice the consumer has within a product or product category. Depending on the chosen positioning, stores with around the same number of product categories can still have totally different range depths. At a regular supermarket with 15,000 or more products, the consumer will basically find the same product categories as at a hard discounter that only offers 600 products. The supermarket however has a deeper range because it offers a lot more choice in each product category. On the tea shelf for example, there are not only the usual flavours, but also many speciality teas: from pomegranate to jasmine, and from chamomile to peppermint. Apart from that, retail companies with a bricks-and-mortar store will always lose to their online colleagues when it comes to breadth and depth of their range. The space is always limited, no matter how big the store. In some sectors the available product range doubles every five to ten years, but shelves are not elastic. Not everything launched on the market by manufacturers gets shelf space in the store. An online retailer does not have that space limitation. In principle, it can offer an endless range. For example, there is no bookstore in the world that has an range comparable to Amazon's.

Large ranges of stock are not completely advantageous. They push up purchasing and logistics costs for the retailer, and the consumer does not always want to be confronted with an enormous selection either. People want choice, but not confusion. Food and drug discounters can also be successful with their very limited merchandise mix. Exactly how much choice the consumer wants depends largely on the product category and the situation the consumer is in, but in general the consumer requires the retailer to make a preselection from the enormous number of alternatives. It is the retailer's job to help the consumer make the best choice. Through the internet it is easy for a retailer to offer the consumer tailor-made information about preselected products.

Customers who are confronted with too much choice will look for independent advisors, or will simply choose the cheapest product. However, they will most likely choose a store that is a strong retail brand. By trusting the retailer's preselection, consumers make it easier to deal with the enormous number of products. Thus they save a lot of time and simplify their lives. Mothercare, the English retailer for babies, young children and their parents, narrowed down its range by about 30 per cent for that very reason. At the same time Mothercare focused on buying in its best-selling items in greater depth. This strategy resulted in greater choice and clarity for its customers.

4.4 Brand-mix brands

Consumers never buy everything from one brand. Depending on the type of product, opportunity, available budget and lots of other factors, consumers mix and match multiple brands. So a retail brand can also position itself by the choice of brands. It can choose to stock either private brands or specific manufacturer brands to create an important competitive edge. Marks & Spencer, C&A, the Gap, Ikea, Hema and Victoria's Secret are examples of one-brand store formats that sell only their own private brands, which are not sold anywhere else.

For years, retailers were selling products that were made at their request. These products sometimes had a 'fantasy' name, and sometimes a brand name that was identical to that of the company. But in both cases they were usually private labels and not private brands. After all, there was no strategic brand strategy. The brand name was only used as a sign of recognition, and the products were not aligned with certain brand associations. There was no emotional bond between product and customer. However there has been a big change here in the past few years. Retailers, like manufacturers, now develop brand strategies for their own products. These products are used as strategic weapons in building a strong retail brand. That is why in many cases private labels have turned into private brands.

Many retail companies sell both manufacturer brands and private brands. Sears in the United States, Carrefour and Decathlon in France, Albert Heijn in the Netherlands and Tesco and Boots in the UK are examples of this. They create the necessary shelf space for their private brands by delisting manufacturer brands that have a weak position in the consumer's mind and/or are less profitable for the retailer. Another solution is not to delist manufacturer brands, but to allocate less shelf space to them than they might deserve on economic grounds.

Range-oriented retailers that strongly depend on manufacturer brands for their sales will usually have to strive for distinction through a unique mix of manufacturer brands and shopping environment. The British department store Selfridges and the American Neiman Marcus are good examples of this. Besides their own private brands they also sell a large number of well-known manufacturer brands. Selfridges proclaims a dazzling mission to create and operate stores filled with brands and experiences that inspire and excite its customers, and has forged a 'house of brands' identity (Wood, 2003: 18–19). Selfridges has many varied price points and happily mixes concessions with own-bought merchandise, stocking TopShop's fast fashion alongside exclusive labels such as Louis Vuitton. There are 3,000 brands in total. Selfridges gives these brands space to express themselves. It does not force a standard shop-fit on brands, as customers already have their image in their head from the specific manufacturer brand advertising. These manufacturer brands have spent millions of pounds developing their identity to differentiate themselves, and Selfridges is happy to go along with that. Of course, the brands really like that kind of freedom because it gives them much more control over how they are presented in the store as well.

It is easier for a retail company to build up its own, differentiating positioning with private brands than with manufacturer brands. A private brand is almost indispensable for establishing a differentiating range. After all, manufacturer brands can also be found in other stores. A retail company that does not have its own strong private brand becomes almost like an anonymous distribution centre for manufacturer brands. That is why retail brands more often use private brands to position themselves.

A private brand is specifically produced for one retail company (or group of companies). This company has legal ownership and also puts it on the market. It is possible for a private brand to have any of several different types of brand names.

Company name

The private brands of Albert Heijn in the Netherlands, Sainsbury's and Tesco in the United Kingdom and the Gap in the United States belong to this category. With these types of brand names the direct identification with the retail brand is strong. After all, product and store have the same brand name. Of course it is then also necessary for the positioning and personality of these private brands to exactly match that of the retail brand.

Fantasy name

Clockhouse (for C&A), Per Una (for Marks & Spencer) and George (for Asda) are examples of this kind of brand name. A fantasy name can be chosen if it concerns products with strong emotional appeal. The brand name of the retail company might detract from the perceived value of the product. In practice however, it appears that private brands with a fantasy name can be just as strongly connected with a particular retail brand as those that use the company name.

A fantasy name can also be chosen if the product is of inferior quality. To prevent the retail brand having an association with this inferior quality, a fantasy name is used. This happens with the price-competitive brands sold by many supermarkets, for example. Sainsbury's first used the brand name Value for a product range in the lowest price segment. This name was focused too much on price, though, so the brand name Basics was introduced instead, with an emphasis not only on price but also on a certain quality. The copy on the packaging explains why the products are cheaper but still of great quality. Copy lines include, for fresh tomatoes, 'All shapes all sizes', for cooking apples, 'No lookers, great cookers', and for canned peeled tomatoes, 'Some peel, still appealing'.

A third reason for choosing a fantasy name can be that multiple retail brands (which might or might not belong to the same group) want to develop a shared private brand because of economies of scale. For practical reasons, a fantasy name is usually chosen that is not associated with any of the individual retail brands. An example of this is the low-priced Euroshopper brand, which is sold by a number of supermarket companies throughout Europe.

Well-known designer or character

H&M, which enables people without much money to still afford high fashion and look good, once had Karl Lagerfeld very successfully design a special collection for it. Target has a permanent clothing line specially designed for it by Isaac Mizrahi. Ikea sometimes uses the name of the designer as a brand name for its furniture. Kmart sells home decorating products from the famous lifestyle adviser Martha Stewart. Hema has a range of children's clothing and products branded with the characters Jip & Janneke, who are very well known in the Netherlands. These types of brand names are mainly chosen because the well-known name will give the products added value.

4.4.1 PRIVATE BRAND FUNCTIONS

Private brands are no longer overshadowed by manufacturer brands. Private labels have become private brands. Until a few years ago retailers could create a private label by just putting their name on products: it was not about creating brand associations. The brand name acted as the label. Today however, many retailers are managing their private brands in the same way as manufacturers manage their national brands. Private brands now have a clear function in the retailer's total marketing strategy.

The functions a private brand can have for a retail company are numerous. Usually however they are a combination of the ones mentioned below.

More differentiation

For multi-brand stores it is more difficult to create a strong retail brand, than it is for stores that only sell their own private brand. Fashion retail companies like H&M, Zara and the Gap have built their strong retail brand partly through the help of their private brand range. The clothing these retailers sell is not sold anywhere else. In increasingly many stores the private brand is becoming the most important distinction from the competition.

Higher margin

Margins in retail are under pressure because of the growth of low-price and high-value retail brands. Private brands can help gross margin. Because of the internet, market transparency is higher and it is easier for consumers to find the store with the lowest prices. Retailers are often confronted with lower margins because of this, and therefore try to compensate by putting private brands on the market. The gross margin of a private brand is higher than that of a manufacturer brand, because the private brand manufacturer does not incur marketing costs: those are at the retailer's expense. Moreover, manufacturers often use overcapacity in the factory to produce a private brand, and the cost-price calculation then only includes direct production costs. However, a higher gross margin does not necessarily mean a higher net margin. After all the costs the retailer incurs to establish a private brand are taken into account, a different picture can develop. In general, though, a large range of private brands will have a positive influence on the company's profitability.

Own price strategy

A private brand gives a retail brand the opportunity to compete on price without giving up too much margin. A private brand gives a retailer more control over pricing. The retailer can completely independently determine the sales price of a private brand. That is not always the case with manufacturer brands, especially in product categories where the power is still with the manufacturer and the retailer has to stick to the manufacturer's price rules. However, with private brands a retailer is not entirely free to determine the price. After all, it has to prevent the price of the private brand from getting too close to the price of competing manufacturer brands. In many sectors a minimum price difference of 10–15 per cent is observed. If, in a price war, a retail company is forced to lower the price of manufacturer brands, this will of course also have consequences for the price proposition and margin of its private brands.

Before the American supermarket company Kroger will carry a private brand, it must meet three tests. First, the quality of the private brand must be equal to or better than that of the national brand. Second, Kroger must be able to sell the private brand at a retail price lower than the national brand equivalent. And finally, Kroger must be able to make more profit per item. Kroger private brands are sold in three quality levels:

- Private Selection is the premium quality brand, designed to meet or beat 'gourmet' or 'upscale' national or regional brands. Ten of these Private Selection products have earned the Good Housekeeping Seal, one of the most widely recognized symbols of quality and value in America.
- The Kroger brand, which represents the majority of the private brand items, is designed to be equal to or of better quality than the national brand, and carries a 'Try it, like it, or get the national brand free' guarantee.
- FMV (For Maximum Value) is the value brand that is designed to deliver good quality at a very affordable price.

Other retailers also use three price points for their product offer: a good, a better and a best product. Marks & Spencer clothing for example has the Essentials range for its lowest price point, the Perfect range for its core business in the middle of the market and for the more pricier products it has the private brands Per Una for the younger, more fashion-conscious customer and Classic for more mature customers.

More buying power

A private brand can also indirectly improve the retailer's margin. In categories where the retailer has a high share of private brands, it can achieve a higher margin on manufacturer brands. After all, private brands make a retailer less dependent on manufacturer brands, and therefore its negotiating position with suppliers becomes stronger. That is particularly important if one or two major manufacturers dominate a product category. On the Dutch coffee market Douwe Egberts, part of Sara Lee, has a market share of about 75 per cent, for example. Therefore Dutch retailers might become strongly dependent on this coffee manufacturer. In order not to become completely dependent on Douwe Egberts, Ahold has its own coffee factory.

Own product strategy

A private brand enlarges consumer choice. It offers consumers an alternative to manufacturer brands. That is why in-store choice can be made easier for them. A retailer is closer to customers than a manufacturer. It can use the increasing amount of information available on customers' shopping behaviour to develop new private brand products. The designers for the US brand Abercrombie & Fitch visit colleges, concerts and other places its target group frequents, so they can keep in touch with trends. In addition, they organize group discussions with their customers and retrieve lots of information from salespeople in the stores. These salespeople are recruited from local colleges.

In order to gain full benefit from their own product strategy, some retail companies choose vertical integration in brand development. They control the whole production and marketing process, from product design through to production and then distribution to the stores. Apart from that, having private brands rarely leads to important product innovations. The investments needed for that are too high for a retailer. Moreover, retailers might well have the customer knowledge, but they often lack the specific product knowledge to develop real product innovations.

More flexibility

In fashion it is necessary to be able to react fast. Styles and colours change constantly. With a private brand it is easier to react to such changes than with manufacturer brands. With a private brand a retail company can readily produce items according to the demand of the moment. Because of the shorter supply chain, this process occurs a lot faster with private brands, so the range can be more up-to-date. In addition, the markdown on poorly performing products need not be as much. In combination with higher gross margins, this enables retail companies only selling private brands to usually obtain higher profitability than those that mainly sell manufacturer brands.

Cleaning up the range

In many sectors product ranges are becoming larger and larger. Sometimes they double every ten years. The average sales area, however, does not grow that fast. That is why every retail company needs to look very critically at the size of its range. In many product categories there is only room for two manufacturer brands alongside the private brand. Brands that do not differ much and only represent a small share of the market will run a particular risk of being delisted. Multiple small brands will then need to be replaced by a private brand.

C&A only sells private brands. To help customers find the fashion that suits them best, its range is conveniently grouped into recognizable and exclusive sub-brands, each serving a distinct group of consumers and their needs. Each private brand has its own distinctive character and personality, meeting individual customer requirements. The Clockhouse collection, for example, is for young adults aged around 18 to 20. This brand is perfect for this target group because the range is 'street credible', fun, affordable and frequently updated to match the latest trend innovations. The Your 6th Sense brand on the contrary is for stylish women. High quality and understated exclusivity are important features of this classic-style collection. Your 6th Sense is tasteful, elegant, sensible and wearable, never brash or loud. It is designed as an expression of individuality rather than a statement of the collective. The most well-known C&A private brand is Canda. For millions of Europeans, Canda is the prototypical C&A brand. Reflecting C&A's core values, it is C&A's main private brand. Canda offers a complete range of competitively priced quality clothing for men and women. It is easy to wear, everyday clothing that values practicality, durability and lifestyle essentials rather than courting some exotic fashion dictate. Canda garments represent good value for money and offer high levels of comfort and performance.

Completing the range

Just as a private brand can be used to clean up a range, it can also lead to an extension of the range. If it is impossible to obtain a good range of stock with only manufacturer brands, then a gap in the range can be filled up with a private brand. Subsequently the retailer can offer the consumer more price variety, for example.

4.4.2 SUCCESS FACTORS FOR PRIVATE BRANDS

Private brands can be a very important tool, particularly for retail brands positioning themselves on range or price. They can improve profit for the retailer and value for the consumer. That is why retailers are more professional now when it comes to private brands. Low-profile private labels have been transformed into well-positioned private brands. Manufacturer brands are consequently having a hard time defending themselves against these private brands. Many consumers assume that private brands are produced by well-known manufacturers, and make no, or hardly any, distinction between these and manufacturer brands. That is why Procter & Gamble has recently started to mention on its Dreft detergent that it does not produce private brands.

However, not every retailer is equally successful with a private brand. The success of a private brand largely depends on the following market conditions.

Retail brand strength

To successfully put a private brand on the market, the retail company itself has to be a strong brand. This condition is even more applicable for the introduction of a premium private brand. After all, the private brand has to compete with well-known manufacturer brands that are supported by heavy advertising. Only a strong retail brand can take the consumer's doubt away, as the retail brand gives the private brand credibility. The brand values of the company can be transferred to the private brand. Manufacturers are afraid that a low price will harm their brand image. Retailers however prove with their private brands that despite a low price, a strong quality image can still be built up.

Size

Scale and size are important drivers for a private brand's success. The retail company needs to be of a certain size to be able to negotiate successfully with the manufacturer for favourable terms. In countries like the UK, the Netherlands, Belgium and France, which have a high retail concentration, it is often easy to see the large share held by private brands. But in countries like Spain and Italy where there are not so many large retail chains, private brands have only been able to obtain a small market share, for the time being anyway.

Product complexity

The products a retail company wants to sell as a private brand should be easy to produce. With complex products, specialist manufacturers are constantly able to gain a technical lead. Continuous product innovations make it difficult for private brands to acquire a strong position. Retailers usually do not have access to the required technology. In the sports shoe sector for example, large manufacturers continuously launch product innovations onto the market. It is then difficult for retailers to compete with the manufacturer brands. Manufacturers that have unique product know-how will not use this knowledge for the production of private brands.

Type of product

A private brand will have a higher chance of being successful with functional products than with products that have a strong emotional value. It is easier to sell a private stationery brand than a cosmetics one. A retailer can only communicate about the private brand in generic terms, since budget-wise it is impossible to create a separate advertising campaign for every product category. The retailer cannot actually say much more than 'Our private brand is of first-class quality and is much cheaper.' On the contrary, a manufacturer can focus all its communication on one product (category). That is why a manufacturer is more able to communicate the specific and relevant values of its brand. Nevertheless, a shift is also taking place here. Baby food, for example, has always been a product with strong emotional value. Consumers want the best for their babies and do not want to take any risks. But gradually even in this product category, more private brands are entering the market.

Strength of manufacturer brands

The sales opportunities of a private brand depend on the strength of competing manufacturer brands. If there are no strong manufacturer brands in a product category, it will be relatively easy for a private brand to launch in the category. In the mid-price fashion market, in both Europe and in the United States, there are only a few strong manufacturer brands. It is therefore be an relatively easy category for a retail company to introduce a private brand into, and this would give a higher profile to its store brand as well. This is more difficult in markets that are dominated by one or more strong manufacturer brands.

Private brand quality
In the past, the quality of private brands sometimes left much to be desired. This was reflected in the packaging, which looked simple and often communicated the message 'cheap'. The private brand was a bad imitation of the manufacturer brand. Consumers were regularly disappointed in the quality. In the last couple of years, however, the quality of private brands has made a lot of progress. The differences between private brands and manufacturer brands have begun to blur. Retail companies now also use strong quality standards. Hema is a good example of this. Because Hema does not want to run any risks when it comes to safety, all products are tested in its own laboratory. That is why Hema products often test well in consumer tests.

Quality is now also emphasized in the packaging and advertising of private brands. A private brand can even build up so much consumer franchise that it ends up being sold through channels other than the retailer's own stores. The British car accessory and bike retailer Halfords, for example, sells its private brand products through BP forecourt shops.

Price gap
If the price gap between the private brand and manufacturer brand is big, this makes opportunities for the private brand. These opportunities will be bigger, of course, if this price gap is not justified by additional functional or emotional benefits from the manufacturer brand. Manufacturer brands that do not regularly innovate and do not maintain their mind position are particularly vulnerable to attacks from private brands.

4.4.3 FUNCTIONS OF MANUFACTURER BRANDS

Private brands are becoming a very important force in retailing around the world. A private brand can contribute to the profitability of a retail company, and can also be very important for building up a strong brand identity. Nevertheless, it can be meaningful for a retailer to (also) sell manufacturer brands. After all, strong manufacturer brands can perform several different functions for a retailer.

Adding to positioning

The quality level of the manufacturer brands a retailer is selling can have an influence on the store's appeal. A store that sells premium manufacturer brands will inevitably attain a strong qualitative appeal itself. Strong manufacturer brands can also contribute to the desired positioning on range. A store that only sells unknown brands has a different appeal from a store that mainly sells well-known premium brands. Manufacturer brands can also be used to fill in a positioning on price. By selling well-known manufacturer brands far below their usual price, a retail company can clearly position itself on price. Apart from that, manufacturer brands and retail brands mutually influence each other. The manufacturer brand not only influences the store's positioning, the converse is also true. The stores in which a manufacturer brand is sold influence the positioning of that manufacturer brand.

Price benchmark

A private brand often needs a price reference. The comparable manufacturer brand is the benchmark for setting the price of the private brand. However, there are some private brands entering the market that have a higher price than manufacturer brands. Loblaw, a Canadian company, was the first to launch a premium private brand onto the market under the name President's Choice. Loblaw was so successful with this private brand that it also sells the product in a large number of American supermarkets now. In Canada it has become one of the most trusted brands.

Creating traffic

Manufacturer brands with a strong consumer franchise create store traffic. Retailers cannot afford not to sell strong manufacturer brands;

otherwise they run the risk that consumers will go to another store to buy their favourite brands.

Margin improvement

If a manufacturer still controls price-setting, a retailer should be able to earn a high margin on manufacturer brands. However, if that control is not there, well-known manufacturer brands might just be used to attract customers. The price will then be so low that no or hardly any money is made on them.

Brand stretching

In the case of products with strong emotional value it can be difficult to put the store's brand name on a private brand. This is especially so if the retail brand is not that strong, as the company brand name would then only harm the quality appeal. It is then wise to choose a well-known manufacturer brand instead, or to put the private brand on the market under a fantasy name.

Lively store

To maintain and strengthen their market position, manufacturers need to introduce product innovations on a regular basis. Consequently retailers constantly have the opportunity to show their customers something new. This keeps the store exciting and alive. Customers like to return to a store where there is always something new to be found.

4.5 Product-mix brands

Flowers and chocolates in a store in London, perfumes and tea in a store in New York, and a Belgian supermarket company that sells cars: some stores differentiate themselves by their merchandise mix. In general, retail companies still assemble their range of stock in a traditional way. They sell what they have always been selling. There are no or hardly any changes to the range. That is why lots of retail brands' ranges look so much alike. As a result, a retail brand can create a competitive advantage by choosing a different, distinctive mix of product categories. For example, Staples sells everything for the office:

from computers to coffee, from notebooks to toilet paper. To complete its service to small businesses and home offices, and save its customers time, Staples also offers various services: insurances, payroll servicing, copying, telecom services and shipping.

The Container Store is devoted to helping people streamline and simplify their lives by offering a mix of storage and organization products. The concept is to sell multi-functional products that save customers space, and ultimately save them time. The store layout is divided into lifestyle sections marked with brightly coloured banners such as Closet, Kitchen, Office and Laundry. Employees in blue aprons are ready to help solve everything from the tiniest of storage problems to the most intimidating organizational challenges. So the Container Store positions itself not only through its merchandise mix, but also through convenience, by offering perfect service, an important supporting attribute. Customers receive great service along with fresh ideas and a very interactive shopping experience.

With strong product-mix brands, there is a clear connection between the various product categories. The consumer must experience the chosen mix as logical and relevant. In particular, the end-use should be the trigger for the understanding of this connection. Everything the consumer needs for a given situation is sold under one roof. At Staples it is everything for the office, at Container Store everything to solve storage problems. Home Depot sells not only do-it-yourself products, but also electrical appliances for the kitchen and products to decorate the house.

The White Company offers a product mix that is especially well known because almost everything in it is white. Founded in 1994, The White Company specializes in supplying a wide range of stylish home accessories and clothing, principally in white. The company, that began life as a 12-page mail-order brochure, has become one of the UK's fastest growing multi-channel retailers. With over 410,000 customers, it produces eight brochures a year, operates a highly successful website and has recently opened its eleventh store in the United Kingdom. The idea for the company began when its founder, Christian Rucker, identified a gap in the market for beautiful but affordable home accessories in white. The market at the time was polarized between low-quality cheap designs and the unaffordable 'designer' end of the market. A comprehensive collection of white bed linen, towels and napkins was really hard to find. So the idea for The White Company was born. To address a national market, without retail premises overheads, the ideas of white products and mail order were combined. Once the mail order business was fully established, and so that customers could see and touch the products they were buying, The White Company opened its first store. Now its 11 stores are proving to be just as successful as mail order. In addition, the website is providing yet another successful channel for sales. Although some signature colour pieces were introduced into the range to add seasonality, the core product range remains in timeless and impeccable white.

Recently, a place called The Pottery Bakery opened up in the Aventura Mall in Miami. At the storefront customers can enjoy a sandwich, a salad or something else light to eat, while at the back of the store they can learn how to paint pottery. For kids and other parties, eating and painting can of course be combined. The experience of painting something is almost as important as the unique product-mix of food, beverages and pottery. It is hard to determine what the differentiating and supporting attributes are in this case. The range and the store experience balance each other.

4.6 Target-group brands

A retail brand can also stand out from the competition by offering the added value of a unique selection of products related to a specific target group. The target group might for example be characterized by certain physical attributes. In London you can find the Left-Handed store, which sells everything for left-handed people. Mothercare focuses completely on pregnant women and women with babies and toddlers. Lane Bryant is the most recognized brand name in the United States for plus-size clothing.

American Girl Place sells historic dolls to girls up to 12 years old. Its mission is to serve the developing interests and intellectual and emotional needs of girls aged from 3 to 12. It sells premium, age-appropriate products and experiences that educate, entertain, reinforce positive social and moral values, and build self-esteem. Its stores in

Chicago and New York are filled with all the things these girls love, providing a place where these girls can nourish their spirit, create lasting memories, and celebrate their interests through products and experiences designed just for them. American Girl Place offers a full range of historic dolls, doll accessories and books. The dolls are about US$50 more expensive than a typical Barbie. Girls can visit a photo studio and get their picture taken, and it is then put on the cover of a personalized souvenir issue of the American Girl magazine. They can also see a one-hour show in the intimate 150-seat theatre. There is also an American Girl Café, which offers fancy dining with delicious girl-sized menu choices that are fun for girls, their mothers and their dolls. There are special seats for the dolls, so they can sit at the table with everyone else. In Chicago the American Girl store is an important tourist spot and one of the highest-performing retail brands. The range is the strong differentiating attribute, but the store experience is almost as appealing to customers.

For older consumers looking for a convenient place to shop for groceries, the Adeg Aktiv Markt in Austria has become a popular choice. It is Europe's first supermarket designed specifically for the mature shopper. This '50 plus' market features reduced-glare lighting, wider lanes, signs in larger type and reading glasses for customers in need of them. Instead of shopping trolleys with seats designed only for toddlers, the market offers an array of trolley and basket options, including one that attaches to a wheelchair and another with a fold-down seat. According to Adeg Aktiv Markt the supermarket is not meant to exclude any category of shoppers, but is just a place where seniors can feel particularly at home. In addition to the store amenities, Adeg Aktiv Markt has geared its staff towards their target demographic by only hiring employees aged 50 and above. While the initial belief was that this might be seen as a liability, the result has been quite the opposite. Although older employees command a higher premium, the chain has been rewarded by lower turnover, less absenteeism and an overall better work ethic. Without workers over the age of 50, the concept would only be 50 per cent of what it is now ('Market for seniors matures in Austria', The Natural Grocery Buyer, summer 2004, cited on www.aarp.org). The convenience of this store supports the positioning for this specific target group.

A positioning based on a specific target group only achieves the desired results if that target group provides sufficient sales and profit potential, not only in the short term but also in the long term. Creating a niche will not bring in enough for a retail brand with many stores to realize sufficient growth. Niches are generally only of interest or suitable for retail brands with a limited number of stores.

4.7 Speed brands

It is more difficult to predict consumer behaviour than it was a few decades ago. Retail companies have to be able to react fast to trends. Consumers want to be constantly surprised. They want to see new merchandise every time they visit the store, so retail brands can use speed to their advantage. Particularly in the fashion sector, the survival of the fittest is turning more and more into a survival of the fastest. In other sectors too, speed to market can be a strongly differentiating positioning attribute. Trends and hypes spread around the world quickly, not only in the fashion sector but in the electronics sector, for example. The lifecycles of digital cameras, MP3 players and other electronic goods are much shorter than they used to be. In the food sector, logistic systems have improved to help reduce stock and create fewer out-of-stock situations. In other sectors, these logistic improvements have mostly been made so that a retail brand can adjust its range faster in relation to changes in consumer demand. In the past, fashion retailers used to work with four to six collections a year. However, those times are definitely over: the fashion cycle is becoming faster and faster. Besides fast food there is now fast fashion.

The Spanish Zara, with around 900 stores in more than 60 countries, and the Swedish H&M, with about 1,200 stores in more than 20 countries, have drastically changed the rules in fashion retail. These fast-fashion stores have a new range every couple of weeks. They offer the consumer a new shopping experience every time. Modified variations of the clothing that famous designers show on the catwalk will appear in their stores within a few weeks. At Zara and H&M the lead time for new designs is on average four weeks, and sometimes only one or two weeks. Every time customers visit Zara or H&M they will see something new, so consumers have a reason to visit the store frequently, and they know that if they do not buy an outfit today, chances are it will be gone tomorrow. This knowledge does of course increase sales. Because Zara and H&M can react so flexibly to demand and stock turnover is very high, markdowns stay very low. At many fashion stores around 50 per cent of stock is eventually marked down, but at Zara the proportion is only 10 to 15 per cent. That is why positioning on speed to market is not only appealing to the consumer but also great for the retail brand's profit, because there is no or hardly any dead, unsaleable stock. Zara is able to react quickly to consumer demand, because it produces about half of its collection in its own factories through a vertically integrated supply chain. Zara is both a retailer and a manufacturer.

On a daily basis Zara has 250 designers designing new collections. On a yearly basis around 11,000 different designs are made. Because Zara controls the entire production process, the time between design and distribution to the stores is very short. At H&M the entire process takes a bit longer, because a large portion of H&M's clothing is manufactured in the Far East. However, this means it can be somewhat cheaper than Zara, and that is also why in its positioning mix, price is more important than it is for Zara. Retail companies like Marks & Spencer and C&A are much less innovative. They change their ranges far less often. This lower speed of change is undoubtedly one of the reasons that these retail companies are going through difficult times.

Hot Topic, an American chain with around 600 stores, also positions itself on speed to market. Founder Orv Madden realized in 1988 that no other retailers were taking timely advantage of the direct correlation between music videos, alternative artists and teenage fashion. Music is one of the primary influences driving teen fashion preferences. That is why Hot Topic puts a strong emphasis on listening to both customers and the music they listen to. The company takes its fashion cues from music videos, MTV, television programmes, concerts and music magazines, and is always ahead of the curve. The stores specialize in music-licensed and music-influenced apparel, accessories and gift items for young men and women principally between the ages of 12 and 22. Approximately 50 per cent of the range consists of music-licensed T-shirts, hats, stickers and posters branded with musicians' logos and CD artwork. The remaining 50 per cent is music-influenced, and includes both branded and private-brand products inspired by the clothing and accessories worn by modern rock bands and artists.

Following the philosophy of being 'first to market' with products, soon after an artist wears an item in a video clip, in a club or on stage, the item will appear in a Hot Topic store. Hot Topic's 'secret weapon' is its connection with its customers. Through thousands of report cards filled out each week by customers and sent directly to the headquarters, together with a 'talk to us' feature on its website, the company hears directly from consumers. Clearly inspired by what is happening in modern rock music, Hot Topic is quick to identify a new band or new product featured on an artist. Reacting quickly to the inspiration is key; 30 to 60 day lead times with domestic vendors ensure timely product flow.

Most people on holiday spend time sipping red wine and sightseeing, not staring at the ground, but Australian Hype DC founders Daniel and Cindy Gilbert were fascinated by the feet of passers-by. Their foot fetish inspired countless hours of shopping in the streets and stores of Europe, checking out the latest styles, brands and colours. They discovered edgier streetwear styles were a point of difference that was missing in Australia, and a retail concept was born. In 1998 they opened a store offering footwear for customers who are style initiators, not followers. Five years on, the fact is that the funky footwear business is still driven from influences from outside of Australia, so Hype DC is still about bringing the latest styles from Europe and making them available in Australia. Hype DC is all about emerging trends, being first with tomorrow's shoe fashions, and displaying them in a store that looks very much like an art gallery, where the shoes are the pieces of art, displayed with care. Hype DC is now Australia's premier retailer of the freshest footwear and accessories, with nine stores in Sydney and Melbourne, bringing customers faster, sharper and closer to the edge products from around the world.

Although speed to market is a differentiating attribute quite particular to fashion retail brands, other retail brands can also position themselves around the speed in which they can change their range. Tchibo, which has around 800 outlets in Germany and a couple of hundred in the UK, Austria, Switzerland and the Netherlands, has developed a unique retail format. It sells via four channels: its own stores, concessions in supermarkets, the internet and catalogues, and coffee bars. Tchibo's positioning is mostly based around the speed at which it can change its range. This positioning gains even more power through the low prices at which its products are offered. The stores have a small coffee bar and also sell packs of coffee. Most striking however is the range of innovative non-food products, which changes weekly. These products are produced exclusively for Tchibo and marketed under the company's private TCM brand.

Originally Tchibo only concentrated on selling coffee. Now however, Tchibo is most well known for the 25 non-food items it launches every Wednesday. Each week these non-food items follow a certain theme: kitchen, garden, sport and so on. In each case, only one version of each product is offered. For example, there is only one iron, not 20 from which the customer has to choose. That saves the consumer the hassle of having to make a choice. Presented in this way, each item becomes an unchallenged 'star' in the selection. It is important that the various products follow a single theme, and harmonize and relate to each other. This allows the creation of a new experience at Tchibo every week, mirrored by the window dressing and shop decor, TCM magazine and television commercials. It means that each week Tchibo is transformed into a specialist store, if only briefly. Many products sell out in a few days. Customers have to act fast, because the offer is deliberately limited. This stimulates a 'need', a phenomenon proven by the fact that most purchases are in fact spontaneous. In one week for example, 800,000 pairs of jogging pants were sold. At Christmas, Tchibo is Germany's biggest jewellery company, and every second woman in Germany wears a bra from Tchibo.

4.8 Ideology brands

No retail brand operates in a vacuum; stores are an indispensable part of our society. They have relationships with consumers, employees, suppliers and neighbours, and retail brands of course also influence the economy and the environment of a region or country. So every retail brand has a responsibility with regard to society. More than ever, people do not trust retail companies and their management. But retail companies are certainly not the only big organizations that are under attack. There is a tendency to dislike every big organization: big is bad. Therefore Wal-Mart and other retail brands are trying to regain trust. But retail brands can go one step further by selecting a merchandise mix based on a social ideology. Social responsibility is then not just something that comes along; it is the core of the brand. A social ideology is what differentiates this type of brand from its competition.

American Apparel is a vertically integrated manufacturer, distributor and retailer of T-shirts and related products, which disassociates itself from the poor working conditions in much of the textile industry. All of its garments are cut and sewn at its facility in downtown Los Angeles. The company is committed to making clothing of the highest quality while pioneering industry standards of social responsibility in the workplace. Its goal is to make garments that people love to wear without having to rely on the cheap labour of the sweatshops. The employees of American Apparel earn the highest wages in the industry and are active participants in the life of the company. Every production aspect of their garments, from the knitting of the fabric to the photography of the product, is done in-house. By consolidating this entire process, the organization is able to pursue efficiencies that other companies cannot because of their over-reliance on outsourcing. American Apparel's downtown Los Angeles factory, now considered the largest sewn-products facility in the Unites States, is a design lab where creative ideas, efficient manufacturing techniques, and concepts for designing and selling T-shirts are developed and put to the test. While apparel is a universal necessity that transcends almost all cultural and socio-economic boundaries, most garments are made in exploitative settings. American Apparel hopes to break this paradigm. The company is as much a capitalist success as a social success.

The Body Shop is another example of an ideology brand. It does 'business as unusual'. Right from the start The Body Shop tried to break all the conventions of the cosmetics market. The Body Shop was founded by Anita Roddick who, in 1976, started retailing home-made naturally inspired products with minimal packaging. The ethical cosmetics company rapidly evolved from one small shop in Brighton, on the south coast of England, with only 25 hand-mixed products on sale, to a worldwide network of shops. Today The Body Shop operates in around 2,000 stores across 50 countries. The Body Shop's mission statement gives a good impression of the ethical principles it strives to meet:

> To dedicate our business to the pursuit of social and environmental change. To creatively balance the financial and human needs of our stakeholders: employees, customers, franchisees, suppliers and shareholders. To courageously ensure that our business is ecologically sustainable: meeting the needs of the present without compromising the future. To meaningfully contribute to local, national and international communities in which we trade, by adopting a code of conduct, which ensures care, honesty, fairness and respect. To passionately campaign for the protection of the environment, human and civil rights, and against animal testing within the cosmetics and toiletries industry. To tirelessly work to narrow the gap between principle and practice, whilst making fun, passion and care part of our daily lives.

This mission statement steers all the activities of The Body Shop. The Body Shop is a retail brand that is committed to a strong set of ethical principles. Even now, while The Body Shop is struggling to hold its market position, these ethical principles are unchanged.

Brands like Ben & Jerry's exist not only to make money, but also because they want to contribute something to the world through the way they do business. Ben & Jerry's, the Vermont-based manufacturer of ice cream, was founded in 1978 in a renovated gas station in Burlington, Vermont, by childhood friends Ben Cohen and Jerry Greenfield, with a US$12,000 investment (US$4,000 of which was borrowed). It soon became popular for its innovative flavours, made from fresh Vermont milk and cream. Over the following years, Ben & Jerry's moved from being a single-parlour operation to manufacturing tubs of its increasingly famous ice cream for distribution to retail outlets. The company currently distributes ice cream in the United States and other countries through supermarkets, grocery stores, convenience stores, franchised Ben & Jerry's scoop shops, restaurants and other venues. However, despite the growth, both Ben and Jerry made sure they did not forget one of their original mottos, that 'business has a responsibility to the community in which it operates'. Ben & Jerry's is an anti-establishment, values-driven company. The founders' social mission is to operate the company in a way that actively recognizes the central role that business plays in society, by initiating innovative ways to improve the quality of life locally, nationally and internationally. A few years ago Ben & Jerry's was bought by Unilever. However when selling, the founders negotiated to ensure their strong company values remained untouched. This was a demand Unilever had no problem meeting. After all, the core company values are the foundation of the Ben & Jerry's brand.

Virgin, the third most respected brand in Britain, is involved in planes, trains, finance, soft drinks, music, mobile phones, holidays, cars, wine, publishing, bridal wear and lots of other activities. What tie all these businesses together are the values of the brand and the attitude of its staff. All companies under the Virgin brand are built on the same ideological values. The brand always positions itself as the consumer champion, which competes on behalf of the consumer with the large, established companies that are too expensive. Virgin began in the 1970s with a student magazine and small mail order record company. The company now operates over 200 companies worldwide, employing over 25,000 people. The Virgin brand stands for value for money, quality, innovation, fun and a sense of competitive challenge. These brand values are applied to most of the new activities. The company often moves into areas where customers have traditionally received a poor deal, and where the competition is complacent. With its growing e-commerce activities, Virgin also looks to deliver 'old' products and services in new ways.

The growing influence of ethical values is related to the growing cynicism about the way companies do business. Social issues are gaining more influence in customers' perception of a brand. Honesty and integrity are playing a more important role in their choice of store. Big retail companies are especially being challenged about their social responsibility. So a retail brand that truly stands for a certain social ideology can create a competitive advantage for itself over stores that merely exist.

5. POSITIONING ON PRICE

Because of the strong competition no retail brand can afford to be seen as expensive. A manufacturer brand with a high price can be a market leader, but in retail that is impossible. The market leader is never a retail brand in the highest price segment.

A positioning on price can be chosen in several ways:

- Low-price brands always try to be the cheapest. All other positioning attributes are of minor importance.
- High-value brands do not necessarily have the lowest prices. They offer consumers low prices, but combine these low prices with added values, such as a wide range and a pleasant shopping environment.
- One-price brands offer a very heterogeneous range. Their merchandise mix depends on the question of whether something can be sold for the chosen price point(s) or not.
- Premium brands are appealing because of their very high prices and extreme exclusivity.

Many consumers are not looking for the lowest prices. They are looking for a store that offers a number of other benefits besides low prices. Therefore, high-value brands will enjoy very strong growth in the near future.

5.1 The importance of price

The power of the brand cannot always be measured by the higher price the consumer is willing to pay for that brand. Manufacturer brands can often ask a premium price if they are market leaders, but that is impossible in the very competitive retail environment. The retail brand with the highest market share never has the highest price. In most retail sectors price is at least a competitive attribute. Therefore, the power of a retail brand primarily has to be measured by its position in the consumer's mind and not by its premium price. A store with low prices can also be a very strong retail brand.

Sometimes it seems like retail brands only talk about price. The low price is often emphasized in advertisements, sale after sale occurs, and price wars have become a fact of life in retail. In some sectors there are just too many stores. Consumers are continually looking for a good price, often because of the activities of retail brands themselves. They want to save money on commodities so they can spend more on premium shopping goods. Therefore, a positioning on price can give a retail brand an important competitive advantage. Price will be decisive especially if consumers see no difference in range, convenience or store experience. For many retailers however, price is hardly a conscious decision. The decision to go for low prices is usually the result of a lack of distinction on other positioning attributes.

It is often very tempting to lower prices. Every retailer knows that a price reduction will attract customers, and a price reduction can be realized quickly and easily. In the short term, a price reduction almost always works. This does not mean, however, that price can also be the foundation for a positioning. Competing on price is a tough road. More is needed for a positioning on price than just lowering a couple of prices. After all, there will always be other retail brands that can lower the prices of these products even more. In the long run, continual price promotions can even harm the positioning and cheapen the retail brand. Price promotions often only attract cherry pickers. When the promotions are over, the customers will also be gone. In the long run there is no or hardly any effect. Customer loyalty cannot be bought. A retail brand that positions itself on price will also have to build up an emotional bond with its customers. Low prices should not only result in saving money, but should also offer the consumer an emotional benefit, like for example the feeling of being a smart buyer. If there is no emotional bond between the customer and the retail brand, loyalty will remain an illusion.

Many retail brands try to position themselves on price. Sometimes price seems to be the only strategy that works. Supercentres like Wal-Mart and Target, wholesale membership clubs like Sam's Club and Costco, dollar stores like Dollar General, discount stores like the Dutch Kruidvat drugstores, Zeeman textile supermarkets, the German Aldi and Lidl and lots of other retail companies all use price as their most important weapon. However, in every sector only one can be the cheapest, so for other retailers it is difficult to also base their differential advantage on price. However, every retail brand has to make sure that its price image is good. No retail brand can afford to be seen as (too) expensive in the current competitive battle. Partly because of economic developments in the last couple of years, consumers have become more price conscious. Not only do the less wealthy pay attention to price, more affluent consumers also find price to be important. Buying in a low-price store is completely accepted. Young, old, rich, poor: everyone pays attention to price. Because of the internet, information in newspapers and elsewhere, consumers are much better informed about the price levels of various stores, and it is no longer the expensive store that acts as a reference, but the store with the lowest prices. Other retail brands are compared with that store, so having fair prices has become an absolute condition for every successful retail brand. It is at least a qualifying attribute, but it will become a competitive attribute in more and more sectors.

Depending on the way in which positioning on price is implemented, four types of price brands can be distinguished in retail: low-price brands, high-value brands, one-price brands and premium brands.

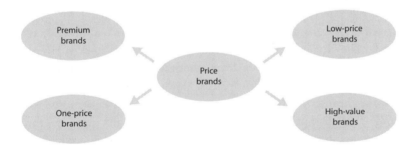

Figure 5.1 Types of price brands

Within each of these four types it is necessary of course to differentiate quite specifically from the competition. This can be achieved either through different supporting, competitive and qualifying attributes, or through a unique interpretation of the price positioning. For example both Aldi and Wal-Mart use price as a differentiating attribute. Both retail brands focus on price-conscious people, who think low prices are more important than an appealing store experience. However, both store formats are very different because they implement their price positioning differently, and because they also handle other attributes of their positioning mix completely differently. Range, location, store interiors and service are totally different at both retail companies. Therefore, the total positioning mixes of Wal-Mart and Aldi are not particularly comparable.

5.2 Low-price brands

A retail brand that chooses a lowest-price positioning has a very clear strategy: wanting to be the absolute cheapest in the market. All other positioning attributes are completely subordinate to this. The range is limited and new products will only be added if they have been successful somewhere else. Store design and visual merchandising are as simple as possible, and the function of the salespeople is limited to filling up the shelves and working the cash registers.

A strong operational excellence is a condition for a low-price brand. In the long term, a retail brand can only charge the lowest prices if it also has the lowest costs. The entire business culture needs to be focused on lowering costs where possible. These are real no-frills retail brands. They focus on only essentials, and things are kept as simple as possible. They are often newcomers that try to carve out a place in the market with their extreme low prices. Nowadays, the influence of these low-price brands on the rest of the retail sector is enormous. Retail brands that do not want to position themselves on price are forced by these low-price brands to keep their prices down as well. Because of these low-price brands, traditional supermarkets have developed private fighting brands. The Belgian Delhaize introduced 365 and Ahold launched Euroshopper together with its foreign colleagues.

5.2.1 ACTUAL PRICES VERSUS PRICE PERCEPTION
The actual prices a retailer charges do not always have to correspond with the consumer's price perception. After all, consumers base their image of the price level on many factors. Some of the most important ones are as follows.

Price of price-sensitive products

Consumers do not know all prices by heart. The price perception of a retail brand is determined by a limited number of products and brands. These reference products are usually products that are easy to compare, with a high purchase frequency and/or a high purchase amount. So it is of the utmost importance to every retailer to know which products and brands are the most price-sensitive to its target group. With these products it definitely needs to ensure it charges the right price. If the retailer succeeds in that, it can strengthen its price image as much as possible in a cost-efficient way. Some retailers use internal price rules of conduct to guarantee this. These rules mention exactly what price should be charged for specific products compared with the store's most important competitors.

Brands and service

The type of brands and the customer service can give a store an expensive or less expensive appeal. Stores that sell expensive brands and offer an excellent customer service are almost automatically considered to be expensive.

Store environment

Consumers also use non-price-related cues to form an idea about price. Store design and visual merchandising have a big influence on this price perception. Low-price brands clearly communicate low prices with their simple layout, bright lighting and straightforward product presentation. On the contrary, a department store like Nordstrom with its pianist, thick carpets and pleasant lighting undoubtedly makes a much more expensive impression.

Communication

In-store and out-of-store communications also strongly contribute to the price image. A retail brand that positions itself on price will talk exclusively about low prices in its out-of-store communications, and pursue an aggressive image. In public relations and advertising it regularly confronts its competitors, and profiles itself as the defender of consumer interests, for example by emphasizing how hard it bargains with manufacturers that are claimed to charge too-high prices. In in-store communications it works with powerful, big price signals, and guarantees that consumers will not find the same goods cheaper anywhere else.

Temptation

In a low-price store with its limited range and simple visual merchandising, consumers are not really tempted to buy more than is on their shopping lists. This does however happen in a department store, and in other stores with a much bigger and more surprising range and much more inspiring visual merchandising. But if, after coming home, consumers review what they have spent, this could influence their price perception of the store.

Merchandise density

The merchandise density in the sales area also has a big influence on the price perception of a retail brand. As the merchandise density increases, the store appeal will cheapen. In stores that position themselves on price, there is always a high merchandise density, because the lower profit margins will have to be compensated for by higher sales per square metre. Expensive stores with high margins can afford to present products spaciously. Because of their low merchandise density they undoubtedly give an impression of luxury and expensiveness.

The Dutch Zeeman is an example of a retail brand that chose a lowest-price positioning. Zeeman is an established retail brand in the European market. Zeeman's mission is to be a first-class retailer and number one in household textiles and basic clothing. The company, which was founded in 1967, has about 1,000 stores in the Netherlands, Germany, Belgium, France and Luxemburg. Zeeman has a strategy that can be described in one word: simplicity. It has no expensive packaging, no fancy store interiors, no elaborate sales pitch. All stores have the same layout and the same range. Most of the products are presented on display tables. Zeeman is a kind of covered market, where the products are laid out for the customers to see. At Zeeman you pay just for the products, not for all kinds of extras. Zeeman runs its business processes in-house as far as possible. The short lines of communication and the high level of automation enable it to operate very efficiently. That cuts costs, and that means low prices. As Europe's biggest textile supermarket, Zeeman places the biggest orders, so it can get the lowest prices.

To emphasize their positioning as the lowest-price stores, but also to really increase their sales, Aldi and Lidl use stunt promotions for their general merchandise. The biggest part of their advertising is now focused on computers, cameras, televisions, T-shirts and other general merchandise. Each week there is an exclusive selection of weekly specials, which are very popular. Customers know they are 'when it's gone it's gone' offers, so they are already in line early in the morning to buy the promotions.

5.2.2 EVERYDAY LOW PRICES OR HIGH/LOW

Some retail companies, like for example Wal-Mart, choose a strategy of everyday low prices (EDLP) for their price positioning. Other retail companies prefer a high/low price strategy, in which promotions play an important role. These promotions can bring excitement to what is supposed to be a dull, routine task, and can tempt consumers to react quickly. In that way, a retailer can also get rid of less successful merchandise, so price promotions have a clear function for fresh products and fashion products. However, price promotions do not create loyal customers. They often only result in a temporary sales increase, but in the long term, sales are not influenced by this strategy. Stores with an EDLP strategy try especially to attract consumers who have no time or do not like comparing different promotional advertisements and brochures. So EDLP is particularly appealing for low-cost, speedy replenishment shopping.

It can be assumed that more and more retail brands will (partly) choose everyday low prices as their strategy. Especially with routine purchases, consumers want to take less time and effort to figure out where and when best to do their shopping. EDLP creates a feeling of transparency. Consumers prefer to buy at a store where they pay a fair price every time: a price that is as low as possible and does not go up and down frequently. Retailers that continually mark down their products and sell nearly all of their merchandise at promotional prices lose part of their credibility. Consumers will no longer be prepared to buy at the regular price, but will count on the fact that the product will soon be marked down, so they just wait for the next sale. More and more consumers do not want to pay full price any more. About 15 to 20 per cent of sales in Dutch supermarkets are now achieved through promotions, and it is no longer exceptional for 30 to 40 per cent of sales of a product to be on promotion. A retail brand that is confronted with this problem would be wise to align its initial prices more closely to the prices it eventually charges, otherwise it will lose its reputation for price integrity. For example, the American department store Nordstrom has no more than five chain-wide sales per year. Other special events, like special size events, trend shows, loyalty events and personal appearances, focus on adding value, not discounting prices.

Carphone Warehouse in the United Kingdom chose a striking price strategy (*Retail Week*, 2005). In the fast-moving mobile phone sector, it has been a source of frustration to customers that prices can fall just after they have bought a new phone. To counteract this, Carphone Warehouse launched the Ultimate Price Promise. The retailer proactively contacts customers a month after they have left the store. If the price of the product they bought has dropped in the interim, the letter encloses the difference in price in the form of a voucher.

The trend for EDLP will also continue because EDLP is the most cost-efficient price strategy. In particular, logistic and personnel costs weigh heavily upon the profitability of promotions; this is a problem manufacturers also face. Consumers benefit from promotions by purchasing extra stock, but this will be at the expense of future purchases. Consequently sales show high fluctuations. However, sales are more steady with an EDLP strategy, and inventory management can be far easier for retailers and manufacturers, resulting in fewer out-of-stock situations. The retailer also incurs all kinds of additional expenses to run price promotions: changing prices, building displays and so on, but because the interests of retailers and manufacturers are the same in this situation, both parties can form a partnership to eliminate the inefficiencies of a high/low price strategy.

Despite these advantages, EDLP will never entirely oust price promotions. Many retailers that choose EDLP still have a number of price promotions, to keep the store dynamic and surprising, to attract more consumers to the store, and/or for stock clearances. Aldi for example uses an EDLP strategy coupled with general merchandise promotions to boost store traffic and raise margins. Tesco also uses a hybrid price strategy. It combines the cost advantages of EDLP with a high/low strategy. It uses a cunning customer relationship management (CRM) programme to ensure price promotions are focused mainly on existing loyal customers. For some products Tesco is more expensive than for example Asda, a supermarket company which is part of Wal-Mart and, like Wal-Mart, works mainly with EDLP. However, Tesco compensates for this by running more promotions.

In general, a positioning on price is easier to obtain with EDLP than with promotions. Because of the consistency, an EDLP strategy is easier to communicate than a high/low strategy. With a high/low strategy the price positioning needs to be proven each and every week. With an EDLP strategy on the other hand, the message is the same every time; therefore the low-price message comes across much quicker. However, the advertising message is not exciting. After all, the messages in out-of-store and in-store communications are always the same. That is another reason for an EDLP strategy to be coupled in practice with a few price promotions.

5.3 High-value brands

High value and low prices are not the same to customers. Value means more to a consumer than just low prices. It is also about quality, range, store experience and other, intangible attributes. Low prices do not have to be reflected in poor quality and messy, unattractive stores. Consumers have become more demanding, and realize they can expect value as a matter of course. They want more for less, and compare the benefits of a store with the financial and other burdens they experience when visiting it. They do not always want the lowest price, but do always want the highest value. Buying at high-value retail brands is all about smart buying, because high-value retailers offer a balance between very low prices and other positioning attributes. Compared with the total store benefits, the price is a pleasant surprise.

Wal-Mart is known for its very low prices, but Wal-Mart also has a very wide range, quality merchandise, friendly salespeople and provides a pleasant shopping experience. So Wal-Mart offers a high-value positioning of 'more for less'. This proposition is only possible through improved productivity and high operational excellence.

Price is no longer the only distinction for high-value brands. The very low price is the differentiating factor in their mix of positioning attributes, but a high-value brand also performs well on other attributes. Besides low and fair prices, it also offers consumers an extensive range, a pleasant store experience and high shopping convenience. Therefore high-value stores, especially supercentres, mass merchandisers, warehouse clubs, dollar stores and big-box stores, offer consumers a strong consumer proposition (McKinsey, 2003: 3). This strong consumer proposition has created a virtuous cycle for high-value formats. The growth in both traffic and basket size has given them a much higher sales productivity (that is, sales per square metre). This higher sales productivity results in very attractive store-level economics, which in turn enables high-value retailers to reinvest some of their surplus returns in even lower prices and, in contrast to popular belief, more labour hours in the store. This, of course, results in improved stock situations, better merchandise presentation, and thus an even more compelling shopping experience for customers, leading to an even higher sales productivity.

This cycle enables high-value retailers to have lower gross margin percentages (lower prices) but a higher gross margin per square metre than their more traditional competitors. Likewise, these high-value retailers have significantly lower selling costs as a percentage of sales (well beyond the advantages conferred by lower wage rates), but more employees per square metre (more labour hours in the store). Over time, this virtuous cycle will place increasing pressure on traditional retailers that lack similar sales productivity levels, leading to diminishing service and presentation and/or an increasing gap in pricing, reinforcing value players' consumer advantage.

High-value retail brands usually position themselves somewhat above the lowest-price retailers. Such a positioning can be unclear if the retail brand cannot find the right mix of low prices and added value. The danger for high-value brands is that they continue to improve the range and look of the stores, and forget the real differential advantage of their retail brand. By upgrading the range and the stores, they might lose contact with their customers. However, in most sectors, high-value brands succeed in obtaining a strong market position, and these retailers will probably strengthen their position even more in the future. Consumers do not want to have to choose between low prices or added value. They want it all, and high-value retail brands offer it all. That is why high-value retail brands currently belong to the most successful retailers.

Ikea is a high-value retail brand that has turned the home furnishings market completely upside down in a very short period of time. Its positioning mix of high value and a distinctive range has given Ikea an entirely unique place in the market. Its concept of self-service, self-assembly and the involvement of the customer in the whole process changed the furniture and home accessories market completely. Ikea offers consumers attractive products for the home and does not make them wait three months or more for delivery. The Ikea business idea is to offer a wide range of home furnishings with good design and functionality, at prices so low that as many people as possible will be able to afford them. However, to manufacture beautiful, durable furniture at low prices is not easy. It requires a different approach. Finding simple solutions, scrimping and saving in every direction except on ideas, Ikea's business model is based on a partnership with the customer. First Ikea does its part. Its designers work with manufacturers to find smart ways to make furniture using existing production processes. Then the buyers look all over the world for good suppliers with the most suitable raw materials. Next Ikea buys in bulk, on a global scale, so that it gets the best deals and customers can enjoy the lowest prices. Then customers do their part. Using the Ikea catalogue and visiting the store, customers choose the furniture themselves and pick it up in a self-service warehouse. Because most items are packed flat, customers can get them home easily, and assemble them themselves. The customer thus becomes a kind of co-manufacturer. Ikea does not charge customers for things they can easily do on their own, so together they save money for a better everyday life. By doing all this, Ikea differentiates itself from all other furnishing stores.

At Wal-Mart, everything it does is also about high value: finding it, making it and sharing it with customers. Its business is to see how little it can charge for a product, not how much; how easy it can make it to shop at Wal-Mart, not how difficult. Wal-Mart's high value also comes from staying true to its core philosophy of offering low opening price points: the lowest price available for an item of any kind. Here, you will find 88 cent toothpaste, US$10 cookware sets, a gas grill for less than US$100, DVD players for under US$50 and microwave ovens for less than US$35. And right down the aisle, you will find merchandise that is one step up in quality for just a little more. Wal-Mart is the home of respected national brands, but when the company sees an opportunity to create better value it will add a private brand product to the mix, providing brand quality at a lower price.

Wal-Mart does not compromise on quality to sell for less. Consumer-testing laboratories ensure the products meet recognized industry standards and government regulations, regardless of the price. But if the customer still has a problem with a product, Wal-Mart has a return-and-exchange policy that is one of the most liberal satisfaction guarantees in the business. The incredible range at Wal-Mart, featuring up to 150,000 different items in its biggest supercenters, is also an important value in and of itself, helping customers get everything they need in one place. And with its seasonal items, Wal-Mart stores actually creates an ever-changing shopping list for customers.

At Target, the fourth largest retailer in the United States with more than 1300 stores, creating high value for the customer is also at the core of the strategy and vision for the future. It is inherent in Target's 'Expect More. Pay Less' brand promise. Its annual report gives some examples of the values Target offers customers:

- the value of low prices on film and flip-flops, lozenges and lampshades, diapers and DVDs, all under one roof;
- the value of designers like Mossimo Gianulli, Michael Graves and Liz Lange at exceptional prices;
- the value of bright lights, wide aisles and quick checkouts;
- the value of a fast, fun and friendly shopping experience;
- the value of choices;
- the value of a credit card that earns rewards, saves you money and raises funds for your child's school while you shop;
- the value of complex technology that simplifies your life;
- the value of receiptless returns, shopping online at midnight and a store that understands your preferences;
- the value of trend-right timing;

- the value of the merchandise you want on the shelves when you want it;
- the value of a helping hand or a caring smile;
- the value of contributing more than US$2 million every week to support schools and students.

Over time, customers' definitions of value and their expectations have evolved, but Target's commitment to delivering high value remains as clear and unwavering as it has always been.

Carrefour, the French retail company with about 10,000 stores in 30 countries, builds its high-value marketing strategy for hypermarkets on five pillars (Pinto, 2004):

- providing the lowest prices every day;
- providing the best value for money in every price category;
- providing as much information as possible about the products Carrefour sells;
- making shopping a faster, more practical, more enjoyable experience;
- respecting people and the environment.

Together, these five pillars have formed the proposition with which Carrefour has grown into the second biggest retail company in the world.

Hema is a Dutch example of a high-value retail brand. This company, which started in 1926 with a one-price-for-everything formula, now has about 300 small department stores in the Netherlands, Belgium and Germany. Hema's mission is to stand for surprising simple solutions for as many people as possible. Hema distinguishes itself by having all products sold under the Hema brand name itself. The range includes products for daily use, and is divided into four groups: fashion, hardware, food and services. Every group includes products in which Hema has been very strong since its beginnings, like picture frames, underwear, cosmetics and fresh pies. All products and services are tested extensively. Besides durability, user-friendliness and choice of materials are also very important. Because Hema focuses on a large group of consumers, the most relevant style directions are always present. Starting points for the Hema style are functionality and simplicity, in combination with modern design. Changes in the market and trends are quickly transformed into practical and usable solutions that make daily life easier and more fun. The stores have a simple appeal and look clean. Costs are kept as low as possible, without harming quality. The result is a unique combination of good quality, modern style and relatively low prices.

5.4 One-price brands

The implementation of a differentiating price attribute with a one-price-for-all strategy was developed many decades ago. Hema in the Netherlands, Monoprix in France and lots of other variety stores positioned themselves about 75 years ago by using just a small number of price points for their goods. At first, Hema only had three price points: all products cost 5, 10 or 25 cents. Dollar General and Family Dollar in the United States, and the 100 Yen shops in Japan, are contemporary successful examples of this way of price positioning. Every product in the store costs a dollar or 100 yen.

All these one-price retail brands target the lower-income segments. The most important criterion when determining the range policy is whether an item can be sold for a dollar or 100 yen. The result is a wide variety of merchandise, including many kinds of everyday consumer products. All products have only one thing in common: they all cost the same. Apart from that, these stores position themselves not only on price, but also on the supporting attribute of convenience. Stores are always located in residential areas, so customers do not have to spend a lot of time to get to them.

Stores like Family Dollar Stores, Dollar General, Dollar Tree and 99 Cents Only Stores in the United States are examples of this fast-growing price segment. They have even grown so fast that they have forced Wal-Mart and Target to also offer dollar-priced merchandise in special aisles. Limited-range grocery retailers like Aldi are also experiencing more and more competition from the dollar stores, because these stores are adding more food and consumables to their range. Dollar stores typically sell unbranded products or private-label brands, written-off or liquidated merchandise, or redirected merchandise, goods intended for another buyer that did not complete the deal. Dollar stores also sell imported items, ranging from 30 per cent to 60 per cent of inventory, depending on the chain (Schoolcraft, 2003). To further increase their number of customers, they have extended their range and cleaned up their product presentation. In that way they attract not only the lower socio-economic classes, but everyone who is in for a bargain. That appeals to a larger target group, because everyone likes bargain hunting. This appeal becomes even stronger if the dollar stores succeed in exploiting their supporting attribute of convenient locations well. Because of their small, low-cost concept of neighbourhood stores, they can offer the consumer a unique mix of price and convenience. This proposition would be retained even if inflation forced them to ask more often for more than just a dollar. Some dollar stores price their merchandise for example in dollar increments: $1, $2, $3 and $5.

With more than 8,000 stores, Dollar General is one of the leading retail brands in this segment. Its formula for success consists of 10 crucial factors (Crawford and Mathews, 2001: 55):

- Dollar General accepts only cash to eliminate credit-card fees and technology expenses.
- Dollar General does not advertise regularly, except to announce the opening of a new store.
- Dollar General features limited price points to make shopping easier for customers, and accounting and stock control easy for employees.
- Dollar General carries predominantly in-house and private-label brands for the lowest consumer prices and maximum margins.
- Dollar General focuses on fast-turnround consumables to drive sales volumes.
- Dollar General operates 'no-frills' stores with inexpensive fixtures and displays.
- Dollar General uses its network of district managers to help determine where to open stores, and a small cadre of real-estate professionals to close lease or sale transactions quickly.
- Dollar General signs low-rent, short-term leases to minimize real-estate costs.
- Dollar General uses only basic technologies that help boost operational efficiency.
- Dollar General locates stores as close as possible to distribution centres to minimize transportation costs and reduce replenishment time.

Economic developments in the past few years have resulted in a rise in low-price and high-value retailers, causing price to become an important success factor for differently positioned retail brands. The internet also adds extra transparency. Consumers can compare prices between different retailers on various sites. Therefore, a retail brand that does not position itself on price also has to make sure that its price difference from the low-price and high-value retailers does not get too big. The prices of reference products are of the utmost importance. After all, consumers use the prices of reference products to get an idea about the overall price level of a store. Every price difference from the competition will have to be compensated for by a substantial distinctiveness elsewhere in the positioning attributes: a better range, more convenience or a surprising store experience. Only if a retail brand offers a clear added value compared with other brands can a small price difference can be justified. In all other cases a more expensive brand will lose the battle with competition.

5.5 Premium brands

More and more people are trading up. Consumers save on commodities in order to spend more money on luxury products. Because of increasing prosperity, luxury products are now within the reach of a lot of people. Luxury has become democratized. Even people with a lower income can sometimes shop at more expensive stores. Therefore, a positioning on price does not only have to be about low prices: a choice of higher prices is also possible.

Premium prices are paid because they are an indication of good quality. However expensive, exclusive brands are not only bought by consumers because of their quality. The price at which a product is offered also has a communication function. Some people buy expensive, luxury brands just because they are expensive. A pair of limited-edition jeans for more than US$600 is an example of conspicuous consumption, which serves to express a (desired) identity and to differentiate the buyer from other people. It is a signal to other people: you are what you buy.

Premium retail brands are used in the same way. These retail brands can help customers to obtain admiration from other people, so the challenge for them is to stay very exclusive. A store that everyone knows is very expensive and exclusive can help consumers to demonstrate their sophistication. Buying at such a store is not meant to be for everyone. It gives the customer extra status. The premium price is a sign of wealth. It shows who the consumer is or wants to be. Without the high price, part of the attraction of the retail brand would disappear.

Premium brands have a positive price elasticity: the higher the prices, the higher the appeal of the retail brand. However, buying at an exclusive store does not always have to be used to communicate something to others. Glamour shopping can also be a kind of reward to a consumer for a hectic, busy period at home or at work. So besides premium prices, service and store experience are important positioning attributes for this type of retail brand.

The stretch of shops and boutiques on Rodeo Drive in Beverly Hills is only three blocks long, but those three short blocks constitute the most famous shopping district in America, and probably the most expensive three blocks of shops in the world. It is here that the rich and famous do their shopping, and tourists window-shop while trying to spot movie stars on the fabled street. The most celebrated clothing designers in the world have boutiques here: Armani, Gucci, Christian Dior, Coco Chanel, Ralph Lauren, Valentino, Gianni Versace, Tommy Hilfiger and others. The jewellery stores boast names like Cartier and Tiffany. In fact, Rodeo Drive is home to the single most expensive store in the world, Bijan. You must make an appointment in advance just to shop at Bijan (which was named after its Iranian owner). On a typical visit, Bijan's average customer spends about US$100,000 on men's fashion, which ranges from a US$50 pair of socks to US$15,000 suits.

The enormous price competition in retail results in prices from the low-price brands and retail brands in the middle of the market coming closer together. For example, the low prices charged by high-value brands will deviate less from the lowest prices of discounters, because the prices of high-value brands will go down further. On the other hand, the difference between these brands and premium price retailers will become larger. To keep their high-end positioning, these premium brands will only sporadically have price promotions. Products unsold are offered to loyal customers at a discount at special private shopping events, or they go to bargain brand outlets, usually after removing the brand name. Because of this increasing price distance from other retail brands, premium price retail brands are becoming even more exclusive. Customers are not able to just walk into a very exclusive store. They have to ring a bell, then a doorperson decides whether they will be let in or not. If they are indeed admitted, this will give them a feeling of satisfaction.

Comme des Garçons has a very exclusive store in New York, in the trendy Chelsea district. No one would expect to find such a store in an area, alongside slaughterhouses and garages. And to top it all, the store even camouflages itself with incorrect company signage. What you see is a brick facade, an iron fire escape ladder, a hole in the wall and above it a scruffy sign 'Heavenly Body Works' announcing a car repair shop. Initiated customers are not put off and bravely step into the hole. There they find themselves standing in a metal tunnel with a glass door at the end. But how do you open it? What is the magic 'Open sesame'? First you have to reach through a hole in the glass door, then the door will revolve around an invisible axis and you practically slip through (Mikunda, 2002: 121).

Tiffany & Co, the internationally renowned American jewellery retailer, is another retail brand that positions itself on premium prices. The company's mission is to be the world's most respected jewellery retailer. Tiffany was founded in 1837 when Charles Lewis Tiffany opened a store in downtown Manhattan. His first day of business brought in a mere US$4.98. Today, more than 100 Tiffany & Co stores and boutiques serve customers in the United States and international markets. In 1887 Tiffany shocked the world by purchasing the French crown jewels. From then on, Tiffany became the world's authority on the finest diamonds. The company even became the subject of a book and a movie: Truman Capote's best-selling novel *Breakfast at Tiffany's* was published in 1950, and Paramount later released a movie based on it, starring Audrey Hepburn. Over the years, the finest families and heads of state worldwide came to prize Tiffany diamond jewellery. Hollywood and sports celebrities have always had a passion for Tiffany creations. The premium prices of Tiffany, with for example diamond engagement rings that are priced up to US$1,300,000, become a recommendation rather than an obstruction. Combined with a distinctive range, these premium prices create a very strong retail brand out of Tiffany.

A positioning on premium price can be even more extreme. The De Luxe Alliance, a worldwide group of luxury goods and services companies, plans to open a store in Moscow with the ultimate cachet: it will sell only products costing more than US$1 million (New Paper, 2005). It is calling it the multi-millionaires' 'supermarket'. It is a one-stop shop offering every oligarchic accessory, from luxury yachts and private jets to Pacific islands and Arabian thoroughbreds. The project is aimed at multi-millionaires. Its slogan is, 'Millionaires are not allowed in. If you only have one million, you can't afford it.' The company said its research shows that there are up to 20,000 potential customers in Moscow.

6. POSITIONING ON CONVENIENCE

Time is becoming an important driver for the retail sector. Consumers constantly lack time and prefer to do their shopping hassle-free. They are shopping for time, so to speak, so there is clearly a need for retail brands that focus on convenience. When focusing on convenience, just as with range and price brands, different approaches can be chosen:

- accessibility brands offer the customer maximum accessibility to the store, the website and/or the call centre;
- efficiency brands optimize the speed and ease of the total buying process;
- service brands make shopping easier by offering the customer perfect service.

6.1 Time as a driver

Time and money are key drivers of store selection. Consumers pay a lot of attention to price, but they also have limited time. They want to spend as little time as possible on everyday chores, and have more time left for things that are more rewarding. That is why consumers look for retail brands that make shopping easier: less time, less effort and less stress. These are retail brands that offer not only products, but solutions. Stores that are close to people's homes and convenient to get to have a strong positioning attribute, as do stores with long opening hours. Location is sometimes even the most important factor for store choice. The shift towards convenience can also lead to an increase in new formats, like internet grocers for example.

Consumers are prepared to pay more for a retail brand that offers a solution to their time problems. They want to buy time, because their lives have become increasingly busy. Therefore convenience can become a differentiating attribute for a retail brand. A retail brand that eliminates irritations for the customer and increases shopping efficiency will be rewarded with increased patronage. Especially when it comes to grocery replenishment shopping, it is all about an easy location. The store should be close to customers' homes. However, convenience is about more than a spacious store in an easy, accessible location. Products have to be presented in such a way that they can be found easily, too. Employees should help customers if necessary. Paying has to be efficient, and if there are complaints at any time, they have to be solved quickly and without any problems.

Any retailer should not underestimate the importance of convenience. A differentiating positioning is always based on a mix of four attributes: range, price, convenience and experience. A retail brand should always offer the customer a certain level of convenience, even if it positions itself primarily via one of the other three attributes. Offering a certain level of convenience, like a fair price, is a condition for every retail brand.

A great location allows for easy access and attracts large numbers of customers. That is why Dollar General, the American high-value retailer that primarily positions itself on price, has also identified location and six other factors to help keep its stores accessible to busy families and older customers alike (Crawford and Mathews, 2001: 64–65).

Small outlets
At about 7,000 sq ft, the typical Dollar General store is smaller than most competitors' outlets.

Eye-level focus
In every Dollar General store, nothing (fixtures, signs, merchandise) is above eye level. The uncluttered 'airspace' enables customers to stand at the store entrance and have an unobstructed view of every area of the store.

Streamlined checkouts
To keep the checkout lines moving, Dollar General installed new flatbed scanners to allow cashiers to ring up items quicker than with the previous hand-held models. In addition, the company removed impulse-buy items such as gum, candy and tabloids from the front-end area.

Clearly marked prices
One of the basic tenets for competing on access is clarity and visibility

of item prices. At Dollar General, the price of every product is clearly marked right on the item. So there is no need for large price signs on the shelves or hanging from the ceiling.

Clean and well-stocked stores
Dollar General also excels in making it as easy as possible for shoppers to navigate its stores. All stores are clean and well-maintained, with no dirty floors, or boxes and crates strewn in the aisles.

Limited choice
The company keeps a tight rein on its stock-keeping units (SKUs), limiting itself to just 4,500, compared with around 35,000 SKUs offered by Wal-Mart. Adding more SKUs would crowd the look of the stores, making them feel less inviting and accessible.

Convenient location
Although access today is more about internal navigation, a pleasant store does not mean anything unless consumers can get to it. That is why Dollar General tries to locate its stores in the heart of small towns or on major public-transit lines in larger cities.

Depending on the focus of the convenience positioning, three types of convenience brands can be distinguished in retail: accessibility brands, efficiency brands and service brands.

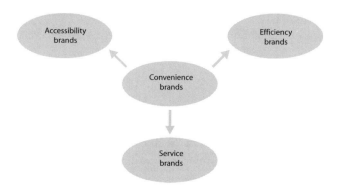

Figure 6.1 Types of convenience brands

6.2 Accessibility brands

Positioning on accessibility is all about the ease with which the consumer can reach the store, website or call centre. Important elements here are store location, parking facilities, opening hours and the speed at which the website or call centre can be reached. With the arrival of new store formats like category killers and other stores situated in the outskirts of cities, the importance of distance seems to have diminished. Other positioning attributes in turn compensate for an increased distance. To ensure location is still a strong differentiating attribute, it has to meet very specific requirements. Some brands, like Coca-Cola for example, are just there when you need them. A retail company like McDonald's has restaurants in just about all town centres and along most highways in the United States, not to mention most other countries as well. Neighbourhood stores also derive a large part of their appeal from their location.

Since 1927, 7-Eleven has been a leader in convenience retailing. 7-Eleven pioneered the convenience store concept at the Southland Ice Company in Dallas, Texas. In addition to selling blocks of ice to refrigerate food, an enterprising ice dock employee began offering milk, bread and eggs on Sundays and evenings when grocery stores were closed. This new business idea about opening hours produced satisfied customers and increased sales, and convenience retailing was born. Today, 7-Eleven is the undisputed leader in convenience retailing, with more than 27,900 stores operating in the United States and 17 other countries. Each store focuses on meeting the needs of busy shoppers by providing a broad selection of fresh, high-quality products and services at everyday fair prices, along with speedy transactions and a clean, safe, friendly shopping environment. The stores have expanded their food service offerings with a proprietary line of deli items and baked goods, which are prepared and delivered fresh daily. 7-Eleven also offers convenient services based on each neighbourhood's individual needs, including automated money orders, copiers, fax and automatic teller machines, long-distance phone cards and lottery tickets, where available. So the convenience of the location, the opening hours and the speedy transactions are strengthened by a range that is also completely based on the convenience concept.

Instead of trying to compete with Wal-Mart and other high-value retailers, Walgreens emphasizes convenience across all elements of its business. It expanded rapidly to make its drugstores ubiquitous, meanwhile ensuring that most of them were on corner locations with easy parking. In addition, Walgreens overhauled its in-store layouts to speed consumers in and out, placing key categories such as convenience foods and one-hour photo services near the front. To protect pharmacy sales, the company implemented a simple telephone and online pre-ordering system, making it easier to transfer prescriptions between locations around the country, and installed drive-through windows at most of its freestanding stores (Frank et al, 2004).

Positioning on convenience can mean having to go where the customers are. Instead of waiting for the customer to come to the store, retailers might have to go after the customer. Retail brands could therefore open up stores where consumers live, work or spend their leisure time. Albert Heijn in the Netherlands and Sainsbury's and Tesco in the UK offer the customer a variety of formats to maximize access at different times and to suit different shopping modes. Among other things, they are opening up neighbourhood stores close to people's homes, and city stores close to commercial offices.

6.2.1 MULTI-CHANNEL RETAILING

A retailer that chooses convenience as its differentiating attribute has to make sure it is always very accessible. The target group require 24-hour accessibility and instant satisfaction. They want to be in control and want to decide for themselves when and through which channel they will gather their information or conduct their purchases: call, click or visit. Because of the internet consumers can now gather much more information than they used to, and without visiting a store, they can now make purchases everywhere in the world. The location of the retail company is not important any more, because products are delivered to the home. That is why consumers are more empowered. The power that first shifted from manufacturer to retailer is now more with the consumer.

The number of retail brands that offer products and/or information via a website has increased dramatically in the last few years. However, many e-commerce companies have been mistaken in their calculation of the costs of internet shopping. In a traditional store, some of the activities are carried out by customers themselves. Customers collect together their own groceries, and takes them home themselves. The staff of an e-commerce retailer have to do these things, and this of course results in higher costs in addition to the already high IT costs. Despite lower accommodation costs, internet supermarkets in particular have a hard time succeeding in offering the customer the low prices that they have come to expect from internet suppliers. However, that seems to be less important for food than for other products. E-commerce for daily groceries is more a matter of ease than of low prices, as opposed to products like CDs and books, where low prices often tip the scales in the purchase decision. Retailers have also learnt that doing business via the internet requires skills other than those of a traditional store. There are fewer impulse purchases, and setting up the technology and the logistics costs a lot of money. That is why Amazon sometimes sees itself more as a technology company than a retailer.

Consumers shop across various channels. Stores, websites and catalogues can therefore complement each other. Before consumers go to a store, they can first take their bearings extensively from the internet. In the store there is then the opportunity of personal contact, and the product the customer has seen on the website or in the catalogue can be checked out in reality. If customers like the product they can buy it immediately. That is faster and can save possible forwarding charges. In addition, customers can go back to the store if they have any complaints or problems. That is why a multi-channel retailer has to make sure that online and offline are integrated into one marketing approach that addresses customers' needs no matter where they shop. Consumers who use both online and offline channels should experience a consistent brand positioning and brand personality across all those channels.

Lands' End has created a virtual salesperson in its My Personal Shopper feature, which encourages consumers to compare styles, colours, patterns and fabrics. The online salesperson then helps them make selections that match their individual tastes. Because the retailer understands that shoppers are more likely to buy when they have a friend along to encourage them, the site's Shop with a Friend feature allows two people in different locations anywhere in the world to navigate the site together, look at the same screen and discuss the options. Shoppers can also 'try on' outfits by filling out a questionnaire about their measurements and body types, then seeing the outfit they select displayed on a model who resembles themselves or a famous person. Unlike most of its competitors, which offer little more than special-occasion reminders and address lists for gifts, the Lands' End site is a true extension of the brand promise that customers have come to expect from the company's catalogue and outlet stores (Boston, 2001).

Multi-channel retailing should actually become integrated-channel retailing. Customers should have a consistent experience. However, different channels may have different strategic roles in building the brand. Every channel has its specific characteristics and opportunities. If these characteristics and opportunities are used well, the different channels can strengthen each other. Every channel, based on its own opportunities, can communicate the brand positioning and personality. With a well-integrated marketing approach, multi-channel retailers can benefit from all synergies and use the power of the different channels to strengthen their brand:

Trust
Offline retailers that start with a multi-channel strategy can capitalize on their existing brand strength. The familiarity of the offline retail brand provides consumers with extra trust if they want to buy something via a website or catalogue. Even though they do business at a distance, the brand is still trustworthy. For this reason offline retailers with a strong brand image will also become important online retailers. Compared with online retail brands without any stores of their own, multi-channel retailers have an advantage with their bricks-and-mortar presence.

Information
The advantage of a website is that an enormous amount of information can be provided. Sometimes consumers even know more than the salespeople. But a website, a catalogue and a store can also complement each other in a different way. Staples, REI and Office Depot have in-store kiosks. Via these kiosks the customer can see which products are

new in the store. They are no longer dependent for in-store product information on the availability of a salesperson. All the necessary information is available at the in-store kiosk, and if the customer wants to order something that is not in stock, that is also possible. In addition, before visiting the store, customers can look up the information online at home.

Consumers mainly seek information for purchases bearing a large financial, social or health risk, or if there are many retail brands with similar propositions and it is difficult for them to make a choice. For example, the majority of American consumers that visit a car dealership have often done extensive research beforehand into various models, options and prices.

No physical limitations

A retail brand can use the internet to extend its range enormously. The internet is the biggest mall in the world. With a click of the mouse the consumer can order products and services from all over the world. Websites are virtual megastores that can compete with every offline retailer on range. Stores and catalogues are not elastic. The quantity of products they can offer is limited. That does not apply to e-commerce retailing. In addition, less successful products with high margins can be offered via the internet, as there only has to be a central supply from one location.

Multi-channel retailing also offers a wider geographical reach. Retailers with a strong brand but only a few stores can grow very quickly via the internet. New markets can be entered without opening up new stores. The market area can be extended with low investment. However, this means the competition becomes more intense as well, as there are no more geographical barriers. Every retail brand, anywhere in the world, can now be a competitor. The cost of entry is relatively low for an online retail brand. The small speciality stores of the past have partly disappeared but they are being replaced by lots of websites for small retail brands.

Tailor-made product

We are living in a world of mass customization. Starbucks for example has thousands of ways to serve a cup of coffee. In the shoe stores of

Florence Kooijmans in Cannes and other French cities, the consumer can combine every desired model with every heel height and every colour. In this process of mass customization, a multi-channel retailer has an advantage over offline competitors. Through the knowledge it has of its customers, it can tune its products and service to the customer's individual needs. There are no more standard products, but customized products that are made completely according to the customer's demands.

An intensive relationship with customers

Through their databases, web-based retailers can know a lot about their customers. That is why they can build up a solid, personal relationship with them. For example, they can remind customers of their regular weekly purchases, so nothing need be forgotten any more. A web-based retailer can also immediately check if the product is in stock, and continually gets feedback from customers as well. Successful two-way communication is happening. Through the website the retailer can also determine what the consumer is particularly interested in.

Stronger brand positioning and personality

Multi-channel retailing offers more opportunities to promote the brand. After all, the number of contacts with the consumer increases. More and more consumers explore the internet or the catalogue first before they buy something in the store, so a website or a catalogue can have an enormous influence on the positioning and personality of a retail brand. Brand awareness increases as before customers even visit the store, they already have a good understanding of the brand's proposition.

Lower costs

Through e-commerce additional store sales can be generated for only minimal extra costs. Tesco, Asda and Sainsbury's for example use a store-choice model for their online business, as all online orders are delivered from their supermarkets. Moreover, if the retailer is in direct contact with customers via the internet, there will be less waste in the communications budget.

Better timeliness and flexibility

Compared with a catalogue, the range on a website can be more up to date. Via a website it is possible to react quickly to market changes. If it is necessary, the offer on the website can be adjusted within a short period of time. Products that are not available any more can be deleted from the website straight away. It is also possible to try to launch products on the website that are not yet in the store. Because of these product launches, the retail brand stays up to date and flexible.

All channels can work together to intensify the relationship with customers and to increase sales through every channel. The advantages and strengths of each sales channel can complement each other. By being present in all sales channels, the retailer will have more marketing opportunities. Awareness and use of the website and the catalogue can be promoted through in-store communications. A website can enrich the brand promise and provide information that is not available in the store. Online then becomes one more way to be in contact with the consumer. It does not compete with the other channels. The analysis of JC Penney's customer spend by channel in Table 6.1 shows that a well-executed multi-channel strategy is exponential, not additive.

Channel	Average yearly spend (US$)
Internet	157
Store	195
Catalogue	201
Internet and catalogue	446
Internet and store	485
Catalogue and store	608
Catalogue, store and internet	887

Source: DFWIMA presentation 2003, JOP figures, cited in The Smart Marketing Report, June 2004, Doubleclick.

Table 6.1 JC Penney's customer spend by channel

Multi-channel retailing can result in incremental sales. After all, internet sales are growing faster than retail sales via stores. A JC Penney triple-channel shopper (catalogue, store and internet) is worth more than four times as much as a store-only customer. The mix of shopping channels strengthens the relationship with the customer.

American Girl, one of the top direct marketers, children's publishers and experiential retail brands in the United States, is not only a good example of a retailer with a very specific target group, it is also a nice example of a multi-channel retailer with a fully integrated market approach. Since the first catalogue debuted in 1986, American Girl has provided products for each stage of a young girl's development. From her preschool days of baby dolls and fantasy play through to her teen years of self-expression and individuality, the product range features books, dolls and accessories. In 1992 the company launched the *American Girl* magazine, an age-appropriate, advertising-free publication. With over 650,000 subscribers, the magazine ranks among the top ten children's magazines in the United States, and is the largest magazine dedicated exclusively to girls.

In 1995 the range was extended with toys and clothing. American Girl opened its first store in 1998 in Chicago. The main reason was that the company got a lot of requests for places where customers could see and touch the products. The store in Chicago was such a success that the company opened another store in New York. Both stores, as well as the magazine, show that the company really understands little girls and knows how to create a unique experience. All American Girl products are marketed and distributed through the company's award-winning catalogue, its website and American Girl Place, its proprietary retail stores. The books are also available in bookstores nationwide, so customers can shop with American Girl in just the way they want.

The English retailer Argos also offers customers a multi-channel approach, allowing people to shop in stores, over the phone, through its website or by mail order. A catalogue is published twice a year. Customers can order via the internet, the call centre or by mail. The majority of Argos's range is also available in its stores. Argos is the UK's leading general merchandise retailer. It is the UK number one retail brand for toys and small electrical appliances, and a leading player in many other markets including do-it-yourself and gardening, consumer electronics and furniture. Argos has over 650 stores throughout the UK and the Republic of Ireland. Approximately 98 per cent of the UK population live within 10 miles of an Argos store. There are also several Call and Collect stores, offering the full Argos range on 'order today – collect tomorrow' terms in small catchment areas. Argos also has an award-winning website and an Argos Direct home shopping division. All these shopping channels are fully integrated. Orders made via mail, call centre or internet can be picked up in the stores, and possible problems can be solved there too.

The Sharper Image is an American leading speciality retailer of innovative, high-quality products that are useful and entertaining and designed to make life easier and more enjoyable. The company is known for its unique range of products across categories such as electronics, recreation and fitness, personal care, housewares, travel, toys and gifts. More than 75 per cent of its revenue comes from The Sharper Image private brands and exclusive brands. The Sharper Image is trying to expand its customer base by offering products with popular price points and by attracting younger customers through its internet offerings. The stores, the catalogue and the internet are now three synergistic selling channels for The Sharper Image. The stores are good for almost half the total sales. The catalogue represents about 30 per cent and the internet about 15 per cent. The direct response expertise The Sharper Image has acquired over 25 years is now leveraged across catalogue, internet, magazine, radio and television. Catalogues still serve as the primary medium, and 78 million of them are distributed every year.

Traditional retailers like Victoria's Secret and Barnes & Noble in the United States, and GUS and Tesco in the UK, now run successful multi-channel operations. Retailers originally established in the bricks-and-mortar environment will increasingly dominate the e-commerce market. Tesco.com is the most profitable online grocery company in the world.

6.3 Efficiency brands

Convenience is not only about the accessibility of the store, the website or the call centre. A foundation of that nature will often be too thin as a successful differentiating attribute. Only the most extreme implementation of accessibility can lead to a strong positioning.

Accessibility will more often be a competitive or supporting attribute than a differentiating one. There are more opportunities to establish a unique positioning if the retailer focuses on the speed and the ease of the total buying process. Accessibility is only one aspect of it. Customers do not have a lot of time to explore a store extensively. They are looking for efficient retail brands, particularly when it comes to low-interest products. Convenience and one-stop shopping are then more important. Once they have found what they are looking for, they want to leave the store as quickly as possible. A retail brand that saves the customer time will truly stand out from the competition. Consumers try to optimize their total shopping costs. Convenience and price therefore become the most important components.

Efficiency brands should provide convenience in all areas of the business, because convenience is a complete experience. Aspects that are important to the consumer are discussed below.

Easy pre-shopping

Before consumers go shopping, they want to have an idea about the merchandise mix and the prices the retailer charges. They want to have that information when it suits them. The internet can play an important role in this, but so too can the call centre, by answering possible questions for example.

Easy accessibility

The opening hours have to meet the customer's wishes. The store or the website has to be easily accessible. For some consumers that means a large category killer or hypermarket at the edge of town. Other people however would prefer to go to a nearby store. For large, important purchases consumers are generally prepared to go a little further out of their way than for commodity purchases. The proximity of other stores can also make a location more appealing. The store entrance and the website's homepage have to be inviting, and parking at the store has to be sufficient and convenient. The safety of the parking area is also becoming more important. It is of course even easier when customers do not even have to go to a store any more Shopping from home or the office at non-store retailers, combined with door-to-door delivery, makes this possible.

Easy navigation

Customers should be able to find what they are looking for quickly and easily, on the internet, in the catalogue and in the store. Layout, visual merchandising and signage should be clear, and lines of sight should be established within the store to ensure optimal visibility. A layout that forces customers to follow a prespecified route causes irritation. Ikea used to do this, but is now experimenting with routes through the store that are less dictatory. After all, customers want more freedom and a better overview. The aisles should be wide enough and the circulation easy, without congestion. Products for immediate use should be close to the entrance. Products that are used together should be presented together. That is why in its concept stores, Sony presents large television screens in fully decorated living rooms. This enables customers to get an idea of how these televisions might look in their homes.

A convenient range and services

Stores can help customers save time by offering more one-stop shopping. Supermarkets for example are now offering services like photo developing, ATMs and telephone services. However, a store can also make shopping easier in another way. Consumers have more choice, but less time, so giving them good product information makes things easier for them.

It can also be an advantage for a retailer to offer a limited number of versions of each product. Product ranges have been extended enormously in the last few years. Customers cannot see the wood for the trees. The supply of products has become so large and unclear that a consumer really needs help to make the right choice. The range is likely to increase further in the next few years. Consumers have too little time and too many choices, and even though they can acquire extensive product information from a retailer's website, they often do not have time or do not feel like doing so. They would rather trust the preselection made by the retailer. If consumers get the feeling the retail brand understands exactly what they need, they will leave searching for the right products to the retailer. In the store is of course where they will find what the retailer has selected as suitable for their tastes. Some department and exclusive clothing stores will go even one step further. As soon as clothing comes in that meets a customer's taste, a store employee will call the customer to invite him or her to visit the store. A personal shopper then shows the customer the clothes he or she is thought likely to choose.

Availability of products

The products customers want should be in stock or available at the moment customers want them. Once the customers know what they want, they should be able to get the product quickly and easily. At the French optician chain Grand Optical, glasses are ready for customers within an hour of the decision to purchase. At other opticians customers might have to wait a week or longer.

However, in many stores customers are still often confronted with out-of-stock situations. For example, according to AC Nielsen the average stock-out level in Dutch supermarkets is 5 per cent, but at peak moments it can be as high as 20 per cent. The Gap invests in high inventory per square foot to ensure its stores can carry many units in each size, and avoid disappointing customers.

Easy information

Store employees should be knowledgeable, product information should be relevant and present at any desired moment, and prices in the store should be clearly marked, so customers can see how much the products cost straight away. Restoration Hardware, a fast-growing retail company in the United States, offers a very well-merchandised world of high-quality textiles, furniture, lighting, bathroom goods, hardware and unique 'discovery' items. These are products of lasting value and classic design, and are all from brands that speak of good taste and free-spirited individuality. The stores are known for their eloquent signs posted next to each item. The signs tell a story about each of Restoration's products, and provide detailed information about the item's construction, components and functionality.

In its produce department Target provides information about the purchase, storage and preparation of the various products. More and more stores are installing price-check devices as well, so customers do not have to look for employees to figure out what the price is. And the drugstore chain Walgreens offers prescription labels in larger print for older customers.

Easy choice

In many fashion stores customers can only take three items into the fitting rooms, because this enables stock to be controlled more easily. That is not a rule at Victoria's Secret, though, because it wants to avoid obliging women to get dressed again and walk out into the store in order to obtain another item to try on. Moreover, there is always an employee stationed at the fitting rooms to get customers a different size if necessary. The fitting rooms are also bigger than in other stores.

In REI sport and outdoor goods stores, customers can test all the equipment in real-life situations. There are a climbing wall, a mountain bike track and lots of other opportunities to test all kinds of products. In supermarkets customers can taste products they are not familiar with. In Apple stores customers can experience for themselves all the different computer models and other equipment, and at Amazon customers can get an impression of a book they are interested by using the 'search inside the book' feature on the website.

Availability of employees

The role of employees is determined by the retail concept. In some stores that role is limited to replenishment of the shelves and working at the checkout. In other stores, employees have a clear sales and advice role. But no matter what the role of the employees, they still have to be there when the customer needs them.

Easy use

Some products require extra information or directions for use, or perhaps even installation in the customer's home. A retail brand can help by giving sufficient and relevant information to consumers so they know exactly how to install and use the product. That information can be provided by employees or via useful and accurate information points, located near the products.

Easy checkout

Fast checkout is critical for an efficiency brand. Once customers have selected their purchases, they want to leave the store as quickly as possible. Contact at the checkout is the last contact the customer has with the retail brand. If queues at the checkout are long, that last contact will leave a negative impression. Especially if not all checkouts are open, customers soon become irritated about the wait. One possible solution to long queues is self-scanning, something several multiple retail brands are currently experimenting with.

Easy post-purchase procedures
Once the product is bought, it still has to be taken home. If customers cannot take it home themselves, the retailer should offer a solution: hiring out trailers or a home delivery service, for example.

If a product does not live up to expectations at any point, the customer's problem should be solved quickly and without any hassle. It should therefore be irrelevant whether customers bought the product in a store, on the website or from the catalogue. What is important is that the retail brand is flexible and can adapt to their needs. Apparel retailer Banana Republic's return and exchange policy for its online sales is very clear, for example. It wants customers to love what they ordered, but if something is not right, Banana Republic gladly accepts returns of unwashed, unworn or defective merchandise. It will send customers another colour, a new size or an entirely different style. If they would rather have a refund, it will take care of that too. Banana Republic online offers several convenient ways to return or exchange merchandise, and customers can either go to a Banana Republic store to return merchandise purchased online, or simply mail it back.

Super Fast Pizza in Wisconsin in the United States positions itself on the speed of the buying process. It delivers really hot pizzas in about 15 minutes, a positioning mix of speed and quality it can only achieve by using new technology and by streamlining its entire process from order to delivery as much as possible. First, it specialized. It identified the seven most popular types of pizza. If a customer wants a pizza that is one-quarter anchovy, one-quarter pineapple and half bacon, for example, it can't help. Second, it focused on the most popular size of pizza, medium. And since some people like their pizza cut in slices, and some prefer squares, it doesn't cut the pizza. It does however give customers a free cutter with their first order.

The pizza is cooked while the driver is delivering it. Super Fast's high-tech mobile pizza kitchens are licensed restaurants, and are fitted out with custom ovens that can cook pizza at a speedy 600 degrees. Its mobile kitchens utilize the latest in wireless internet technology, and produce enough electricity to power a typical home. And because they cook the pizza while driving to the customer's home, the 30-second trip from the oven to the door ensures the pizza arrives hot every time.

To keep everything as easy as possible, the pricing structure is also very simple. Super Fast Pizza prices all its pizzas the same, and since it is already coming to customers' homes, it offers them a second, third, fourth or fifth pizza at a real bargain price. When customers order online, they help the company to deliver their pizza even faster, so they are rewarded with a free Pepsi for each pizza they order. And since repeat customers are easier to find, the company offers a discount for repeat orders.

Staples, the American office supplies superstore chain, opened its first store in 1986. The company now has approximately 69,000 associates serving customers through about 1,800 office superstores, mail order catalogues, e-commerce and a contract business. Staples operates in the United States, Canada and a number of European countries. Its superstores offer everyday low prices on more than 7,500 office supply items, including business machines, computers and peripherals, furniture and communications equipment. All stores offer a copy centre that provides on-site copying, printing and binding services, and stores in the United States also feature a business technology centre where customers can obtain computer upgrades, software installations and consultations with specially trained staff. The US superstores also have internet access points to Staples.com, expanding their available offerings to 45,000 products and dozens of business services.

In selected locations, Staples operates its superstores 24 hours a day. Staples' goal is to provide small business owners with the low prices on office supplies that were previously enjoyed only by large corporations. To these customers time is very important, so Staples' business strategy is to provide an easy shopping experience. This positioning on convenience is further extended with its supporting attribute of low prices. It wants to be the retail brand that makes life easier, saves time and delivers products consumers need and trust. Buying office supplies should be as easy as possible. That is why Staples' advertising tagline is 'Staples. That was easy.' It proves this promise in many different ways: easy access, clear layout with a technology solutions department in the centre of the store, informative signage, knowledgeable salespeople and short queues at the checkout. In addition, its mobile technical services department installs computers in customers' homes and offices.

Staples has also introduced an ink and toner in-stock guarantee programme. Based on customer research, 84 per cent of small businesses surveyed said a critical aspect of shopping for office products was finding the toner or ink cartridge they needed in stock. Staples now guarantees in-stock availability of every inkjet and toner cartridge currently offered in its stores. If a cartridge is out of stock, it will deliver it direct to the customer at a 10 per cent discount.

Buying a used car can be pretty complicated. Customers tend to be insecure about the quality and worried about having to negotiate the price with the dealer. CarMax, America's leading speciality retailer of used cars, has simplified the buying process considerably. In 1991 it surveyed consumers to find out what those buying cars liked and disliked about the process. Unsurprisingly, buying a used car was right up there with going to the dentist for a root canal treatment. Customers asked for the following:

- Do not play games. Let me know the price straight away, not after hours of haggling and mind games.
- Do not waste my time. Have one salesperson work with me from start to finish. And do not make me drive all over town to find the right car.
- Provide security. Inspect and recondition all cars and back them with a limited warranty so I do not have to worry what will happen when I drive off the lot.
- Make car buying fun. Be helpful, not pushy. Buying a car should be as much fun as driving one home.

With this wish list in mind, CarMax opened its first store in Richmond, Virginia in 1993. Its used car superstores and new car locations have quickly become the largest chain in the United States. Best of all, its customers really appreciate the convenience. In fact, 93 per cent of its customers would recommend CarMax to a friend. So CarMax proves what its slogan promises: 'The way car buying should be.'

Shopping can also be made easier through perfect visual merchandising. If everything customers need for a certain purpose is presented together, they will be able to find everything a lot quicker. About 12 years ago Rooms To Go opened its first two furniture stores in Orlando, Florida. The plan was to create a totally new way of buying furniture. Rooms To Go would simply make furniture buying easier. The founders were convinced they could sell good-looking furniture at affordable prices every day, if they sold enough of it. To do that, they created a new way of displaying their furniture: in complete, easy to see room settings. Each room is displayed and accessorized to the last detail. Rooms To Go designs and coordinates each room, so its customers do not have to. It carries enough stock, so delivery comes in days, not months. It simply is Rooms To Go. Consumers like the idea of easy one-stop decorating, so much so that Rooms To Go is now the largest furniture retailer in America.

1-800-Mattress and its online store, Mattress.com, are also really efficiency brands. They make buying a mattress as easy as possible. Together, these shopping channels offer consumers advantages and benefits they cannot find anywhere else: a positioning mix of differentiating convenience and a supporting merchandise range. The most important benefits are:

- Best in selection. They have the best and largest selection of the most popular brands in North America. They have the largest selection of the number one brand in the United States and a house special, the 1-800 mattress collection.
- First in service. Customers can order online, by phone or visit one of the showrooms. The company was the first in the mattress industry to offer a 1-800 number for customers to call and order its mattresses. And if customers are unsure about their mattress choice, they can talk to specially trained, skilful bedding consultants. They are always on call, 24 hours a day, 365 days a year. Customers can also browse the site to find information.
- Best in home delivery. 1-800-Mattress offers a fast and convenient delivery service; same day delivery is available in many areas. Fun fact: people in Chicago have called both a Chinese food restaurant and 1-800-Mattress. The mattress arrived before the food did. The drivers give the

customer 'white-glove treatment'. They repackage the mattress on the spot and take it away if it does not suit the customer's health and lifestyle needs.

• What you buy is what you get. From the beginning the company made a practice of selling top-quality merchandise instead of 'no name' mattresses, as many mattress retailers have done.

• Compare and buy. The company does not just tell customers its mattresses are superior, it shows them. It lines up cut-aways of its competitors' products against its own offerings. Customers can see for themselves that 1-800 offers more value every time and at any price point.

• Satisfaction guaranteed. Customers can rest easy knowing that their comfort is ensured by a 60-night comfort exchange policy. 1-800-Mattress offers a comfort exchange when a customer purchases a mattress and boxspring set, or a mattress for use on a platform bed. The customer only has to pick up the phone and call customer service.

By making the purchase of a mattress as easy as possible, 1-800-Mattress has built a very successful business in a cut-throat competitive retail market. Forty percent of new customers are referrals. Many of their customers remember their mattresses because their parents and grandparents ordered them. In fact one customer called the company and confessed that he had crank-called its operators as a child, but was now getting married and wanted to buy a mattress.

6.4 Service brands

A retail brand can also make shopping easier for the customer by offering excellent service. Consumers are increasingly confronted with self-service in stores. The only contact they have with employees is often at the checkout now, and even this is disappearing in favour of self-scanning. Machines are taking over from human contact. It is easy, at any given moment, to order something via the internet from all over the world, and ATMs are fine for people in a hurry. Face-to-face contact is becoming scarce. This therefore results in more opportunities for retail brands that offer good, personal service. The service however needs to be unique and tailor-made, and to be visible and perceptible in every activity: giving customers what they want, when they want it and how they want it.

Almost all retailers believe they offer good service. The question is whether consumers think so too. Often there is a huge gap between what the consumer perceives as special service and what the retailer offers. Some kinds of service belong to the customer's normal expectation level. Home delivery or giving guarantees is no longer enough, as they are nothing more than qualifying or competitive services. Price brands also offer these to customers. An 'ordinary' service level is not enough for a service brand because the customer expects no less. It is often only if a service is not provided that the customers take notice. All the basic services are therefore only potential dissatisfiers. A store that wants to position itself as a service brand has to go further and take the wishes of the individual customer as a starting point. Personal contact is then almost indispensable. The retail brand will have to offer a service that far exceeds the customer's expectations, and this then becomes a satisfier. For example a store might offer not just regular home delivery, but home delivery when it suits the customer best, even if that is early Sunday morning. At the English electrical goods chain Comet, for example, customers can see real-time delivery options on the website and book the time slot that suits them best.

A store can provide better service using customer data from a loyalty programme, for example, but real service is still undertaken by humans. Knowledgeable salespeople can be a real benefit to the customer. For example, buying electrical appliances, with all the incomprehensible abbreviations and technical terms, can be so complicated that customers have a real need for demonstration and assistance in the store, and installation and service at home. That is why Staples in the United States has a mobile technical service to help customers install their computers at home. After-sales service can also lead to a competitive advantage if complaints are solved quickly and without any hassle. If the brand promise is always lived up to, then customers will be surprisingly pleased, resulting in store preference and brand loyalty. Through excellent service, which exceeds the customer's expectations, a retail brand can position itself in relation to the competition. The American department store Nordstrom is an example of this. It is legendary for its associates, who go to the limit to please customers. For example, the story goes that Nordstrom exchanges and takes back products it does not even sell.

So service offers a lot of opportunities for a real point of difference. In retail, service can be a very important differentiating weapon. It is however also one of the most difficult positioning attributes. After all, to provide great service a retailer largely depends on its employees, and unfortunately no retailer is able to completely control its employees. The owner of a small store might be able to observe well how its employees behave, but that is impossible in a larger store. A customer's experience with one salesperson might perhaps determine his or her total perception of the brand, so positioning on service also has to be evident in the retailer's hiring and training programme. If a retailer takes good care of its employees, the employees will take good care of the customers. However, good salespeople are expensive, and wages make up about half the total overheads of a retail company, so where possible retailers try to save on wages, for example by changing to self-service. However, if there are fewer salespeople a retail brand will have to communicate with its customers in other ways. In a self-service store the only contact with the customer is at the checkout, and the customer will then perhaps only remember the long queues.

A lack of (qualified) salespeople can partly be compensated for by offering good, relevant information near the product itself. For consumers who want to do their own thing in the store and for moments when salespeople are busy with other customers, good signage and product information can be very meaningful.

However, a shift has been noticed over the years concerning salespeople. Retailers no longer assume that employees have to take care of the shelves and that the shelves then take care of the customers. Retail companies have realized they cannot endlessly continue lowering wages. Low prices are important but customers also expect a certain level of service. That is why a lot of money is spent on educating and motivating salespeople. The retail brand then has to find the right balance between good service and the costs incurred in providing it.

The common assumption is still that improving service means increasing costs. However this is the old paradigm. The new paradigm concerns improving service and decreasing costs. This sounds like a pipe dream, but in fact it is a portrait of the future. High-performance retailers are becoming increasingly proficient at (GDR, 2004: 25):

- eliminating non-value-adding processes from the service chain;
- improving productivity through technology;
- redesigning the service system to be simpler and more reliable and minimizing the need for a service network;
- empowering service providers, reducing the need for costly supervision and inspection;
- reducing customer defections through improved service and value, benefiting from the cost efficiencies of serving the same customers for longer periods of time.

In effect, the best-managed companies spend a relatively high proportion of their resources on these items, which add demonstrable value to customers. Retailers need not make a choice between superior service and efficient, cost-effective operating practice. Customers want both excellent service and competitive prices.

A retail brand that primarily wants to position itself on service will first have to define what its target group understands by service. The retailer will have to research which services are relevant to the customer, and which really make it stand out from other retail brands. Historically, customer service has been equated with people: smiling, greeting shoppers, and of course heavy doses of 'Yes ma'am, yes sir, thank you very much and have a nice day.' Customers think genuine customer service and courtesy are great as well. They would love to experience that on a more regular basis. However, for them, it is the fourth most important aspect of customer service. Here are the top four issues given by customers when asked to define great customer service (Rice, 2005):

- Having the product they are looking for to solve their needs; and having it in stock. Simply put: sell what I need and actually have it on the shelf when I come to buy it.
- Having a store that is logically laid out so customers can find what they want without wasting their time. This includes easy entrance to and exit from the parking lot, readily available parking, baskets available, and

shopping trolleys that actually work. It also includes the basics of navigation such as logical adjacencies of products, clear signage and clearly marked products. Finally, it includes customer public enemy number one: the checkout lines. They need to be staffed and moving fast; or perhaps in the future, eliminated altogether.

• Having information readily available to answer questions and to help customers decide what to buy: signs, brochures or salespeople, providing the tools customers need to help them make intelligent buying decisions in the store.

• Finally, it is important to have friendly, knowledgeable staff. While many retailers equate great customer service with great people, customers equate great customer service with things that make shopping easier and more efficient. Having great staff is just one part of that.

From its humble beginnings as a small dairy store founded in 1969 with seven employees, Stew Leonard's in Norwalk, Connecticut has grown to become not only the world's largest dairy store, but also one of the most renowned grocery stores. The first store carried just eight items. Stew Leonard's has taken the fresh dairy concept and expanded into meats, fish, produce, baked goods, cheese and wine. Unlike traditional grocery stores that sell an average of 30,000 items, each Stew Leonard's store carries only 2,000 items, chosen specifically for their freshness, quality and value. The success of this family-owned business and its legion of loyal shoppers is however largely due to its passionate approach to customer service: 'Rule 1 – The customer is always right; Rule 2 – If the customer is ever wrong, re-read rule 1.' This principle is so essential to the foundation of the company that it is etched in a three-ton granite rock at each store's entrance. In order to create happy customers, Stew Leonard's is also recognized for its management philosophy: 'Take good care of your people and they in turn will take good care of your customers.' It is this philosophy that has helped Stew Leonard's earn its ranking in *Fortune* magazine's '100 best companies to work for in America' list for four consecutive years.

The challenge for service brands is that the dividing line between qualifying or competitive service and supporting or differentiating service is becoming more blurred. What is seen as a differentiating service today will perhaps be a competitive service tomorrow, offered by every store: a service that is taken for granted by the customer. To remain really distinctive in the future, service will have to be more tailored to personal needs. A supporting or differentiating service can really delight customers.

Positioning as a service brand will not only influence the way the employees behave, it will influence the entire marketing strategy. The British firm Vodafone, for example, chose a very striking layout for its store on Oxford Street in London. The most prominent and most expensive space on the ground floor is completely used for providing service, as opposed to many other stores where service is hidden in a corner on the top floor. In order to buy telephones and accessories at Vodafone, the customer has to go downstairs. This is perhaps at the cost of sales, but at one of the busiest and most expensive locations in London, this layout makes a very clear statement about the importance Vodafone places on good service. The store design is used to communicate the desired brand positioning.

Superquinn is an Irish supermarket chain that is known for its service. The company opened its first store in Dublin in 1960. It now has around 4,000 employees. With a market share of 20 per cent, Superquinn has a dominant position in the Dublin grocery market, a success that is mostly due to the excellent service it offers its customers. For example Superquinn (Crawford and Mathews, 2001: 7):

- posts a greeter at the door to welcome people, help them get a trolley, offer coffee, or even fetch a wheelchair;
- promotes visibility of store managers in the store instead of in their offices;
- provides umbrellas and a carryout service to customers' cars;
- posts signs around the store explaining the nutritional content of fruit and vegetables to help customers make more informed choices;
- positions a customer-service counter near the entrance of every store to help customers with questions and complaints;
- will stock special items for customers, even those only normally carried by a competitor, to eliminate the need for them to make special trips for one or two items;
- employs aisle monitors in charge of specific areas of the store to whom customers can go with questions;

• trains fishmongers and butchers in culinary skills so they can help recommend cuts and give preparation ideas to customers;
• operates a child-care centre, staffed by trained professionals, where customers can leave their children to play while they shop.

Top of the priority list of founder Feargal Quinn (until he sold the group recently) was the need to stay close to the customer. One of the ways he did this was through regular stints in each of his stores, packing bags for customers, and attending weekly customer panels at which he listened to groups of volunteer Superquinn shoppers who told him how they thought the company could serve them better.

7. POSITIONING ON STORE EXPERIENCE

When they go shopping, consumers are looking for experiences. Shopping is competing with other ways of spending free time. Therefore, there are plenty of opportunities for retail brands to focus not only on merchandise, but also on store experience. Through the store experience, offline retailers can permanently differentiate themselves from their online competitors, whereas with their range, price and convenience that difference is harder to achieve.

Especially in the future, there will be opportunities for six types of brand experience:

- entertainment brands, which owe their competitive advantage to a unique mix of entertainment merchandise, inspiring visual merchandising, and employees who are, if you like, performers on the retail stage;
- expertise brands, which challenge customers intellectually: customers gain new knowledge and ideas every time they visit the store;
- design brands, where the merchandise as well as the store architecture and visual merchandising have a strong design character;
- hedonism brands, which offer pleasure and stimulation for the senses: these brands are real consumption palaces;
- lifestyle brands, which focus on customers' actual or desired lifestyle, and offer everything for that particular lifestyle;
- bargain brands, which offer the consumer the chance to go bargain hunting: this is not about the lowest price, but about the best bargain.

7.1 More than just products

For many people retailing today is not only about products, but also about experiences, recreation and having a good time. Offline retail brands can differentiate themselves from their online competitors through a store experience with multi-sensory appeal. In order to experience the brand the store becomes a stage. To these brands retailing is not just selling: it is also about telling stories and providing excitement. In every store the consumer undergoes an experience, either desired or not desired. Aldi and Kruidvat offer a relatively dull in-store experience. On the contrary, Victoria's Secret and Zara offer an exciting experience.

Consumers experience the store through all their senses: through touch-points like the range of stock, prices, store design, visual merchandising, employees and many other impulses. An experience develops automatically, as it were. The experience is created by the total of all impressions in the store. What you see and what you feel is what you get. But a store can also consciously try to differentiate itself from other stores by providing a unique store experience. This store experience will be the differentiating positioning attribute. Buying products now becomes buying into an experience. As for an experience brand, it is not only the merchandising that is important for the development of the store format, but the experience of the customer as well. A good-looking store counts for as much as a good range.

In the case of an experience brand, the store becomes a place to spend leisure time instead of just shopping time. The store experience will include the entire retail offer: the merchandise, the customer service, the visual merchandising and the total store atmosphere. All touch-points in the store are orchestrated in such a way that consumers will leave the store having had a unique experience that appealed to all their senses.

Of course it is the intention of the retailer that consumers will also buy something. In order to be successful, the store experience should entice people to spend more money. Consumers who only come to browse are not bringing in any money.

Shopping used to be primarily about buying something. However, it is increasingly about doing something. Stores now have to compete with other leisure activities. Consumers want to be stimulated, entertained and inspired, and they refuse to accept boredom. Each time, the store experience has to be more surprising and more extreme, because customers are always looking for new shopping experiences.

Retailers that respond to this demand for experience shopping have the possibility of creating a sustainable point of difference. The shopping experience can be just as differentiating as the range, price or convenience. A store visit can be a unique and memorable experience rather than the act of simply buying something. A visit to a store can be like a voyage of discovery, in which the shopping context is equally as important as the merchandise offer. For example, Barnes & Noble, the leading bookseller in the United States, believes that a bookstore does more than just sell books. It welcomes its customers to browse, read, chat, think, debate or simply relax with a cup of coffee in any one of over 600 stores across the country. Barnes & Noble is a mixture of a bookstore, a library and a coffee shop. Armchairs are everywhere, so customers are at ease when browsing through books and magazines. The shops also organize all kinds of events. Authors sign their books, salespeople read to small children, and in the music department customers are advised on how to start a collection of classical music. Barnes & Noble has become a sort of gathering place with a multi-sensory experience. This emotional benefit of Barnes & Noble strongly distinguishes it from the more functional Amazon.

No laws require a retailer to be boring. Great experience brands generate customer excitement by offering their customers more than a mundane experience. Customer excitement means (Berry, 1999):

- experiencing genuine pleasure in interacting with the retailer as a result of the freshness and creativity of the store, merchandise and/or employees;
- learning something new from the retailer: a new approach to cooking, a great vacation idea, how to build a deck or put up wallpaper, how to dress better, or how to use the internet more effectively;
- solving an important problem: fixing a car, fixing a tooth, finding a great wedding dress, a stylish pair of glasses or fashionable yet comfortable shoes.
- feeling like a smart shopper who is in control and not wasting money or time.

A retail brand can beat the competition by offering a unique experience to consumers. Such an experience is difficult to imitate, and the better the experience, the more often customers will come back. To provide this experience, the store will have to be exciting, stimulating and memorable. Entertainment, food and drinks, and retailing will then more often be an indissoluble whole, because entertainment, food and drinks can contribute a lot to the retail experience.

In the western world, consumers already have everything they need. Therefore, consumers want to be stimulated emotionally when shopping. They want to be entertained. Disney and Nike offer their customers this experience by turning their stores into theatres. Disney then connects two worlds, entertainment and retail. With Nike it is about the mixture of sports, entertainment and retail. The Dutch department store De Bijenkorf offers entertainment by letting children decorate their own cake on Mother's Day, for example.

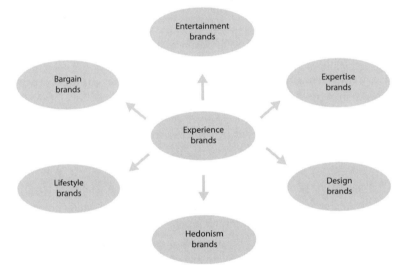

Figure 7.1 Types of experience brands

Store experience is often associated with entertainment. However, entertainment is not the only experience a retailer can offer its customers. A store experience is almost always developed by a unique mix of the range, inspiration-enhanced visual merchandising and highly motivated employees. At the centre of the experience is the merchandise. After all, a consumer visits a store to buy something. But an experience brand does more than offer a unique range. The visual merchandising and the way the employees behave are consciously used to create a differentiating store experience. The emphasis can differ between experience brands. Some experience brands emphasize the range; others try to create an unforgettable store experience through their visual merchandising or employees. In all situations, however, all the components of the in-store experience should be consistent with each other. The store experience can then be created by adventure, aesthetics, culture, luxury or creativity as well as simple entertainment.

In the future, there will be opportunities in retail for six main types of experience brands: entertainment brands, expertise brands, design brands, hedonism brands, lifestyle brands and bargain brands.

Entertainment brands

A retail brand that builds its experience positioning on the entertainment it offers is more or less comparable to amusement parks like Disney World and Sea World. The range held by these entertainment brands is entertainment-related, and the visual merchandising increases the entertainment even more. The store is a kind of stage, and the employees are the performers in the show.

Expertise brands

This kind of retail brand inspires, educates and delivers knowledge. Consumers visit the store to gather knowledge or information. Therefore, some of these stores are a little like a library or a training centre. In visual merchandising a lot of attention is paid to product information. And the employees play an important part when it comes to expertise brands, as they are the undisputed experts in their field.

Design brands

A retail brand can also position itself with its excellent store design and visual merchandising. The commercial side of things is almost of minor importance compared with the aesthetics. In this type of store all products appear as if they are in a museum or gallery, individually presented with special lighting. With design brands employees are mainly there to perfect the visual merchandising.

Hedonism brands

Some retail brands are a real consumer paradise. Enjoyment comes first. The store is a location where the consumer can be pampered in these hectic times. It offers the consumer an escape from daily existence. The merchandise, visual merchandising and employees all communicate pampering.

Lifestyle brands

A retail brand can help consumers to obtain a desired lifestyle, in the same way as a lifestyle magazine does. The emphasis for lifestyle brands is mainly on the merchandise and its coordinated presentation. There is a clear style relationship between all products in the store, and all the products and services that fit a certain lifestyle are presented together.

Bargain brands

Most consumers are not looking for the lowest prices. However, they do like to profit from bargains. Stores that do not sell the cheapest products can still be real bargain paradises because they sell designer labels far below the regular price. The heavily marked-down merchandise is the biggest attraction of this type of experience brand. The visual merchandising suggests that customers are getting real bargains. The employees mostly work on replenishing stock or at the tills.

Some retail brands offer consumers a mix of multiple store experiences. For example, the Christmas display windows of the French department store Lafayette and the British store Selfridges offer entertainment for all ages, but these are also stores that appeal to all kinds of hedonistic feeling. Consumers can buy the most beautiful gifts for themselves or for others. Lafayette and Selfridges are reminiscent of a gallery in which people can admire all the beautiful things. At the same time, they also act like lifestyle magazines, selecting and displaying exactly what they believe customers are looking for. During sales and other price promotions they are a true shopping paradise for consumers. Both department stores offer customers a total experience, but within these broadly similar positioning mixes both department stores have different emphases. Selfridges is, for example, more focused on food than Lafayette is.

Requirements for positioning on store experience

The impact and growth of e-commerce makes visiting a store more and more a leisure activity, so every offline retail brand has to consider which role experience should play in the store. Stores that want to clearly position themselves as an experience brand will have to meet a number of requirements.

Authenticity

The store experience has to be real and honest. It should not be created at random, but should fit well with the store's brand identity. The store experience should reflect and strengthen the brand positioning and brand personality. If that is not the case, consumers will see right through it. The need for authenticity is also an important trend in consumer behaviour. Because of the abundance of products, services and information, consumers have developed a need to identify what is authentic. This authenticity is indispensable for experience brands. The history of the retail brand, the country of origin, the core competence and a number of other factors can be the foundation of this authenticity.

Product related

A store that only offers an experience, but does not offer the right range and other functional and emotional benefits, will not be successful. After consumers have visited the store a few times, the novelty will be gone and they will not go there any more. Planet Hollywood is an example of this. With only an attractive store design and some film memorabilia, Planet Hollywood could not hide the fact that the food and service were sometimes very poor. The basis of the format was missing. So after a while, customers did not show up any more. The store experience has to match the merchandise on offer, and it should preferably be integral with the merchandise itself. If there is no connection between the experience and the merchandise, there is a risk that consumers will only come to browse but not to buy. Ikea is very successful with its playground for kids, but what works for Ikea will not automatically work for other retail companies. Serving free cups of coffee in the corner of a supermarket could work, for example, whereas a storyteller in an American Kroger supermarket sounds like an inappropriate choice. Why not have an area where children can prepare delicious snacks themselves?

Consumer involvement

To really undergo a store experience, consumers should not stand on the sideline, but become part of the experience themselves, and be able to buy products they have contributed to, for example. Consumers should be co-creators, making the experience stronger and more memorable. After all, interactivity results in higher involvement, and the experience becomes personalized. Build-A-Bear Workshop offers customers the opportunity to make their own bear, making them part of the experience. Barnes & Noble enables customers to read books and magazines at their ease, and at some fashion stores consumers can participate in the design of their own clothes.

Frequent innovations

Every season, amusement parks have a new draw to attract customers. After all, consumers get bored easily. Retail companies that want to position themselves as entertainment brands should follow the example of amusement parks. This is something that is only possible if the store design is flexible.

Rainforest Café is a place to shop and eat. The store and restaurant look like a rainforest, with lush surroundings, cascading waterfalls and beautiful giant aquariums. The menu is influenced by the cuisines of Mexico, Asia and the Caribbean. It certainly is a unique concept, but Rainforest Café does not change enough to really profile itself as an entertainment store. Visitors that come to the Rainforest Café for the second time are not surprised any more and do not really see anything new.

Profitability

The store experience is not an objective but a means. It can never be at the expense of sales and profit. If the experience attracts so many customers so that there is hardly an opportunity to buy something, the experience misses its objective. Customers should be not only looking, but also buying. With this positioning retailers can take into account learnings from the movie and music industries, and also the publishing industry. Every year companies in these industries find success with only a few blockbusters or bestsellers. These successes finance the losses from the failures. Retail brands will come to experience that not every store experience will achieve the desired effect.

Experience brands, more so than those positioned otherwise, will have to captivate their customers every time. Each time customers visit the store, it has to be worth their while. This creates high demands on the store design and visual merchandising. Both will have to be very flexible, therefore easily replaceable materials should be used for the store design. Stores can learn from theatres, where the stage set is changed multiple times in one night.

For years, DKNY has been a good retail example for store design and visual merchandising flexibility (Gobé, 200: 89). Its New York store completely changes its look and feel every month or so, to tell an entirely new story. If the story is themed around 'Spring', for example, the theatrical lighting is adjusted, the store redecorated and completely remerchandised to also communicate the same 'Spring' look and feel.

No matter how much experience a store offers a consumer, it should never be forgotten that the store also has to meet a number of operational demands. The store experience is the differentiating attribute. Range, price and convenience are the supporting, competitive or qualifying attributes. The range and price should be right, and customers should also be able to find the products they are looking for easily in an experience store. When they have found these products, paying for them at the till should be a hassle-free experience.

Disney parks are a good example of this. These parks not only offer the experience they are known for, they also ensure everything else goes smoothly. For example, if there are queues at certain attractions, everything is done to make the wait as pleasant as possible. In the same way, experience stores have to make sure they achieve the right balance in their positioning mix between emotional and functional benefits. After all, customers will judge the store on both aspects.

7.2 Entertainment brands

Entertainment brands offer customers a mix of unique entertainment merchandise, inspirational visual merchandising and employees who are, if you like, performers on the retail stage. This mix differentiates entertainment brands from stores, where entertainment is only an extra added value for the customer. Attracting customers with free entertainment will always be an option, especially as long as there are department stores. For example, in stores that offer customers free music and fashion shows, retail and entertainment are combined. The retailer wants customers to stay in the store as long as possible. The longer customers stay, the higher the chance of their spending money, so the retailer has to give the customer reasons to stay longer. A children's playground for example, where customers can temporarily drop their children, enables easy and potentially more pleasant shopping. Entertaining music, surprising lighting effects, a pleasant temperature, interactive displays and video monitors can make shopping more fun. Cafés and food courts can play an important role in making shopping more pleasant as well. Because of the entertainment in the store, a retail brand can build up an emotional bond with customers. However, retail brands that position themselves on entertainment achieve even better on this attribute. These brands have a completely integrated entertainment offer consisting of merchandise, store design, visual merchandising and employees.

In Las Vegas retail meets entertainment in the best way. The city itself has become a retail destination. Together with a casino and a hotel, the Forum Shops are part of Caesar's Palace in Las Vegas. The mall was opened in 1992 and continues to be the most successful mall in the United States, with sales per square metre that are about four times higher than the national average (Ryan, 2002: 14–15). With its mock-Latin slogan, 'Shoppus 'til you droppus', the mall's tongue-in-cheek Roman theme includes fountains, toga-clad entertainers and an artificial sky that shifts hourly from dark to dusk. One of the reasons for the success of the Forum Shops is the application of the traditional flair shown by the Las Vegas casinos for display and presentation.

At Times Square in New York, Toys'R'Us has a flagship store of more than 10,000 sq m. Toys'R'Us itself calls this store 'the Centre of the Toy Universe', but the store does not only impress with its size and enormous range. The store design is also impressive, as it features amongst other things 20 manufacturer brands all represented by their own shop. A 20 m high Ferris wheel is the centre of the store. Tickets for the ride are a few dollars. This money is given to charity. Manufacturer brands are grouped around the Ferris wheel. Other attractions include a Jurassic Park with a roaring dinosaur 6 m high and 12 m long, a two-storey Barbie doll's house, an Empire State Building, Statue of Liberty and Chrysler Building made from Lego, an ET shop and a Microsoft X-Box. This enormous range supports the store's positioning on experience.

The NBA store on Fifth Avenue also has many of the characteristics of an amusement park. Consumers can not only buy shirts from all the well-known basketball clubs, but also have a go at getting the ball into the basket themselves. They can have their picture taken with famous players and buy all kinds of basketball souvenirs. In short: it is a real experience for basketball lovers, just as the NBC Experience store at Rockefeller Center is an experience for fans of certain television programmes. In this store, customers can not only buy all sorts of products branded with well-known television programmes, but can also take a studio tour, for example.

Build-A-Bear Workshop is another example of an entertaining retail brand. The company was founded in 1997 and it now has about 230 stores in the United States and other countries. Build-A-Bear is an interactive store, where young and old children personally experience the joy of creating their very own teddy bear. Mass customization for a clearly defined target group has been turned into an interactive experience, where people spend hours choosing the materials for their one-of-a-kind bear. From the moment people walk in the door they know they are in a magical world. They are greeted by a Master Bear Builder associate, who guides them through all the bear-making fun. First they choose a furry friend to make from more than 30 animals, starting at US$10. Next they can let their 'friend' do the talking by recording their 'beary own' message, or choose from prerecorded sounds or songs. Then it is off to the 'stuff-station', where the stuffing is added with the customer's help and a hug test is given to make sure it is just right. Next customers select a heart, warm it up in the palms of their hands, make a wish, and put it inside the bear. This magical moment brings their furry friend to life and creates an unforgettable memory.

After the bear has been stuffed, hugged and given a heart, it is time to help stitch it up. Then it is given a spa treatment and its fur is brushed. Next it is time to name the new friend and create a personalized storybook or birth certificate. This is also where the bear is registered in a tracking system which helps lost animals find their way back home. The staff help customers to choose from hundreds of fashion clothing and accessory choices, and finally they walk out, hand-in-paw with their new best friends in an exclusive carry case, and with lots of smiles as well. Visiting a Build-A-Bear-Workshop is indeed a real experience. The store experience is supported even more by the unique range of self-made bears.

Stores that offer the consumer a mix of shopping, food and drink, and entertainment are starting to look more and more like amusement parks. The Disney stores offer consumers an experience with their merchandise featuring characters from Disney movies. In addition, in Disney stores all the visual merchandising is aimed at making the store look like a theatre. There are sets, movies and music, and the products and employees are the actors in the Disney fairytale world. Shopping and entertainment go hand in hand.

7.3 Expertise brands

People also enjoy shopping because they get a chance to see new products and new ideas. A store can challenge customers intellectually and broaden their outlook. It can be a place for ongoing education. This can be achieved via the extensive knowledge of the salespeople or by the inspiration that is created by the visual merchandising. Products can be presented in such a way that customers think of ideas on how to use them. Information enclosed with the products also adds extra value. Through the store's expertise, the customer not only makes a better choice, but also goes home with additional knowledge and ideas. These retail brands implicitly communicate their expertise; for example by pointing out how long they have been in business they are reassuring their customers of their credibility.

Williams-Sonoma, the American kitchen supplies retail company, is synonymous with culinary expertise. In the store, consumers get all the information and inspiration needed to prepare tasty meals and snacks at home. Williams-Sonoma positions itself as the first and still foremost source for cooks. For over 45 years, Williams-Sonoma stores have been shaping how people think about and cook food. The first store opened in 1956, selling a small array of cookware imported from France. Since then, the brand has expanded to hundreds of products from around the world, more than 250 stores, a direct-mail business that distributes millions of catalogues each year, and a successful e-commerce site.

Williams-Sonoma now sells everything for the kitchen and the kitchen table. In everything it does, it communicates absolute authority. There is an enormous cooking island in the centre of the store, which is not only where customers pay, but also where cooking lessons and kitchen demonstrations are given and different kinds of olive oil can be tasted. The perfect product information and the way the staff are dressed are also methods for Williams-Sonoma to communicate that it is extremely knowledgeable when it comes to cooking and eating. Because of that, the cooking store almost becomes a cooking school. Together, the range and the store experience are a perfect positioning mix.

To Home Depot, expertise is not the most important attribute, but it is still an indispensable one. In its positioning Home Depot chose to focus primarily on range, and the expertise of Home Depot supports this positioning attribute. After all, Home Depot is more than a store, it is a resource where people can go to learn and dream about home improvement projects. It is a welcoming place to go when people need to 'know how'. The power of the Home Depot brand is in the special relationships their associates have with their customers. Whether it is a professional customer looking for industrial quantities of material and speed of transaction, an experienced do-it-yourselfer who loves to work on projects, or a novice seeking help through the knowledgeable associates, clinics and workshops, their customers view Home Depot as more than just a store. To them, Home Depot is a library, an expert, a teacher, a coach, a neighbour and a friend.

Discovery Channel reaches beyond the television screen to bring the wonder and mystery of our world home to people. Those who like the convenience and product selection of online shopping can browse the more than 2,000 unique products, handy comparison charts and customer product reviews at Discovery Store.com. And when they find something they like, they can have it shipped straight to their door. Those who prefer to touch, see and play can visit one of Discovery Channel's American stores. Die-hard catalogue shoppers who enjoy perusing pages of powerful photography and informative product descriptions can sign up for the latest Discovery Channel catalogue. All these shopping channels bring consumers a broad array of products to help them explore the world and entertain their brains.

For over 30 years, Early Learning Centre in the UK has been creating toys: toys that help develop vital skills, toys that help children get off to the best possible start, and toys that are great fun. It develops toys to bring out the very best creativity and inspiration in children. When it designs them it works closely with experts, child psychologists and children themselves. It now has about 360 stores in the UK and 13 countries worldwide, including three new out-of-town playstores, which allow children to 'playtest' their toys through themed playzones. Early Learning Centre also runs concessions in Debenhams department stores, and sells selected toys in over 380 Sainsbury's supermarkets nationwide and over 200 Boots stores.

7.4 Design brands

In some stores it is all about design. The merchandise as well as the store architecture and visual merchandising have a very strong design character. There is a real merger between art and retail design. Elements of museums and galleries are brought into the store to offer consumers an aesthetic, cultural experience. Both store experience and range are equally important to the positioning. The novelty-seeking customer can barely absorb all the beautiful things. Beautifully illuminated jackets or skirts are displayed in eye-catching ways. The merchandise density is extremely low because large portions of the floor and walls are not being used. A higher merchandise density would no doubt be detrimental to the desired luxurious brand appeal. Everything is spaciously presented, and lighting plays an important role in dramatizing the products.

This type of experience store is known for its good taste. Delivering an experience to customers is in this case just as important as having a good range. A good example is the store of fashion designer Karl Lagerfeld in Paris. There are pictures on the walls taken by Lagerfeld himself. Only a few clothes, shoes and other accessories are displayed in the store. It is the type of store in which customers automatically start to whisper. The commercial appeal seems to be completely inferior to the aesthetics. The use of art in retail design camouflages, as it were, the store's sales objective.

A store that is really reminiscent of a museum or a gallery is the Prada store in New York. This store has a surface of about 2,000 sq m and cost about US$40 million, but the result is there to see. Because of its unique architecture and store design, it has become a palace for the brand. Shopping in this store becomes a luxurious experience. There is no signage on the outside. However, once inside, the customer is completely surprised by the store design, which looks more like a museum than a store. The most striking part of this Prada store is the enormous wooden curve, a 'half-pipe', that connects the ground floor with the basement. This half-pipe forms a kind of amphitheatre in which 30 mannequins are sharply aligned. The amphitheatre is, among other things, used to present the range of shoes, but after hours it can also be used for performances, lectures and multi-media events. On the ground level, display cages (derived from car manufacturers) hang from the ceiling with Prada products inside them. The walls are mainly used for graphics. Because of this kind of store design and visual merchandising, the store can quickly change to a totally different look, just as a theatre does.

To give the customer a feeling of luxury, the merchandise density is kept very low. Shoes or bags are displayed only here and there, and there is enough room on the clothes racks to also hang monitors on them, which continually show Prada fashion shows. Furthermore, the store has a round glass elevator, transparent fitting rooms with panels, which are darkened by pushing a button, and lots of other design elements using very innovative technology. For example, customers can change the lighting in the fitting rooms to see how a dress would look at night. Every product has a radio frequency identification (RFID) tag. By scanning this RFID tag, employees immediately have all the necessary information about each garment. They can show the customer what the first design sketches looked like and how the clothes were shown on the catwalk. This tag also provides information about the material and other product features. In addition, the sales staff can immediately tell the customer which sizes and colours are in stock. All this together makes a visit to this Prada store a real experience. The fact that the store looks more like a museum than a selling machine is taken for granted by the Prada family. After all, this store and other stores in, for example, Tokyo and Los Angeles, exist mainly to make a statement about the Prada brand.

Just like the Prada store in New York, the Apple stores have many of the characteristics of a museum, but Apple stores are much more sales-oriented. Apple only opens stores if it expects them to be profitable within a short period of time. It always chooses to locate them in the best streets and malls. Apple believes that using a computer should be simple, and so should buying one be. The store layout is simple and logical. Store design and fixtures are kept as simple as possible, so all the attention goes to the products. The store is a white box with a lot of lighting. It uses materials like stone, metal, glass, transparent synthetics and beechwood. Large pictures and glass are used to separate the different departments. All the equipment in the store can be tried out, and all products needed for a specific purpose are presented together. The sales staff help customers personalize their new Macs by setting up their email and internet accounts, installing software, connecting peripherals and more. In addition, the Apple stores have a Genius Bar where customers can talk to Apple whizzkids about technical problems. They also have a theatre where free lectures and courses are held. So the store perfectly matches the most important brand value of Apple: stimulating creativity. That consumers are very interested in this became obvious at the opening of a new flagship store in London. Some customers waited 25 hours in very cold weather to be at the front of the queue to get in.

Felissimo Corporation of Japan is a global marketing company whose core business is a mail order catalogue full of innovative products, which are available for purchase throughout Japan. Felissimo also operates a design house in New York. By encouraging dialogue and collaboration between designers, consumers and enterprises, Felissimo Design House wants to set the tone for how design will be produced, evaluated and experienced. Felissimo wants to challenge the idea that design is based purely on aesthetics, so in the Design House consumers can experience a place where design becomes sensory and tangible. It is a place for the discovery of fresh design inspirations from around the world. The company believes that design cultivates relationships between people, nature and lifestyles. Design should promote happiness and well-being while adding value to everyday life. In a gift shop on the ground floor it sells items from designers featured in the Design House as well as other unique design products. Part of Felissimo's business is charity, so in the shop it also sells charitable products, many of which have been designed by actors, designers and artists.

Art and retail are merging. Retail brands are building cultural programmes into their offer to create emotionally 'sticky' stores (GDR, 2004: 25). Here are some examples.

- Gibo in London: a designer boutique that is part retail space and part art gallery, featuring the work of London artists. The clothing display system folds away to free the floor area for catwalk shows and other events.
- Hussein Chalayan in Tokyo: a high-end store that draws on the fashion designer's Mediterranean roots. The focal point is a cinema area, where experimental art films by the owner are screened.
- The Lounge in New York: a youth-oriented lifestyle store housing a range of fashion and beauty zones alongside a nightclub area with a resident DJ, hair salon, café/bar and art gallery. The store runs a programme of daytime and evening events for the local community.
- Mavi in New York: the US flagship for this Turkish jeans label uses display fixtures that educate and reference the history and craft of the brand. A quarter of the store is dedicated to displaying commissioned art objects and short films by new and innovative directors.

7.5 Hedonism brands

Enjoying life is an important trend in consumer behaviour. In our hectic society everyone sometimes needs a little indulgence as compensation for the stress of daily life. It is all right for people to pamper themselves once in a while, and retail brands can target that need. Hedonistic retail brands give the consumer sensorial pleasure. All the senses are stimulated, and the stores give consumers the feeling that they can really pamper themselves for a change.

On its website, Aveda promotes the Aveda Experience Centers as follows:

Step inside an Aveda Experience Center to enter a world of aromatic pure flower and plant essences. Sip our licorice and peppermint comforting tea. And relax with any of our complimentary sensory experiences. A complete stress-free way to shop, or simply unwind.

These Aveda Experience Centers obviously position themselves as hedonistic stores, in which all senses are stimulated and the customer can escape from the hectic pace of daily life for a while. The store experience is just as important as the products.

Sephora is another hedonistic store where people can pamper themselves. This revolutionary beauty-retail concept from France is rooted in a powerful combination of aesthetics and lifestyle. Sephora really changed the way cosmetics and fragrances are sold worldwide. Each store is designed as an interactive space where customers are offered unparalleled freedom and specialized service. With its stylish, spectacular black and red interior, pleasing lighting and complete range of cosmetics and fragrances, it is an appealing store where customers like to spend time. On entering, customers are automatically confronted with Sephora's private-brand lipsticks and other make-up products. Everything is presented in order of colour, which results in a rainbow of colours. On the walls, more than 300 well-known brands of fragrances are presented in alphabetical order, and skin care products are at the back of the store. The number of brands is much higher than at other perfumeries. Almost all the fragrances have a tester, so the customers can try them out, and most skincare products can be tested as well.

In addition to the cosmetics and perfumes, the walls are filled with small glass containers with all kinds of tools: nail clippers, eyelash curlers and make-up brushes in all sizes. The store has a lot of stylishly dressed, knowledgeable staff who can give professional advice, but will not force themselves on customers. Customers can determine themselves if they want sales assistance, and how much. At the register, all employees wear one black glove, to receive the customer's products with the utmost care. The customer is being spoiled up to the last moment, both by the store experience and by the enormous range.

'Don't you deserve a little indulgence? Treat yourself to tempting chocolate ranges worthy of your devotion.' This is the copy on the homepage of the Godiva website. This brand, the creator of the one of the world's most elegant selections of handcrafted chocolates, originated in Brussels, Belgium. The Draps family introduced Godiva Chocolate to Belgium in 1926. They founded a chocolate and sweet-making workshop. Their 'pralines', typical Belgian filled chocolates, were made for the large shops that were highly fashionable in those days. Later, Joseph Draps opened the doors of his shop on a cobbled street on Grande Place. He named his family's chocolate company 'Godiva'. Draps perfected a unique formula of rich chocolate with unparalleled smoothness. With a remarkable eye for detail, he set forth the standard for Godiva's innovative selection of elegant, European shell-moulded designs and beautiful packaging. Success was not far off. Godiva expanded throughout Belgium, and soon the first shops were opening abroad: in the Rue Saint-Honoré in Paris in 1958, and in 1966 on Fifth Avenue in New York.

Since its introduction to America in 1966, Godiva has continued to be the leader in the premium confectionery category. Today there are more than 200 Godiva speciality boutiques in major US cities, as well as over 1,000 additional outlets in fine department and speciality stores. Godiva was first to create the concept of premium chocolate. It did this by combining an excellent product, stimulating advertising, sophisticated packaging and selective distribution, and most importantly, by positioning itself as a real hedonism brand.

Everyone has their own routines, for everything from brushing their teeth, doing the dishes and taking a bath, to simply making a cup of tea. Rituals often become routines, so sometimes we forget to enjoy the small pleasures of life. The Dutch retail company Rituals, founded in 1998, has changed this by turning daily routines into rituals. Three characteristics of its unique mix of home and bodycare products make Rituals stand apart and make it a unique concept: the top quality of its products, which use ancient ingredients; special and functional packaging; and the most surprising fragrances. Daily routines become fun again.

The world's best laboratories and specialists guarantee the optimum quality of all Rituals products, from shampoo and facial creams to scented candles and fabric softener. Rituals firmly believes in lifestyle and design. More and more attention is being paid to furnishing kitchens and bathrooms, so each Rituals product is beautifully designed to act as an enhancement to the customer's surroundings. The products are so pleasantly aesthetic that hiding them under the kitchen sink or in a cupboard is a thing of the past.

Rituals also has a passion for perfumes. World-famous perfumiers shared their visions and developed exclusive fragrances for everyday products. Customers can experience the collection in the Rituals flagship store in Amsterdam or any of its other outlets. Customers can test, smell and feel the range for themselves, and read all the background information on computer screens. Rituals is meant for all those people who wish to enjoy the small pleasures of life. The slogan 'Enrich your life' perfectly captures this positioning.

So pampering can be done in different ways. Starbucks, with its delicious coffee aromas and armchairs, is also a place where people can be pampered and all their senses are stimulated. Together, the interior, the atmosphere and of course the coffee, create a store environment in which consumers are encouraged to sit back and relax, listen to the music, read a book or newspaper or chat with other people. Starbucks is more than a coffee shop; it is a meeting place for people. Starbucks has become what Howard Schultz, the founder of the company, has referred to as 'the third place': that is, the place between home and work, the place where you go to spend time with friends or to relax a little; somewhat comparable to the former neighbourhood store. And you never have to walk far for it because Starbucks, with its enormous number of establishments, is never far away. Starbucks is a very strong retail brand with more than 6,200 coffee shops in 30 countries. It is so strong, in fact, that the average customer will visit the store almost 20 times a month.

7.6 Lifestyle brands

Socio-economic characteristics like income, age and education have lost considerable meaning as predictors of consumer behaviour. Consumers who are comparable in income, age and education can still have totally different lifestyles. Their lifestyle describes how consumers spend their time, what they consider important in their lives, their opinions on various issues and their interests, and it is reflected in their consumer and shopping behaviour. It also influences what they buy and where they buy it from. People buy what they want, not what they need. What and where they buy are reflections of what they think. Consumers are sometimes less interested in the functional attributes of the retail brand and more in what their choice of it conveys about them.

So lifestyle shopping is a very egocentric way of shopping. Consumers are looking for products, stores and experiences that will be really important to their lives. A store can, like a magazine, help the consumer to live a desired lifestyle. Through the composition of the range a retail brand can integrate itself into the lifestyle of the consumer. By presenting products from different categories together in visual merchandising, the store can communicate specific lifestyles.

However consumers can no longer be characterized by one lifestyle. People do not fit into boxes any more. Consumers are multi-dimensional, with different needs and lifestyles for different moments. The moods of consumers determine their lifestyle at that moment. Multiple lifestyles are mixed together. One moment a person might be extremely health conscious, the next he or she will be eating a huge meal. The same customer can behave differently each time. It always depends on the circumstances and the mood that people are in. Stores can focus on one of these lifestyles.

The chosen lifestyle will determine the range. Stores that position themselves as lifestyle brands do not usually limit themselves to one or a couple of product categories. Their range is drawn from a large number of categories, in order to meet the desired lifestyle as much as possible. Because of that, lifestyle stores more often than not become a new type of department store. The large Armani store in Milan, for example, does not only sell clothing but among other things also has bags and other accessories, cosmetics, flowers, books, chocolate and home decorations. Moreover, the store has two restaurants.

Among the common lifestyles on which retail brands can focus are the fashionable lifestyle, the active lifestyle, the healthy lifestyle and the back-to-basics lifestyle.

7.6.1 FASHIONABLE LIFESTYLE BRANDS

The clothes people wear and the way in which they decorate their homes express who they are and who they want to be. Some consumers prefer to buy many different types of products from the same brand, a brand they feel fits them perfectly. Fashion and style are then the key issues. The American retail companies Urban Outfitters and Anthropologie each represent a clearly recognizable fashion style.

The Urban Outfitters alternative stores offer all kinds of innovative fashion, accessories and eclectic home products to independent younger people. Anthropologie, which is part of the same company as Urban Outfitters, does not just sell clothes and furnishings. It is selling a sense of adventure and originality, and the promise of self-discovery (LaBarre, 2002: 92–96). The chain does not only sell an unprecedented mix of wares (home furnishings, bedding, apparel, antiques, gifts), it provides an assortment of ideas. Of course retailers like Ralph Lauren and Martha Stewart have always sold their sensibility along with their products. But where those lifestyle purveyors tend to model perfection and prescribe one style, Anthropologie offers diverse starting points and a multitude of cues to set customers on their own path. Anthropologie does not advertise, and the merchandising does not highlight products so much as set a mood and create a context. If the stores have an ethos, it is imperfection, eclecticism and quirkiness. If they adhere to an aesthetic, it is 'low country': the humble luxuries of peasant heritage.

To obtain the desired fashion lifestyle positioning, more is needed than just clothing. Therefore, many stores that focus on a particular fashion style gradually extend their range with more product categories. In particular well-known fashion brands like Giorgio Armani, Donna Karan, Calvin Klein and Ralph Lauren are currently doing just that. Besides clothing, they have also started to sell underwear, accessories and footwear, later followed by home decorations, furniture and other products. Louis Vuitton did it the other way around. First it only sold bags and suitcases, but subsequently the range has been extended to clothing, among other things.

All these brands (which were quickly followed by many retailers) developed from pure fashion brands into lifestyle retail brands. DKNY in New York sells clothing, home decorations, magazines, accessories and lots of other products. The music that plays in its stores was especially produced for them and is only available in the stores. The entire range is designed from one angle of incidence. All products have a clear style relationship; they all fit within a particular lifestyle.

This approach can also be seen at Clinic and Fish & Chips in Antwerp, Microzine in London and Colette in Paris, for example. At Colette, a paradise for fashionable luxury products named after the founder of the company, consumers can find the most beautiful, most avant-garde and most expensive design products. The owner of Colette follows her own taste when purchasing. What she likes is added to the range. This range consists of, among other things, clothes, accessories, make-up, music, mini-electronics, magazines and lots of other design products. And the high-tech restaurant downstairs offers tens of different brands of mineral water.

After two years of research and development, the first GOD lifestyle store opened in 1996 in Hong Kong. The company now has five stores in Hong Kong. The stores sell everything to do with the home: furniture, lighting, carpets, dinnerware, kitchenware, glassware, candles, bedding, fabrics, home decorations, plus a few surprises. The prices are affordable and good value for money. GOD is the phonetic sound of the Cantonese slang 'to live better'. With the rise of Asia as a significant economic force, the world will also show increasing interest in Asian lifestyle and culture. GOD reflects on this phenomenon by providing an eastern-derived lifestyle concept as an alternative to the established western way of living. By exploring age-old Oriental traditions and updating them with modern consumers in mind, GOD demonstrates that the techniques and wisdom of past generations in the east still have a place in the future world. The company's mission is to define a new Asian identity. Asia's climate, diet, space and culture are different from the west, so why shouldn't Asians live differently? So the exciting challenge for today's Asian designers is to define a new identity for their community. In order for GOD to present a focused image to customers, it is important that the 'soul' of the brand permeates from every piece of merchandise. Therefore, GOD's core range of products is designed in-house and is not purchased from trade fairs, as is often the case with other lifestyle retailers. By giving craftspeople modern designs whilst respecting their traditional skills, GOD produces products that possess a human quality they call 'soul'. This, together with a touch of humour, is a reaction against today's mass produced and soul-less products. The GOD style, despite being fashion conscious, is always relaxed and casual. Because the company believes that a home should be a place of comfort, home wares should never be extreme in design. GOD products mix comfortably with family hand-me-downs and holiday souvenirs that most people are bound to have at home.

Marathons in New York, London, Berlin, Amsterdam and other cities, attract large numbers of participants. Consumers are encouraged to work out more on television and in magazines, and they increasingly look for clothes, trainers and other products that fit into this active lifestyle. Brands like Adidas, Puma, Nike, Speedo, Decathlon, Sports Authority and REI capitalize on this trend.

In 1938 a group of mountain climbers founded Recreational Equipment Inc (REI). The group formed a consumer cooperative to supply themselves with high-quality ice axes and other climbing equipment. During the past decades REI has grown to be a renowned supplier of specialty outdoor equipment, currently serving more than 2 million members through stores and by direct sales via the internet, telephone and mail. Although the equipment sold by REI today looks much different than it did in 1938, the guiding principles of the member-owned cooperative remain the same. While non-members are welcome to shop at REI, only members enjoy special benefits and offers including an annual patronage refund based on their purchases. REI offers the consumer a taste of an active life. The stores are often noticeable from afar, because there is a giant climbing rock of about 30 metres high in the store, on which the customer can test climbing products. But whether the customer is interested in climbing, camping, hiking, cycling, cross training, travelling, skiing or paddling, REI has it. And if the store does not have it, it can of course be ordered via REI.com. Clinics are organized for all kinds of outdoor activities, and everything can be tested in a realistic setting. There is a Gore-Tex rain room in which customers can test weatherproof clothing underneath the shower. There is a cross court outside the store so customers can literally test which mountain bike suits them best. These features obviously contribute to the store experience. That experience is strengthened even more by the extensive range and the employees. These employees are just as devoted to outdoor activities as their customers.

The legendary Cocoa Beach, Florida-based surf and beachwear retailer Ron Jon Surf Shop is recognized worldwide for its colossal selection of active lifestyle apparel, board sports equipment and dive apparatus. Ron Jon is a leader in the surf and retail industries. The history of the company started with New Jersey surfer Ron DiMenna's passion for surfing. This passion exceeded the availability of home-made boards, so DiMenna heeded his father's advice to buy three, sell two at a profit and use the proceeds to cover the costs of his own. Soon afterwards, in 1961 he established his first shop on Long Beach, New Jersey.

DiMenna began by selling surfboards out of that tiny Jersey shore shop. Today the Ron Jon Surf Shop has grown into a world-famous surfing Mecca. The original store in New Jersey is now a four-level surf emporium, which features the world's largest surfboards (more than 24 ft in length). The 'one-of-a-kind' Ron Jon Surf Shop at Cocoa Beach in Florida is a whole water world of eternal summer fun, encompassing more than two acres, overflowing with more surf wear, sportswear and beach gear than is available in any other single venue. Additional stores in Fort Lauderdale, Florida, and Orange, California bring the Ron Jon surfing mystique closer to loyal followers in those areas. This mystique is based on the positioning mix of an unprecedented range and a unique store experience.

7.6.3 HEALTHY LIFESTYLE BRANDS

Good health is becoming more important to consumers. Health consciousness is increasing and healthy living is becoming a way of life. If you walk into the cvs drugstore in a shopping plaza near Annapolis, Maryland in the United States, you will find the usual displays of cosmetics, toiletries, first aid products, over-the-counter medications and a pharmacy at the back. But tucked into the corner between the greeting cards and a one-hour photo shop, there is something new: a walk-in MinuteClinic, staffed by a nurse practitioner ready to treat a variety of common ailments. To appreciative patients, this miniclinic offers the ultimate in convenience: easy access to low-cost treatment by experienced professionals, with no appointment necessary. MinuteClinic has already 22 miniclinics in the Minneapolis and Baltimore areas, including 11 in Target stores, four in Cub Food supermarkets and three in cvs pharmacies (Rice, 2005).

Feeling good and looking good are closely connected. If you feel good, you look good, and when you look good, you feel good. We are all interested in stopping the ageing process. Everybody wants to be young forever. Even McDonald's and Burger King now offer healthy meals. Stores that offer Asian medical methods and all sorts of medical check-ups are also growing in number. We want to know more about the origin and composition of products, and people are more sceptical about mass production and are losing confidence in the food industry. A healthy life is also about what we eat, so people are willing to pay more for healthy food. Food safety has become an important issue of public concern, and sales of organic products are on the increase.

Founded in 1980 as one small store in Austin, Texas, Whole Foods Market is now the world's largest retailer of natural and organic foods, with almost 200 stores in the United States and the UK. According to its website, Whole Foods Market strives to offer the highest quality, least processed, most flavourful and naturally preserved foods. On a global basis the company actively supports organic farming, the best method for promoting sustainable agriculture and protecting the environment and the farm workers. On a local basis, Whole Foods Market is actively involved in the communities where its stores are located, supporting food banks, sponsoring neighbourhood events, compensating employees for community service work, and contributing at least 5 per cent of total net profits to non-profit organizations.

Whole Foods Market does not sell only food, but also books, vitamins, cooking aids and lots of other products for a healthy life. In some stores customers can also get a massage, and in the newest flagship store in Austin there is the chain's first all-organic clothing department. The fact that prices at Whole Foods are 10 to 20 per cent higher than at other supermarkets does not matter to the target group. To Whole Foods, price is not more than a qualifying or competitive attribute.

The fast food industry is mostly associated with unhealthy, fatty food. This offered Pret A Manger the opportunity to position itself as the healthy alternative. Pret A Manger, which opened its first sandwich shop in London in 1987, was described by The Times as having 'revolutionised the concept of sandwich making and eating'. The company, which offers freshness and speed, has now grown to over 150 shops, not just across the UK but in New York, Hong Kong and Tokyo too. Quality fresh food is Pret A Manger's passion. The company claims to go to extraordinary lengths to avoid the chemicals, additives and preservatives common to many of the 'prepared' and 'fast' foods on the market today.

When Pret A Manger was just starting out, a big supplier tried to sell it coleslaw that lasted 16 days. There and then the founders decided that Pret A Manger would stick to wholesome fresh food: natural stuff, the sort of ingredients the customers would use at home, and they have not changed that policy. The success of Pret A Manger is still built on a strong commitment to fresh and natural products. Fresh ingredients are delivered to every one of the shops overnight. Each of these shops has a kitchen, where the staff make sandwiches, wraps and baguettes throughout the day. Whatever the store has not sold by the time it closes, it offers to local charities to help feed those who would otherwise go hungry.

In 2001 McDonald's bought a 33 per cent minority stake in Pret A Manger. Its international influence and expertise is helping Pret A Manger in its expansion beyond the UK, but McDonald's does not have any direct influence over what Pret A Manger sells or how it sells it; nor would it want to. It has invested in Pret A Manger because it likes what the chain does.

7.6.4 BACK-TO-BASICS LIFESTYLE BRANDS

Life can be very complicated. That is why consumers look for retail brands that can make their life more simple and clear. There is a growing dislike of all the waste in the world, and some people are moving away from luxury. Doing more with less is something many consumers are striving for. Back to basics is their motto. These consumers look for products that go back to the essence, to honest, pure and simple materials and shapes; to natural and authentic products and stores that improve the quality of life.

The Japanese retail company Muji, which also operates stores in England, France and Belgium, was launched in 1980, and captured the spirit of the 1990s with its no-label, value-led, less-is-more concept. Today Muji, which in Japanese means 'no brand, high quality', is known as a lifestyle store for stylish, functional and affordable quality goods that are relevant to all aspects of urban life, whether at work, rest or play. The unique lifestyle range spans furniture, storage, household goods, clothing, luggage, stationery and gifts. All products are faithful to a set of four core principles that remain unchanged to this day:

- Streamlined, functional and minimalist design, eliminating excess decoration and keeping packaging to a bare minimum. This philosophy has important secondary benefits: reduced cost, environmental friendliness, the use of unexpected materials and minimal processing.
- Basic, understated colours guaranteed to blend and never dominate. All products are earth-coloured, white, black or transparent. The stores have neutral decor and fixtures, which also reflect their minimalist style.
- Value for money, the right balance between quality and price.
- A complete lifestyle product range encompassing all elements of life, which dictates the look, regulates the price point and ensures the reliability of each product within the Muji range.

Because of this clear merchandise philosophy Muji has become a strong retail brand itself despite its 'no name brands' ethos.

7.7 Bargain brands

Most shoppers are not looking for just 'cheap' goods. They are in search of bargains, goods that provide real value for money. Enjoying a bargain often gives more pleasure than paying the lowest price. Who does not like to buy branded clothing far below the regular price? Bargain hunting can create excitement. Spending money makes people feel guilty. Getting a bargain does not. Therefore, bargain brands target a basic need of consumers.

Century 21, also known as 'New York's Best Kept Secret', is, just like factory outlets in Europe and the United States, an example of a real shopping heaven. Designer labels are sold at 25–75 per cent below retail prices. The visual merchandising communicates that consumers are getting a bargain. There are only racks of clothing. Closely crammed together, dozens of well-known brands are offered. Nobody seems to care about the presentation. New stock is brought in almost daily. Every time it is exciting for customers to see if there is something appealing on the racks. That excitement results in a store not only full of clothing, but also full of people.

A special example of a bargain brand is Liquidation World. This company, headquartered in Calgary, Alberta in Canada, specializes in purchasing and marketing merchandise from distress situations. Inventories are acquired through insurance and freight claims, bankruptcies, receiverships, buybacks, over-production, cancelled orders: virtually any kind of problem situation. Liquidation World buys these goods with cash and at large discounts. The inventories are then sold to consumers through its chain of over 100 no-frills Liquidation World outlets across Canada and the United States. With over 2 million sq ft of floor space, Liquidation World offers consumers a treasure hunt through aisle after aisle of liquidation merchandise. Thousands of deals are exposed to over 7 million bargain hunters who pass through the outlets every year. Visiting a Liquidation World outlet is like walking into a new store every day. You never know what you will find. It is a shopping experience like no other. It is a treasure hunt. Furniture, food, paint, housewares, hardware, clothing, sporting goods, toys, health and beauty products: Liquidation World sells it all. The fun is contagious and the savings are too.

Bargain hunting is not limited to bricks-and-mortar stores, it also happens on the internet. Auction sites like eBay.com attract large numbers of visitors, who all try to find bargains. Founded in 1995, eBay is the world's online marketplace for the sale of goods and services by a diverse community of individuals and small businesses. Today the eBay community includes more than 100 million registered members from around the world. People spend more time on eBay than any other online site, making it the most popular shopping destination on the internet. On an average day, there are millions of items listed on eBay. People come to eBay to buy and sell items in thousands of categories, from collectibles like trading cards, antiques, dolls and housewares to practical items like used cars, clothing, books and CDs, and electronics. Buyers have the option to purchase items in an auction-style format, or items can be purchased at a fixed price through a feature called Buy It Now.

Retailers have used the bargain-hunting instinct of consumers to their advantage for years, shifting previously unwanted products by discounting them (Lyster, 2003b: 18). However, the role of a sale has changed over the past decade. Sales have become not just a way of clearing stock, but also a marketing tool. Sales are no longer season-specific. With an almost year-round price reduction culture, stores are now competing for bargain hunters' cash as well as for full-price custom. Many customers rank finding a bargain alongside good sales service as one of the top ingredients for a successful shopping trip. These bargain hunters buy products they might not really need. They especially buy them because the bargain was so appealing that they just had to buy it.

Part 3 Retail brand personality

8. DIFFERENTIATING ON BRAND PERSONALITY

Retailers have always given a lot of attention to the functional attributes of range, price, service and store experience. The brand personality, which is mainly based on emotions, largely developed on its own. There was no or hardly any strategy behind it. In the future, however, brand personality will become more important. Consumers now have whatever they need, so purchase decisions are increasingly made on emotional motives. Consumers visit a store not only because of functional attributes, but also because they love the store. They look for stores with a personality that fits their (desired) self-image. Functional positioning attributes can be copied quickly. However, to copy the 'human' personality characteristics of a retail brand is much more difficult. Just as every person is different, a brand personality can also be unique.

There should be a clear connection between the positioning and the personality of a retail brand. The nature of the positioning and the personality should fit together. A distinguishable personality can further strengthen the positioning. In addition, the personality helps determine the look and feel of all out-of-store and in-store communications. The positioning determines the content of all this communication.

8.1 The importance of brand personality

The foundation of every strong retail brand is a distinctive positioning mix of range, price, convenience and store experience. For example, the big success of Tesco is for the large part based on offering choice, high value, convenience and a pleasant store experience. Each and every day Tesco delivers again on those brand promises. Every strong brand identity has a mix of relevant differentiating, supporting, competitive and qualifying positioning attributes as its foundation. These tangible, functional attributes lead to functional or emotional benefits for the consumer: the 'what' of the retail brand. They help customers to rationalize their choice of store.

Many retailers do not get much further than these functional benefits when developing their brand identity. In these cases it is not really correct to speak of a brand, because a brand should also have an emotional bond with customers. However, retailers wrongly assume that consumers only base their choice of store on functional benefits. But if that were the case, consumers could choose from many stores that all pretty much offer the same. In this case functional attributes are less important than emotional ones, and moreover, consumers are not always rational decision makers. They quite often make purchase decisions based on emotional motives.

People are looking for an emotional connection with a retail brand. If the brand personality matches the target group's values, this can lead to the desired emotional connection. The brand personality that the consumer experiences via all sensory impulses can transcend and enrich the functional positioning attributes. Consumers should visit a store not only because of functional attributes, but also because they really love the store.

Strong retail brands offer consumers both functional and emotional benefits. The emotional context in which the positioning takes place is just as important in retail, and sometimes even more important than functional attributes. This context concerns the feelings consumers have about the retail brand. These feelings often determine the emotional bond between customers and the retail brand. They are partly based on the functional positioning attributes – the 'what' – but are mainly based on the brand personality, the 'who' of the retail brand.

The brand personality describes the retail brand in terms of human characteristics. These characteristics determine the way in which functional positioning attributes are offered: the 'how' of the retail brand. This brand personality is reflected in the look and feel of all in-store and out-of-store communications.

Figure 8.1 The what, who and how of a retail brand

A differentiating brand personality can be used to add emotion to the functional attributes and the relationship with the customer. A retail brand can even be built around a strong personality. In many sectors brand personality is the most important tool to create differentiation. The retail brand then positions itself primarily through emotional attributes. Through this, the retail brand establishes a place not only in the minds but also in the hearts of consumers. Retail brands with both a strong positioning foundation as well as an appealing brand personality are consumer favourites.

Brand positioning is mainly about attributes that can have both functional and emotional benefits. These attributes and benefits result in a consumer proposition. A low-price brand might show customers how much money they can save, but it can also portray them as smart buyers. However, creating differentiation by these attributes is very difficult in retail, because imitation by the competition is easy. Consequently a differentiating personality is becoming more important. The retail brand's personality has a symbolic, self-expressive function.

Customers also use retail brands to create their own individual identity and to communicate something about themselves to others. Consumers have an ideal image of themselves. Trying to realize that ideal, they look for retail brands with a personality that matches their own values. They use these brands to manage the impressions they make on others. Patronizing a retail brand might for example serve as a symbol of success. So the personality of a retail brand has to match the consumer's self-concept. The better a retail brand's human characteristics match a consumer's values, the stronger his or her preference for, and loyalty to, this brand will be.

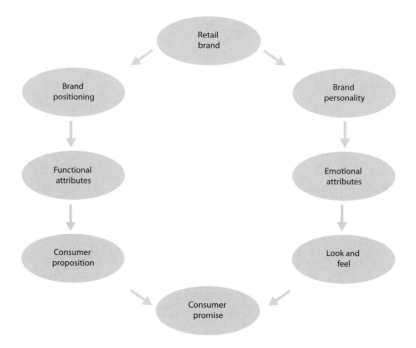

Figure 8.2 Brand positioning and brand personality

Positioning, personality and communication are the three key drivers of a retail brand's identity. The relative importance of each of these three drivers can differ between brands and between markets. Some retail brands, like Wal-Mart and Media Markt for example, derive their brand identity mainly from a strong, differentiating functional positioning. The Body Shop, Ben & Jerry's and other retail brands are more successful because of their emotional personality, and the brand identity of a brand like H&M is to a large extent based on its striking advertising campaigns.

Unilever did some research on the influence of store performance and brand affinity on brand identity. The performance was measured based on a few functional positioning attributes, like range, convenience and service. The affinity customers felt for a supermarket was determined with the help of personality dimensions like trust, caring and prestige. For Dutch supermarkets the functional positioning attributes seem (for the time being) to be more important than emotional personality dimensions. The positioning attributes make up about 60 per cent of the brand identity, while the personality explains almost 40 per cent of the strength of the Dutch supermarket brands. Communications seem to only have a limited influence on the brand identity, which is probably caused by the large extent of uniformity in Dutch supermarket advertising (Bras, 2004).

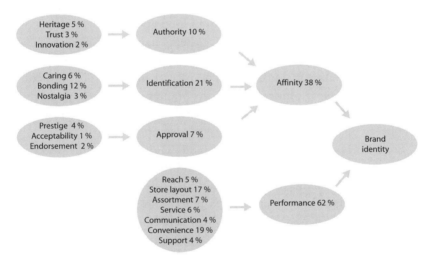

Figure 8.3 Influence of positioning, personality and communication on brand identity of Dutch supermarkets

In France and the United States the personality of supermarkets plays a much bigger role. In these countries affinity makes up 68 and 77 per cent respectively of the total brand identity. The functional positioning attributes in this case are of far less importance to the strength of a supermarket brand.

When choosing a store a consumer is guided not only by positioning attributes, but also by the personality and the behaviour of the company behind the retail brand. This personality and behaviour are reflected in the retail brand's values and, among other things, expressed in the way in which the retail company communicates with its customers. It is made apparent not only through the look and feel of the out-of-store communications, but particularly through store design, visual merchandising and employees. It is in the store that the retail brand is definitively established. That is where customers are confronted most clearly with all elements of the positioning and personality mix.

The brand personality determines the look and feel of the store. Conversely, the look and feel also have a big influence on the perceived brand personality. Retail brands that have a similar positioning can still differ in the way in which they offer their consumer proposition. The look and feel of the store can give a retail brand its own identity entirely. As consumers recognize more aspects of the look and feel of the retail brand that are important for their personal self-expression, a stronger bond will develop between them and the retail brand. Copying a brand personality of another retail brand is then much more difficult than copying a positioning. After all, the brand personality is about the humanization of the brand: the brand as a person, and every person is unique.

Sometimes the person is the brand. Giorgio Armani, Tommy Hilfiger, Calvin Klein, Terence Conran and Richard Branson have had an enormous influence on their brand identities as founders of their companies. Their brands and stores reflect their visions and values. Virgin, the most successful chain of music stores in Britain, has a brand personality that is known for words like fun, innovative and against the grain, for example. These are characteristics that can also be recognized in the personality of founder Richard Branson.

It is difficult for the competition to copy a brand personality, because the origins of a brand personality are mainly in the mission, vision and culture of a retail brand. A brand personality does not just develop, but is reflected in everything a retail brand thinks and does: not only in the present, but in the past and in the future. The brand personality has to match the corporate values and the internal culture. It has to be in the company's genes. The way in which the retail company associates with its customers has to be a reflection of the way in which it associates with its employees. If the internal culture is not good, then the personality that is communicated to the consumers will not be good either.

The brand personality directs all visual and verbal communications with consumers. Sometimes a retail brand will have to adapt its positioning mix to changing market conditions, but the brand personality will always stay the same. The human character and core beliefs of a retail brand should not change. The consumer needs to know exactly what the retail brand stands for. Changes in that can only lead to confusion.

The American mono-brand clothing retailer Abercrombie & Fitch (A&F) has developed a powerful and consistent brand personality, that is fun-loving, independent, and sexually uninhibited: a winning formula with teenagers and college students. To remain familiar with teen tastes and to spark ideas for new merchandise, A&F sends around 30 staff members to college campuses each month to chat with students about what they play, wear, listen to and read. The stores themselves, featuring comfortable armchairs, are designed to be gathering places. They are staffed by high-energy 'brand reps' recruited from local campuses and dressed in A&F clothing. Sales skills are not required; the job is to look good wearing the company's brand and to have fun inside the store.

Evoking powerful associations in the way A&F do is much more difficult for multi-brand retailers, which do not shape and control every aspect of the merchandise they sell or every instance of its exposure to the public. Traditionally, multi-brand retailers have not aspired to the indelible personalities of their vertical competitors, but have instead sought to distinguish themselves through positioning attributes, such as range, price, convenience, and store experience (Henderson and Mihas, 2000).

8.2 Brand personality types

Every retail brand has a perceived personality, which is formed by the positioning and the way in which the retail brand acts and communicates.

It is also shaped by all kinds of external factors, like customer type and the opinion of others about the retail brand, for example. Then the question arises, does the perceived personality correspond with the desired personality? Often this is not the case. An important reason is that in retail the importance of a strong brand personality is still underestimated. A personality develops in a company often by coincidence, as it were. In many retail companies the brand personality is often not, or hardly ever, defined, because these companies mainly concentrate on the more functional positioning attributes. However, in the future, retail brands will learn that a sustainable competitive edge should mainly be established through brand personality. The 'who' is in many cases becoming more important than the 'what'. A retail brand that is not only in the mind but also in the heart has a position as strong as iron. A retail brand without its own, differentiating personality is very vulnerable to competition.

Just as with positioning, some choices have to be made to define the desired brand personality. According to American research, the personality of a brand consists of five base dimensions: sincerity, excitement, competence, sophistication and ruggedness (Aaker, 1996: 144). Together these five dimensions form the personality ring around the positioning mix (Figure 8.4).

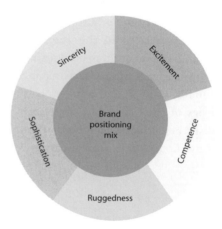

Figure 8.4 Brand personality ring

Every dimension then consists of another couple of factors, to make a total of 15. For the United States this leads to the following brand personality scale:

1. Sincerity
- Down-to-earth: family-oriented, small-town, conventional, blue-collar, all-American.
- Honest: sincere, real, ethical, thoughtful, caring.
- Wholesome: original, genuine, ageless, classic, old-fashioned.
- Cheerful: sentimental, friendly, warm, happy.

2. Excitement
- Daring: trendy, exciting, offbeat, flashy, provocative.
- Spirited: cool, young, lively, outgoing, adventurous.
- Imaginative: unique, humorous, surprising, artistic, fun.
- Up-to-date: independent, contemporary, innovative, aggressive.

3. Competence
- Reliable: hardworking, secure, efficient, trustworthy, careful.
- Intelligent: technical, corporate, serious.
- Successful: leader, confident, influential.

4. Sophistication
- Upper class: glamorous, good-looking, pretentious, sophisticated.
- Charming: feminine, smooth, sexy, gentle.

5. Ruggedness
- Outdoorsy: masculine, active, athletic.
- Tough: rugged, strong, no-nonsense.

This brand personality scale is based on American research. Because of cultural differences, other personality dimensions or factors can be important, or other emphases can appear in different countries. However, these dimensions and factors form a very good starting point for formulating the desired brand personality, especially in more developed retail markets.

Without a good price strategy and a good range of merchandise, the chances for success are minimal. The same goes for a number of personality dimensions. Dimensions like honesty and reliability, for example, are minimum conditions for every retail brand. A brand that is not perceived as honest and reliable will never win consumers' trust. That is why the various personality dimensions are particularly interesting when very different placings along the axis present real options.

In society there is an enormous need for brands that show authenticity. Consumers are looking for real brands and real stories behind the brands. Consumers want things to be real again. They want to buy at stores that are intrinsically ethical, authentic and natural, so brands are facing an enormous challenge. This is true for both manufacturer brands and retail brands. Good quality alone is no longer sufficient. A brand is now judged on values and what it stands for as a company as well. These values need to be expressed in the brand personality and in the way in which the company associates with its customers and other stakeholders; but particularly in the wider role of the company in society. Consumers are more cynical than ever about brands right now. Making as much profit as possible sometimes seems to be more important to companies than manufacturing and selling good, reliable products. Consumers already assume that companies are not always straightforward and honest with their customers. People no longer have an unlimited trust in well-known brands, therefore retail brands also have to deal with this decreasing lack of faith in companies. Consumers are looking for retail brands they can trust: brands that are honest, ethical and socially aware. A retail brand that does not betray this trust will be more successful than competitors that are seen to challenge it. A retail brand that really stands for something will clearly differentiate itself with its personality from all sorts of meaningless, unimportant retail companies.

Consumers are looking for retail brands that match their self-image. Consequently the brand personality of a retail company has to correspond with the values of the target group. These values are the things people consider to be important in their lives. They are ideals of a kind. There can however be big differences in the value systems of different people, therefore every value system is unique.

Values are a guide for all a consumer's actions and thoughts, and together with habit, have a large influence on his or her buying behaviour and store choice. A premium brand's positioning could for example match values like 'power' and 'success'. Consumers effectively compare the brand personality with their own values. Either consciously or unconsciously, consumers want to know how well the brand personality corresponds with their values. Retail brands will more often be judged on the fit of their emotional appeal to the consumer's desired self-image. Just as every value system is unique, brand personality can also be unique. In that case, the retail brand's mind position will mainly be determined by its personality.

Research into value systems in multiple cultures has led to the identification of 10 universal human values (Schwartz and Bilsky, 1987):

- power: social status and prestige, control or dominance over people and resources;
- achievement: personal success through demonstrating competence according to social standards;
- hedonism: pleasure and sensuous gratification for oneself;
- stimulation: excitement, novelty and challenge in life;
- self-direction: independent thought and action; choosing, creating, exploring;
- universalism: understanding, appreciation, tolerance and protection for the welfare of all people and for nature;
- benevolence: preservation and enhancement of the welfare of people with whom one is in frequent personal contact;
- tradition: respect, commitment and acceptance of the customs and ideas that traditional culture or religion provide;
- conformity: restraint of actions, inclinations and impulses likely to upset or harm others and violate social expectations or norms;
- security: safety, harmony and stability of society, of relationships and of oneself.

Some of these values, like for example hedonism and stimulation, mainly have an impressive nature, because they give the customer a good feeling. Other values, like achievement and power, have a more expressive nature. They are values people like to communicate to their social environment. The retail brand's personality will have to match one or more of these human values. Personality dimensions like masculinity and success, for example, will mainly appeal to customers for whom power and achievement are important values. On the contrary, dimensions like trendy and adventurous will appeal to people who consider stimulation to be an important value in life.

8.3 Positioning and personality

The brand personality is, as it were, the connecting link between brand positioning and brand communications. On one hand there is a connection between brand personality and positioning, and on the other there is a connection between brand personality and communications. The look and feel of brand communications are strongly influenced by the brand personality. But the reverse is also true, as the nature of the communication has a big influence on the brand personality as perceived by consumers. The brand personality in turn is closely connected to the chosen brand positioning.

A positioning of multiple retail brands on the same attribute mix does not have to mean that the brand personality of these brands is also the same. In the retail brand cycle the brand personality circles around the brand positioning, as it were. In principle, every brand positioning can be combined with every brand personality. However, some brand personalities will fit better with certain positionings than others. A good brand personality can strengthen the chosen brand positioning even further. For example, it is obvious that the consumer will associate a positioning on price with personality dimensions like down-to-earth, no-nonsense and reliability. If the retail brand does indeed have such a personality, this will strengthen the brand identity. On the contrary, a positioning on store experience will more readily be associated with personality dimensions like exciting, adventurous and glamorous. An experience store that succeeds in communicating such a brand personality will communicate a consistent brand identity to the consumer.

The brand personality dimensions that best fit the four positioning attributes are shown in Table 8.1.

Positioning attribute	Probable brand personality dimensions
Range	Sincerity, competence, sophistication
Price	Sincerity, competence, ruggedness
Convenience	Sincerity, competence
Store experience	Excitement, sophistication, ruggedness

Table 8.1 Brand personality dimensions and positioning attributes

So there is a strong connection between brand personality and brand positioning. A business-like, no-nonsense personality fits better with a positioning on price than a playful personality. Low-price brands have to communicate a no-nonsense attitude in everything they do. The store has to be tightly organized and it has to be clear from all its activities that all the focus is on costs. The same connection also exists between the brand personality and the out-of-store and in-store brand communications. A business-like, no-nonsense brand personality demands a straightforward store design and a similar type of advertising. The stores should take a 'no-frills' design approach and the advertisements should be hardly more than an enumeration of products and prices. On the other hand, a no-nonsense store design and aggressive, businesslike advertising will also contribute to making the retail brand be experienced as cheap. The bare stores and the simple advertising strengthen the price positioning. All touch-points communicate 'cheap'. So the retail brand's personality is the connecting link between positioning and communication. It strengthens the positioning and directs the way in which the positioning is communicated.

Tesco discovered just how important a brand personality is when approaching the baby market a few years ago. Tesco discovered that many new parents chose not to buy their baby products in its stores, but preferred instead to do so at the UK's largest chain of pharmacists, Boots the Chemist. This was despite the fact that Boots was often 20 per cent more expensive than Tesco for key products, so the cause of the problem was not in the price positioning.

In asking its customers why they behaved like this, Tesco discovered something about its relationship with them. The strong bond that the Tesco brand had always enjoyed with loyal customers was very rational and based on functional positioning attributes. The emotional bond, in which the brand personality plays an important role, was much weaker. Trusting Tesco to offer the best for a newborn baby was a big step. The brand personality of Tesco did not match the values of the target group. The authority of the Boots brand in this area was based on its history, its expertise and its cornerstone status on Britain's high streets. Boots had the pedigree that allowed it to command a premium price, to say, 'There are some things money cannot buy.'

Tesco was determined to assert itself. However, this was not simply a case of targeted discounts through mailings, because price was not the problem. Customer feedback told Tesco that mothers were looking for emotional security. The thinking, therefore, was to create a small, targeted Baby Club. The aim was to create the degree of trust in Tesco that Boots enjoyed in this group: enough trust for customers to put Tesco in their 'inner circle' of brands for baby care. Once inside the circle Tesco could compete strongly with its main rival on the positioning attributes price, range and convenience. So Baby Club mailings offered high-value information as their principal customer benefit: the sort of information that new parents need, but do not know exactly where to get. Authoritative, responsible advice on the baby's health, diet and development was more important than promotions. The results were spectacular. Nearly 40 per cent of all British parents-to-be joined the Baby Club. Thanks to the Baby Club, Tesco increased its share of the mother and baby market to almost 24 per cent; a proportion that is now larger than its share of the total grocery market (Humby and Hunt, 2003: 184–93).

The brand personality that a retail company eventually wants to communicate consists of several dimensions, just as does a person's personality. This personality mix can vary widely from one retail brand to another. The eventual mix depends on a number of factors.

Heritage
Except for a totally new retail brand, a retail company never starts at zero. The entire history and vision, mission and values of the company

very strongly determine the brand personality. A brand personality cannot just be invented, and changing an existing brand personality is very difficult and often even impossible. What has been built up over the years cannot just be changed overnight. Very drastic measures and large investments would be needed, and even then there is still the question of whether customers will accept a cultural change or not.

Competition

When determining the desired brand personality, a retail brand also has to take the brand personality of its most important competitors into account. After all, the competitive battle between retail brands will quite often be fought out via the brand personality.

Target group

The retail brand's personality has to match the target group's self-image. Consumers buy from different stores partly to communicate something about themselves to others. There has to be a clear similarity between the consumer's self-image and the retail brand's personality. Consumers who shop at a low-price store will perhaps be afraid others might think they do not have a lot of money to spend. They would prefer others to think they are very smart. Therefore the retail brand's personality would have to communicate this desired canniness.

Product types

The type of products and the matching buying behaviour also influence the retail brand's desired personality. For example, with products that represent a large health risk to the consumer, competence will have to be an almost indispensable personality attribute of the retail brand.

Although the personality of a retail brand has to be in the company's genes, emphases can be made in communication. If there is a difference between the desired and the perceived brand personality, it might be necessary to emphasize certain characteristics of the brand. Large, dominant retail brands, for example, are rightly or wrongly firmly associated with personality traits like arrogant, distant, slow, heavy and not really customer-oriented. It would then be wise to place particular emphasis on traits like leading, renewing, dynamic and customer-oriented. These characteristics will then of course have to be proven by the brand performance.

The brand personality as perceived by the consumer is established by the brand positioning, brand performance and all brand communications in and outside the store. Based on all experiences with a retail brand, people form an opinion about its brand personality. So it is of the utmost importance that all brand communication touch-points communicate the same personality. If that does not happen, it will only cause confusion.

Part 4 Retail brand communications

9. RETAIL COMMUNICATION MIX

Through out-of-store tools (advertising and direct marketing communications) and in-store tools (store design, visual merchandising and employees), a retail brand communicates its positioning and personality. But the nature and way of communicating also contribute to the brand identity. Most retailers have always underestimated this influence. As a result, the communications from most retail brands show few if any distinguishing characteristics. Most retail advertising looks alike, and the stores' offerings show hardly any difference in design, visual merchandising and employee behaviour.

The most important communication objectives of a retail brand are to create store traffic, improve the spend of existing customers and strengthen bonds with customers. Every communication tool plays a specific role in realizing these objectives. However, for every offline retailer the store itself is the most important communication tool. The brand is made in the store.

For most retail brands there is no or hardly any consistency between out-of-store and in-store communications. Most of the time the look and feel of both communication tools do not fit together.

9.1 Communication tools

To many retailers, branding is still equal to communications. Without a differentiating positioning and personality, however, the communications will not be very successful. Only after the desired positioning and personality of the retail brand have been determined can the communications strategy be formulated. To implement this strategy, a retail company uses an extensive mix of out-of-store and in-store tools. The most important of these communication tools are as follows.

Out-of-store communications
- Advertising.
- Direct marketing communications.

In-store communications
- Store design.
- Visual merchandising.
- Employees.

Together, these have to communicate the desired positioning and brand personality. But the reverse is also true: the content and the look and feel of the communications strongly influence the consumer's image of the store's positioning and personality. Therefore, there should be a close connection between the three rings of the retail brand circle. When this connection does not exist, a strong brand identity can never be developed.

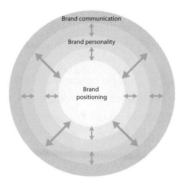

Figure 9.1 Brand communication and the retail brand circle

The brand communications should be an integral part of the brand identity strategy. This brand identity has to be proven in the store. If the store performance does not match the brand communication at all touch-points in and outside the store, most money spent on communications will be wasted. The store is the face and the voice of the retail brand. A consumer who enters the store with the wrong expectations, or has a negative experience in the store, will leave disappointed and might never come back. If the brand promise and the brand performance are not aligned, there can never be a strong retail brand.

Consumers are drawn to the store through the brand promise in the out-of-store communications. When entering, the consumer turns into a browser, and the in-store communications then have to try to convert the browser into a buyer. Finally, the entire in-store performance, both rational and emotional, will have to ensure that this buyer becomes a loyal customer, but this will only be successful if the brand promise and the brand performance are at least equal to each other. Better still, the brand performance should exceed the consumer's expectations. This process can be illustrated as in Figure 9.2.

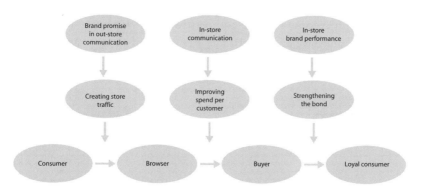

Figure 9.2 From consumer to loyal customer

All in-store and out-of-store communications have two aspects: their content, and their look and feel. It is especially the positioning mix of the retail brand that determines the content of the communication. This content has to consist of clear, often functional consumer benefits. All the retail brand's touch-points with the target group, both inside and outside the store, will have to communicate the positionings for range, prices, convenience and store experience with which the retail brand wants to tempt them to purchase. The brand personality especially influences the look and feel of these touch-points. In order to communicate the desired brand personality clearly and consistently, a unique brand communication tone and style will have to be developed for the retail brand. This tone and style will have to give the retail brand its own look and feel. It will have to be determined which tone of voice, colours, typography, illustrations, materials and shapes should be used for the retail brand. This visual and verbal identity needs to be a clear reflection of the desired brand personality. A unique, consistent brand communication language that consumers will experience everywhere (from the advertisement to the store design, from the truck or the website to the salespeople's outfits) can give the retail brand a distinguishable identity.

This consistency can, for example, be obtained through using a dominant colour, as Vodafone does with red. In its advertising, direct marketing communications, store design and all other in-store communications, the dominant use of red determines the look and feel of Vodafone. In a way, communications can make sure that the retail brand acquires a clear competitive edge. However, most retail brands do not have any consistency between out-of-store and in-store communications.

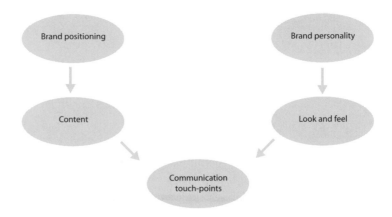

Figure 9.3 Content and look and feel of communication touch-points

Together, the content and look and feel of all communication touch-points can play a big role in building up a unique brand identity. Both the content and the look and feel of the communications will have to appeal to the target group. Appealing content that is being communicated in a way that does not match the personality of the retail brand will confuse the consumer. Conversely, an appealing look and feel to the communications will not be able to hide a lack of strong content. Therefore, it is necessary to make a clear distinction between the content, or consumer proposition, of the touch-points on one side, and the look and feel on the other. Both elements of communication will have to be checked for relevancy to consumers, and will have to match the retail brand's identity. Only when both elements are aligned will there be successful communication.

The content and the look and feel of the various out-of-store and in-store communication tools are mainly about the aspects outlined in Table 9.1.

Communication tool	Brand positioning Content	Brand personality Look and feel
Advertising	Customer proposition; product, price, convenience, store experience	Creative concept; tone and style
Direct marketing communication	Tailor-made customer proposition	Creative concept; tone and style
Store design	Location, size, layout, convenience	Materials, colours, shapes, lighting
Visual merchandising	Product density, method of presentation, number of displays, information on in-store signage and graphics	Multi-sensory communication; sight, sound, smell, taste, touch
Employees	Role of employees; kind of contact with customers, expertise	Behaviour of employees; availability, appearance, friendliness, eagerness

Table 9.1 Translation of brand positioning and personality into content and look and feel of the communication

Determining the tone and style effectively, and then aligning the look and feel of all the communications, will guarantee consistency between the various touch-points. If there are no tone and style principles, or if they have not been precisely formulated, the look and feel of the communications will go in various directions. The chances that consumers will experience incorrect emotional associations will then be very high.

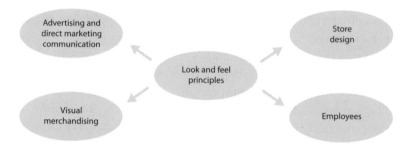

Figure 9.4 Consistency in look and feel of all consumer touch-points

While the designs vary in any particular store to match the local market, the typical Starbucks works around a planned mix of organic and manufactured components: light wood tones at the counters and signage areas, brown bags, and a green icon that features a female figure with long flowing hair, all create a natural, environmentally conscious feeling. These organic-inspired elements are blended with more sleek, modern touches: the wood has a very smooth surface that makes its 'natural' tone seem finished and comfortable; polished dark-marble counter tops seem imposing and high-tech; glass shelves, thin modern white track lighting, and pure white cups all create a contemporary feeling. The logo's human figure also delivers the double organic/modern message: she is earthy looking, yet she is rendered in a modern-looking abstract-representational form, in black and white with a band of colour around the centre only. The colours of the lamps, walls, and tables mimic coffee tones, from green (raw beans) to light and darker browns. Special package and cup designs are coordinated to create livelier, more colourful tones for holidays (Schmitt and Simonson, 1997: 82).

9.2 Objectives and tools

All tools in the retail communication mix have their own specific possibilities and restraints. Out-of-store communications attract customers, and in-store communications try to increase the spend per customer. Therefore, depending on the objectives, it is of the utmost importance to choose the right mix of communication tools. The most important objectives of retail brand communication are as follows.

Creating store traffic

First of all, the retail communication mix will have to make sure that enough customers visit the store or the website. Communications tell customers what to expect from the retail brand. Some stores almost automatically have high store traffic. The location of the store has a big influence on that. A store situated in a high-traffic location will often not have to use a lot of advertising to draw customers in. When a retail brand is located next to or close to another store with enormous appeal, it can benefit from that. The budget for out-of-store communications can then be very low. Good speciality stores that are located close to a large, successful hypermarket will often be more successful than those located further away because they benefit from the store traffic the hypermarket has created.

Improving the spend of existing customers

The exterior of the store can also have an influence on attracting passers-by. A striking and inviting exterior can communicate a clear message to consumers about what the store will be like inside. The interior of the store can then influence buying behaviour. Once consumers are inside, the retailer can try to turn browsers into buyers, with the store design, the visual merchandising and the salespeople, therefore increasing sales per customer. In principle, there are many opportunities to do this as after all, about 40 to 80 per cent of buying decisions take place in the store.

Compared with a bricks-and-mortar store an online retail brand has the disadvantage that not all the senses can be influenced, resulting in fewer impulse purchases. However, there will be much more information available that is relevant to customers' buying behaviour. Because of that, communications can be better targeted. For example, Amazon can offer customers books that exactly match their interests, based on information about their buying behaviour.

Improving the spend of existing customers can happen in three ways, for both online and offline retail brands.

Penetration

One of the objectives of in-store communications is to have existing customers buy more product categories: for example, by drawing customers' attention to new product categories to encourage cross-selling. Among the strategies that are often chosen are product demonstrations, sampling and cross-merchandising. A salesperson can let a customer try a new product for free, and customers can also be persuaded to try certain products through on-pack promotions or very drastic price promotions.

Frequency

Retailers can use visual merchandising and other in-store communication tools to try to persuade customers who already buy a certain product category to buy more of it and to buy it more often. Strategies that can be used in this framework are, among other things, savings programmes and multi-packs, which inspire customers to buy extra of the particular product.

Conversion

The profit margins of a retailer can differ by product and by brand. It could therefore be beneficial for a retail company to have the customer choose a different product or brand. For example, retailers often try to persuade customers to buy their private brand instead of a manufacturer's brand.

Strengthening the bond with existing customers

Attracting new customers costs ten times as much as retaining existing ones. But existing customers also shop in other stores, so retailers pretty much always have to share their customers. Customers who are 100 per cent loyal to a retail brand hardly exist. Even if we talk about a certain loyalty, that will often be based on habits and the lack of a better alternative. In order for the customer to feel at home in a store, an emotional bond should develop between the retail brand and the customer. This bond will mainly develop when the brand positioning is proven by the brand performance in the store or online. The promise to the consumer has to become reality, or even better, be exceeded. The store design, the visual merchandising and the employees for an offline retail brand play an important role in proving the brand promise. For an online brand, the website design and the fulfilment of the order are important in strengthening loyalty. The bond with existing offline and online customers can of course be strengthened via a loyalty programme. This programme, however, will never be able to substitute for solid brand performance. At most, a good loyalty programme is an extra stimulant to customers to go to the store more often. Alternatively when the performance is not good, a loyalty programme will not be able to prevent customers turning their backs on the store.

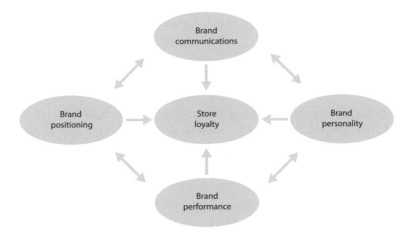

Figure 9.5 Factors that influence store loyalty

There is a clear order between the three communication objectives. First, the customer will have to be drawn to the store or the website with advertising, direct marketing communications and by the store exterior. Next, the retailer must try to persuade the customer to spend as much as possible, and finally, a bond with the customer must develop and the buyer must become a loyal customer. The realization of the three successive communication objectives may acquire the use of different strategies and different tools. Depending on the objectives, the communication tools outlined in Table 9.2 might be used.

Communication objective	Communication tools
Creating store traffic	Advertising
	Direct marketing communications
	Store design (exterior)
Improving spend per customer	Store design (interior)
	Visual merchandising
	Employees
	Direct marketing communications
Strengthening the bond	Employees
	Direct marketing communications

Table 9.2 Communication objectives and communication tools

The store is the most important medium for a retailer. Every day retail companies get lots of opportunities to build their brands through their in-store communications. The brand is made in the store. Nevertheless, a retail company might need other touch-points to make contact with its target group. Store traffic mainly needs to be created through advertising, direct marketing communications and the store exterior. Large numbers of consumers can be reached through advertising in newspapers, circulars, television and other media. Advertising can make sure that the store will be on the consumer's shopping list. Direct marketing communications are usually about smaller, specific target groups. Because direct marketing communications can define the target group very well, the message can be better targeted than with advertising through mass media. It can be completely tuned to the target group.

Making good use of a store's location can also create more store traffic. If the exterior is striking and inviting enough, passers-by will decide to take a look inside. Every Ikea store, for example, is noticeable from afar because of its yellow and blue colours; and additionally, the company uses the exterior of its stores to communicate in-store promotions.

Once consumers are in the store or logged on to the website, they will then have to be inspired via other touch-points to purchase one or more items. In general, the total costs of out-of-store communications (including price reductions and handling and other costs) are not earned back through the extra sales of the advertised products. It is therefore important that once in the store customers are also confronted with other products and spend more than they had planned: for example, by buying a product that is complementary to a special offer. Improving the spend of these existing customers means using different communication tools than those for attracting customers. The positioning and the personality of the retail brand will have to be communicated clearly and memorably through the store design, the visual merchandising and the employees.

In addition, a lot of attention needs to be paid to the range of stock. Customers need to be inspired to purchase something. Customers come into in the store because they already have a certain interest in the retail brand proposition. In the store they are actually confronted with the range of merchandise, and they walk through the brand, as it were. This physical confrontation with the brand has much more influence on buying behaviour than any other communication tool.

Employees especially can have a big influence on strengthening the bond with the customer. This bond should result not only in customers returning to the store repeatedly, but also in the way that they come to feel emotionally involved with the retail brand. Because of this, dependence on price promotions will not have to be as high. Customers will be less inclined to choose another retail brand, and a promotion from another store will be no match for the emotional bond that the consumer already has with the current retail brand. The mind position of the current retail brand is too strong to be influenced.

So in principle, the possibilities of the various communication tools are very different. Every offline and online retailer will have to choose the right mix of tools. The emphases can differ a lot from retailer to retailer. Retailers that have a perfect location with lots of traffic will most likely not have, or hardly have, any out-of-store communications. They will mainly use their budget to optimize their store. Other retail companies, like for example specialist stores in the higher price segment, will pay a lot of attention to the quality of their salespeople. However, the employees of an online retailer will have little or no contact with customers. Therefore the web design, which is comparable to the store design of an offline retailer, will receive the most attention, together with fulfilment. How the available budget is eventually divided between out-of-store and in-store communications depends on the question of where the biggest opportunities for future sales growth lie: attracting new customers or increasing the spend of existing customers.

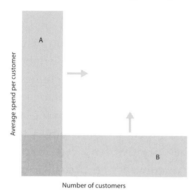

Figure 9.6 Opportunities for future sales growth

Many (super)specialists find themselves in situation A in Figure 9.6. A retail brand in this category does not have many customers, but instead obtains a very high spend per customer. It would therefore not be very meaningful for this brand to try to increase the average spend per customer even more. Future sales growth would best be obtained through new customers. This category of retail brands has to try to use out-of-store communications to attract more customers.

In contrast, department stores for example almost always find themselves in situation B. Department stores have a lot of browsers, but a lot fewer buyers, and additionally, sales per customer are very low. Visitors to stores in situation B also buy a lot at other stores. These retail brands first of all have to try to increase the spend and loyalty of existing browsers and customers. Apart from adjustments to the range or the prices, in-store communications are the most obvious way. Through the store design, the visual merchandising and the employees, browsers need to become buyers and loyal customers, and then eventually the spend per customer will need to be increased.

10. OUT-OF-STORE COMMUNICATIONS: ATTRACTING CUSTOMERS

The objective of both retail advertising and direct marketing communications is to attract customers. There is a considerable difference between the communication objectives of a retailer and those of a manufacturer. For a manufacturer it is very important to create a strong brand preference even before a consumer visits a store. Once the consumer is in the store the manufacturer has hardly any opportunity to influence the buying decision. For retailers the situation is completely different. They primarily want to attract customers through out-of-store communications. Once consumers are in the store, the store design, visual merchandising and employees can turn visitors into loyal customers. For a retail brand the store itself is the most important communication tool. It is in the store that the brand is made or broken.

10.1 Retail advertising

It is almost impossible for a manufacturer to build up a strong mind position for a fast-moving consumer good without advertising. Advertising plays a less dominant role in retail, however, because for a retail brand the store itself is the most important medium. In the store the retail brand has direct contact with the customer. Therefore a large advertising budget is not absolutely necessary for a successful retail brand. If the location and proposition are strong enough, a relatively low advertising budget can often be sufficient. For example, Starbucks became one of the most powerful retail brands in the world without significant communication budgets. Zara also spends very little on advertising: only about 0.3 per cent of the sales total, as opposed to 3 per cent or more for other fashion retailers. Almost every week Zara has new clothes in its stores, and consumers are curious enough about these new collections to visit the stores on a regular basis even if they have not seen any advertising. Locations and store windows are Zara's most important communications media. Consequently it only opens stores in the very best locations. However, H&M, one of Zara's biggest competitors, regularly uses advertising. H&M is especially known for its advertising campaigns with famous models and actresses.

A retail company builds its brand mainly via its stores. For example, most customers visit their supermarket weekly and spend about 30 to 45 minutes in-store, during which time the retailer has every chance to communicate its brand positioning and personality. The shopping experience customers have while walking around the store, seeing and touching the products and being in contact with employees, is many times stronger than the messages they receive through advertising. Therefore proving the brand promise every single day is the challenge for every retailer.

Before that can happen, though, the customer first has to be drawn to the store. Advertising and direct marketing can play an important role in that process. In almost every category the consumer can choose between many different stores. That sets high expectations on the message content: the stronger the proposition, the stronger the communication. The mix of positioning attributes has to be better than that of the competition. Consumers have to make an effort to go to the store, and they will only be prepared to make that effort if they has the feeling that they will do better there than elsewhere. So consumers have to be convinced by strong arguments. That is why retailers who want to create store traffic almost always use concrete products and special offers. These special offers are brought to the target group's attention via mass communications and direct marketing, in the hope that they will motivate consumers to visit the store in the very near future. The extent to which this really happens determines the advertising's success.

Retail advertising that does not succeed in attracting customers to the store in the short term will probably not work in the long term either. If it does not sell this week, it probably will not sell next week. The advertising must stimulate customers in the short term, otherwise it will not meet its most important goal: creating store traffic. Advertising that is only thematic and does not communicate, for instance, that there are special bargains or other strong benefits, will usually be less effective and efficient for a retail brand. This kind of advertising lacks engagement if it does not attract customers to the store and does not turn the store into a brand that is on the top of every consumer's shopping list.

So the strategy that most retail companies adopt to create store traffic is the same: communicating about bargains through the mass media. But it is not only the strategy that is the same. The special offers themselves are also often the same, because every retailer knows which products will be most successful in attracting customers: commodities from well-known manufacturer brands or other price-sensitive products. Consumers reacts straightaway if these products are on sale, hence most retail brands choose the same products for promotions. The price at which these products are offered is usually around the same as well, because after all, competitors keep a close eye on each other. The result is enormous uniformity. Most retail advertisements, circulars and television commercials all look alike, therefore there is no, or hardly any, distinction.

However, there are some ways in which a retail brand can still try to acquire a competitive advantage through advertising content.

Profiling products

A retail brand that wants to position itself through its range can offer a number of 'profiling products', besides the obvious ones. It can select products that sell the store and the brand. A supermarket might advertise not only offer soft drinks, detergents and coffee, but also fresh ready-to-eat meals, for example. A fashion store can become known for always being the first to offer the latest fashion trends. In addition, a retailer can also emphasize its private brand or try to regularly agree exclusive deals with certain manufacturers.

One-off merchandise

Retail brands that want to attract customers regularly offer products that are not normally included in the range. In general, they choose best-selling products from other sectors for this purpose. Price brands with an everyday low price strategy use one-off merchandise to keep their store and advertising exciting. Supermarkets sell computers or televisions, and do-it-yourself stores offer home training equipment and toys. No or hardly any money needs to be made on these special offers, because the most important goal is to attract customers. Once in the store, other more profitable products can be brought to the customer's attention through effective visual merchandising and various other methods.

Added value

Customers can also be drawn to the store by added-value offers like free home delivery, or special events like product demonstrations or fashion shows. In this way convenience and experience brands in particular can try to acquire a sustainable competitive advantage.

Lowest price

If a retail brand does not succeed in positioning itself through differentiating products or added value, the only thing left is to offer products at a lower price. However, this strategy, which is mainly used by price brands, can only be successful in the long run if the retail brand has not only the lowest price, but also the lowest costs.

Distinctive content can be strengthened by a unique look and feel to the communications. However, the advertisement, commercial or brochure should then be more than just an enumeration of products and prices. If an original creative concept gives it recognizability, the emotional bond with the customer can be strengthened further. Moreover, an original concept results in extra sympathy for the retail brand.

Figure 10.1 Content, look and feel of distinctive retail advertising

Advertising can help shape the way we think and feel about a retail brand. Strong retail brands are always the result of years of consistent communication of the brand positioning and brand personality. Strong positioning and personality need to be communicated in the right way to create an emotional relationship with the customer. If the retail brand does not succeed in building that emotional relationship, because it has the same special offers as the competition and also advertises these in the same way, then the only thing left would be to mark down the goods, but this does not result in any real building of customer loyalty. It is dangerous because strong special offers and high advertising budgets become the only way to attract customers, meaning that if a competitor has better prices, the consumer will choose that competitor.

The difference between retail and product advertising

A retail brand essentially differs from a manufacturer brand in the way it uses special offers in advertising. In general, retailers have other objectives for their advertising than do manufacturers. For a retail brand it is important to create store traffic. Other communication tools in the store can then take over and make sure that sales per customer increase and that customers are satisfied when leaving the store. To a large extent, their experiences in the store determine the extent to which consumers appreciate the retail brand. The impressions consumers get in the store are much stronger than those received through advertising or direct marketing communications. Most purchase decisions are made in the store, and a retailer has multiple tools to influence the purchasing behaviour. The retailer determines in which store environment the products will be offered and how, and at what price. Moreover, the retailer decides which role its salespeople will play. In talking with customers, salespeople can have a big influence on the brand choice and the customer's ultimate purchase decision.

The situation is clearly different for a manufacturer and therefore advertising plays a totally different role. Through advertising, manufacturers have to make sure their brand awareness and brand preference are as strong as possible, before the consumer enters the store. In the store the consumer is confronted with lots of brands. At that moment a manufacturer has very little opportunity to influence the consumer's buying behaviour. It can try to attract attention through packaging, but has little or no say about the way in which the remaining in-store media are used: it depends on the retailer's support. So it is of utmost importance to the manufacturer that the consumer goes into the store with an existing strong brand preference. Consequently manufacturers' advertising is more thematic and more focused on the long term than is retailers'.

In their advertising, manufacturers try to communicate functional and emotional arguments why their brand is better than that of other manufacturers. The advertising rarely involves reductions in price, for instance, as manufacturers most likely will not even know what price their brand is offered at in the store. Functional and/or emotional product features are communicated in the advertising. A manufacturer has to build up a brand particularly through mass advertising in consumers' homes, and in other locations as well. The opportunities in the store are just too limited. Therefore a manufacturer's brand-building process is the reverse of a retailer's.

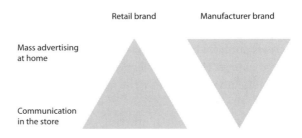

Figure 10.2 The brand-building process for retailers and manufacturers

Retail advertising only ever looks like manufacturer brand advertising if a retailer uses thematic advertising for its private brand. A retailer will then find itself in the same position as a manufacturer, because it will have to try to convince consumers that its brand is better than others. The arguments a retailer uses for that are mainly functional. The retailer will focus on emphasizing that its private brand is just as good as a well-known manufacturer brand, but much cheaper. The private brand's price is often directly compared with the manufacturer brand's. A retailer hardly ever uses emotional benefits when advertising a private brand. This is actually a disadvantage for private brands, especially in emotion-driven product categories, as well-known manufacturer brands often try to acquire customer loyalty based on emotional benefits. However, on the contrary a retailer can always give its private brand extra support in the store, through good shelf presentation or extensive demonstrations for example, which a manufacturer cannot.

For years, manufacturers have used mass-media advertising to build their brands. However, this has become much more difficult because of media fragmentation. Communication through traditional mass media is in many cases ineffective and costly. In addition, the allocation of the manufacturer's communication budget is out of proportion to the consumer's buying behaviour. When buying fast-moving consumer goods in particular, the consumer is led by in-store communications to a large extent. However, manufacturers still do not spend enough money on in-store communications. By allocating only a small part of their budget to in-store communications, manufacturers are in fact missing out on sales opportunities. That is why they are now looking for other ways to get in contact with consumers. They especially look for more cooperation with retailers. Through effective trade marketing they try to motivate the retailer to pay optimal attention to the manufacturer brand in the store. So slowly a shift is occurring in the allocation of the manufacturer's communications budget. Expenditure on trade marketing is rising at the cost of expenditure on consumer marketing, therefore manufacturers are also trying to work on their brands in the store through cooperation with the retailer.

Because retail advertising clearly has a different function from manufacturer brand advertising, retailers have to meet a couple of specific rules, for content as well as for look and feel. The main points that need consideration are as follows.

Recognizable concept

Advertising by retailers has a much shorter lifespan than advertising by manufacturers. Retail advertisements are typically only placed once, and television commercials are generally only broadcast for one or two weeks. That is why a retailer's advertising messages do not have as many opportunities to build up recognition, because the consumer is confronted with a new advertisement or commercial every time. With each new advertising message the retail brand has to start all over again, as it were, in building up that recognition. To minimize this problem, it is of the utmost importance for a retail brand to work with a very recognizable, consistent creative concept in all its advertising. If it uses the same music, the same character or spokesperson, the same location or other consistent elements, consumers will more readily recognize the advertising for a specific retail brand. All the individual advertisements and commercials then begin to add up until eventually the retail brand can enjoy instant recognizability.

Maximum hit probability

The most important objective of retail advertising is to attract customers. Retail advertising has to create store traffic. To maximize this chance, the mix of special offers has to be put together in such a way that it contains enough stimuli for the target group to visit the store. In general, television commercials and other advertising communicating only one special offer will not achieve that. In retail advertising it is better to work with multiple special offers, or category or store-wide promotions.

Local approach

Just as for a manufacturer, it is impossible for a retailer to please everyone. When determining the target group a retailer will, besides other factors, have to consider local residents. After all, in retail all business is local. The market area of a store is much more limited than that of a manufacturer. Distance is still one of the most important factors in store choice. A manufacturer covers an entire country, or even multiple countries with its brand. On the contrary, a retailer always operates in a much more limited area. Even with a large number of stores there will always be areas that are not catered for, therefore a retailer, more so than a manufacturer, is forced to use local media to reach potential customers. If necessary the content of the advertising can be adjusted to local market conditions.

Customers' language

A retailer is much closer to the customer than a manufacturer is. This relationship needs to be a consideration when determining the way in which it communicates to its customers. The tone of retail advertising has to be more mature and human. A retailer has to communicate with customers as if they were neighbours. Consumers are still often addressed like small children in retail advertising, being encouraged by loud copy to visit the store straightaway. After all, that is where the special offer of the century is waiting for them. Retailers sometimes forget that there are more important things in life for a consumer than a cheap detergent or a marked-down drill set. Slowly however, more and more retail brands will begin to choose a more relaxed tone of voice. After all, retail advertising that does not feature loud copy also seems to be successful. H&M, Ikea, Albert Heijn, Diesel and lots of other strong retail brands prove that on a daily basis.

Realism

Within certain limits, a manufacturer can control its product quality because that quality is determined in the factory. For a retail company however, it is much more difficult to prove the brand promise each and every day. A retailer depends more on the performance of employees than a manufacturer does. Promises made in advertising have to be proven in the store. Over-promising and under-delivering cause consumers to walk out of the store. Therefore it is important to not promise too much. Promises in advertising are better off being quite realistic.

Integration

A manufacturer will always have to wait to see what kind of support its brand will get in the store, but in contrast a retailer in principle controls the entire process. Out-of-store and in-store communications should correspond closely. The picture that is created in advertising should be reinforced in the store. The products offered in the advertising should be easily found in the store.

Consistency

A retailer sits at the top of the market. Each day it is exposed to a lot of information regarding in-store behaviour. That is probably why retailers tend to change their advertising concepts frequently, more so than manufacturers. If sales are a little bit disappointing, the retailer will probably consider adjusting the campaign. However, in order to build up a strong retail brand it is actually harmful to change a campaign concept too frequently.

Budget for creativity

Profit margins in retail are small. Therefore retailers are very cost-conscious and also want to save on the development and execution of their advertising. After all new advertising has to be developed every week. The number of different advertisements and commercials produced is much smaller for manufacturers. They often use magazine advertisements or television campaigns for months or even years, so it is no problem if development and execution costs are higher. But a retailer can no longer afford to be satisfied with low-cost, moderately interesting advertising. Moderately good advertising does not attract attention any more amongst all the competing marketing messages, or might possibly even communicate the wrong message.

10.1.1 DETERMINING THE COMMUNICATION BUDGET

One of the most important decisions a retailer has to make when formulating its communications strategy is to fix a budget. This budget depends on a number of factors.

Type of merchandise

Retail brands that sell daily essentials such as groceries advertise proportionally less than retail brands that sell durable or speciality goods. The purchasing frequency for essentials is much higher than for other products. For durable and speciality goods the store visit has to be forced, as it were. In addition, sales per square metre are much higher for daily essentials than for durable and speciality products. That also influences the budget, as it can then be smaller in percentage terms.

Familiarity of store

Well-known stores with a loyal customer base can afford to produce fewer out-of-store communications than stores that have just opened up. For new market entrants, customer flow still has to be built up. Stores that have existed for a while can profit from word of mouth advertising.

Positioning

A retail brand that positions itself on lowest prices will usually have an aggressive communications strategy and a higher budget than a store that is known for its excellent service. The proof of low prices at a discounter has to be communicated over and over again.

Competition

More advertising is found in fiercely competitive markets than in markets where competition is not as strong. Budgets will go up especially if there is a price war. In general the budget for out-of-store communications should be in proportion to the market share. A retail brand that has a market share of 10 per cent should also account for about 10 per cent of the communications expenditure in that sector.

Location

Stores in a remote location have to attract customers through advertising, because the consumer has to make a conscious decision to go to that store. There is no flow of general passers-by. In contrast, a store that is located right next to a very popular one can probably survive with very little advertising.

The average US advertising budgets in a number of sectors are given in Table 10.1.

Sector	Percentage of annual sales spent on advertising
Apparel and accessory stores	3.6
Catalogue, mail-order houses	6.4
Computer stores	0.6
Convenience stores	0.3
Department stores	3.6
Drugstores	0,8
Family clothing stores	2.4
Furniture stores	5.9
Grocery stores	1.0
Hobby, toy and game stores	1.8
Hotels and motels	2.3
Jewellery stores	5.1
Men's clothing stores	3.6
Radio, television and consumer electronics stores	3.2
Record stores	1.7
Shoe stores	2.5
Variety stores	0.9
Women's clothing stores	4.7

Table 10.1 Advertising to sales ratios in the United States

Catalogue and mail-order houses that do not have a bricks-and-mortar store have to spend the largest proportion of their sales income on advertising. These retail companies rely solely on advertising and direct marketing communications to attract customers. Convenience stores, drugstores and grocery stores, with their high purchasing frequency, can make do with a considerably lower percentage.

10.2 Direct marketing communications

Costco, the American warehouse club company, is still market leader in the US warehouse club market sector, despite the competition from Wal-Mart's Sam's Club. The company now has about 500 stores and has opened up warehouses in Canada, Japan, Korea, Mexico and the UK, to name just a few. Costco runs a business with extremely low costs, because it has eliminated almost all the costs of conventional retailers and wholesalers. Its range consists of about 4,000 items, compared with the 40,000 to 60,000 of a conventional supermarket. It stocks only products on which it can offer the customer a significant price reduction. These savings are passed on to the club members, which are small businesses and consumers. Costco does not advertise. It uses information from its membership database, and this data on 25.4 million households enables it to target its customers very precisely through direct marketing communications. This process is much more efficient than mass advertising.

Traditional mass advertising does not always produce the desired results because the consumer is overwhelmed with communications. Therefore, retailers are constantly looking for alternatives, of which direct marketing communications is one. In comparison with mass advertising, direct marketing communications are a relatively expensive tool. The costs per contact are high. However, direct marketing communications offer some specific advantages.

Differentiated marketing
With direct marketing communications a differentiated proposition can be formulated for each target group. Marketing investments can be made in the areas where they will create the highest potential return.

After all, not all products and not all customers are equally important to a retailer. Retailers know from experience that 20 per cent of the range is often good for 80 per cent of the sales. Gradually retailers have learnt that this 20/80 rule can be also applied to the customer base: a small proportion of the customers can account for a large part of the sales and profit. So it is of the utmost importance to focus marketing efforts on that particular group of customers.

Customer relationship management is then an excellent tool. For example, data from loyalty programmes can be analysed with the help of advanced information technology. The information that is useful includes recency of last purchase, frequency of store visits, buying behaviour, total spend and all kinds of demographic data. New customers can be canvassed through a specific selection process undertaken in the most promising target groups. The spend of existing customers can be increased via cross-selling, and former customers can be regained through win-back programmes. Each of these three customer groups requires a different communication approach.

Strengthening the relationship with the customer
In the name of efficiency, personal contact with customers has disappeared, but with the help of technology the retailer can develop tailored communications to build up an effective form of customer relationship. A personal conversation with a customer is effectively replaced (to a certain extent) by a personal direct marketing approach. This means that the customer is no longer voiceless or anonymous, and a mutual relationship can develop that goes beyond the traditional seller/buyer relationship. At Amazon for example, customers can not only buy all kinds of books, but also sell used books and other products, and write book reviews for other customers. With direct marketing communications a retail brand can treat a customer as an individual. The customer can be approached in a very personal way, and there is the potential for the impact of the communication to be much more powerful than with mass-media communications. By the way, the direct marketing contact does not always have to take place at home. For example, the message can also be communicated in the store through an on-pack promotion. Buyers of a certain brand can then specifically be approached in a very direct way.

Relevance

Because the communication can be very targeted and specific, the relevance for the customer is likely to be higher. In mass advertising the proposition is tailored to a pretty large, general target group. Therefore it is inevitable that averages are used. Direct marketing communications are focused on smaller and much more specific target groups. So the communication can really be tailor-made and the influence on buying behaviour can be much stronger. The retail brand's proposition can be specifically in line with the target group's characteristics. Therefore, it is important that in direct marketing communications the target group is clearly defined.

Less confrontation with the competition

A retail brand that uses mass media is inevitably confronted with its competition. Advertisements and commercials from many retail brands in the same sector appear in daily newspapers and on television. If one of these retail brands has a distinctive offer, the competition will react with a similar or even better offer as soon as possible. This makes it very easy for consumers to compare the propositions from various retail brands and to determine which has the better offer. If direct marketing communications are used, competitors are not enticed to react as much. Direct marketing communications are less visible to those not targeted by them, especially if they are only used locally.

Actionable and measurable

Through direct marketing communications, the buying behaviour of every individual customer can be directly and continuously tracked and influenced. Therefore measuring the success of the communication is much easier. Moreover, through direct marketing communications the customer almost always receives a concrete offer: information about a special promotion or event in the store, a discount on one or more products, sampling of a new or unknown product or a savings programme. Following this, the retailer can determine how many and which customers make use of which offers. The costs and results of direct marketing communications can be compared. That is much more difficult with mass communications.

Despite all these advantages, direct marketing communications still have a couple of question marks. The most important one is that in retail there is very little proof of the financial benefits of loyalty programmes. All loyalty programmes promise new customers and higher spend from existing customers, but the proceeds do not always counterbalance the costs. For example, loyalty programme costs for a large supermarket chain are usually 0.5 to 1 per cent of sales, because a large customer base is needed to gather the right information. But it is very expensive to keep and analyse this database. Short-term special offers can sometimes be very successful and attract a lot of customers, but the programme needs to lead eventually to stronger emotional customer loyalty. Very few loyalty programmes meet this requirement, because the programme is often not persuasive enough to bring about real loyalty.

Rewarding loyal customers with discounts is in itself not enough. Consumers' wallets are loaded with loyalty cards. The content of most of these loyalty programmes is very similar, and that is also why they are not that successful. They really only offer customers extra financial benefits, and these kind of programmes do not lead to real customer loyalty or positive economic results, because they are not distinctive and lack an emotional component. Buying behaviour is not influenced in the long run. To create a real distinction, a loyalty programme should not only offer discounts but in particular offer the customer all kinds of personal privileges as well. Customers should really get the feeling that the loyalty programme takes their personal desires into account. Personal privileges can make shopping more convenient and more satisfying, and this can help build an emotional bond with the customer: the kind of bond that is needed in order to turn a store into a brand.

However, offering a loyalty card is not an absolute condition for loyalty marketing. A loyalty card is a means and can be a solution, but loyalty marketing can also be applied without a card. A simple savings programme can also collect customer data. However, the advantage of a loyalty card is that the customer's buying behaviour can be tracked more precisely. The information collected through the loyalty programme can be the key to the added value of a loyalty card, but storing and analysing data from a loyalty programme costs a lot of money. Moreover, many retailers do not know what to do with all that data. A supermarket company with a few hundred stores collects an incredible amount of data each week, and if there are no good analysis techniques available, the retailer will be overwhelmed by all the information. High returns on loyalty programmes will only be obtained if cost-efficient differentiated marketing programmes can be set up with the help of customer data, to encourage customers to visit the store more often. So the challenge for a loyalty programme is to reward the customer and still make money at the end of the day. For years, Tesco has been proving with its Clubcard that this is actually possible.

Albertsons, the American supermarket chain, is one of the many retail companies that offer a loyalty card. Like Tesco but unlike many other retailers, Albertsons is satisfied with the results of its loyalty card programme. Its loyalty card allows it to:

- understand the unique needs of its customers better, and deliver the best combination of products, services and value to meet those needs;
- make better overall business decisions and support their category management initiatives;
- grow identical store sales;
- improve their price image with customers;
- prevent market share erosion;
- protect primary shopper loyalty and grow its share of secondary shopper spending.

The information gained from its loyalty card programme enables Albertsons to offer its customers the following, for example:

- Coupons delivered at the checkouts based on the customers' actual purchases. A customer who buys baby food but no diapers, for example, gets a coupon for diapers.
- Incentives for products purchased, such as a competitive brand. So a customer who buys Coca-Cola might receive an incentive to buy Pepsi-Cola the next time.
- Unique household marketing, where participating brands can identify loyal, occasional, never-buy, new or competitor brand users, and work to influence buying behaviour.
- Private brand themes and specific department promotions.

However, even a successful loyalty programme can never be a substitute for good range, the right price, good service and the right store experience. A good loyalty programme can further strengthen a unique positioning, but a weak positioning will not be compensated for by it. And if it starts a loyalty programme a retail brand must be aware that its customers will then have higher expectations of it.

11. IN-STORE COMMUNICATIONS: HIGHER SPEND AND LOYALTY

Most buying decisions take place in the store. A retailer therefore has every opportunity to work on its brand identity in the store, as a manufacturer does not. Retailers face the challenge of focusing on all the senses. Almost all in-store communication is now visual. The result is sometimes visual pollution, and consequently some retail brands miss the opportunity to strengthen their emotional bond with their customers because of all the clutter. However, a strong retail brand will recognize that its personality has to be translated into distinguishable style attributes like colours, shapes, materials, sounds, smells and other sensory appeals. By doing this, a retail brand can develop a distinctive look and feel for its in-store communications.

The design of a store is broadly comparable to the packaging of a manufacturer brand. It should communicate the positioning and personality, add value to the merchandise and be efficient and effective. Visual merchandising means bringing the retail brand to life and dramatizing the merchandise offer. Immediately preceding a purchase decision, visual merchandising can be the most powerful, most effective communication tool for a retailer. In reality however, many stores do not make the most of the opportunity to seduce consumers. Many stores are very boring and predictable.

Employees are the link between the customer and the retail brand. They are almost the brand themselves, and can make a real difference in retail. That is why internal branding is so important. Every employee should know exactly what the retail brand stands for.

11.1 The most important medium

The strong competition in the retail sector leads to very low margins on best-selling items in particular. This downward pressure on price can be compensated for (to some degree) by creating an inspiring and inviting shopping environment. In the store a retail brand can communicate and strengthen its positioning. Through visual merchandising and by using the employees, attention can be drawn to unique products. A cheap-looking store design and a simple product presentation can strengthen a low-price positioning. Clear signage, wide aisles and attentive employees can make the shopping experience easier, and of course, the shopping environment also has a big influence on the overall store experience. A retail brand can build up a unique identity through distinctive in-store communications. In-store communications not only strengthen brand positioning, but can also express brand personality. That is why no other medium has as much influence on buying behaviour. However, by no means all retailers realize this. They still pay more attention to store operations than to the shopping environment.

In-store communications can be a very strong medium for every retailer. Even if the positioning mix of a retail brand is similar to that of other retail brands, store design, visual merchandising and employees can still create a very distinctive brand identity. The conversion rate in department stores is often below 50 per cent, because many browsers are insufficiently persuaded to buy something. But these browsers can be persuaded to become buyers through inspiring in-store communications. About 40 to 80 per cent of all in-store purchases are unplanned, and these are likely to be motivated by different kinds of in-store communications: store design, visual merchandising and employees.

In-store communications can also have a big influence on profit, because they can guide, engage, inform, excite and stimulate the customer. If managed well, all touch-points together will give the desired, consistent brand impression. In-store communications can create an environment that enhances the shopping experience, and can help build a retail brand as well. Appealing in-store communications that reflect the brand personality can provide a very strong differential advantage.

Clear, attractive and inspiring in-store communications can make shopping an enjoyable experience. Customers want to be informed and inspired, and are willing to let their buying behaviour be influenced by impulses in the store. The level of influence any in-store communication has on buying behaviour depends on the extent to which the purchase was planned beforehand, however. Some purchases are entirely planned while for others the consumer might be planning to buy a specific type of good, but not yet have selected a specific variety. Perhaps a consumer knows he wants to eat fish for dinner, but does not yet know which kind of fish. In a similar way, the consumer might have chosen a product category, but not a brand. For example, a consumer intends to buy a television, but she still hesitates between a couple of brands. In-store communications can help to influence the consumer to buy one brand over another, or even one product over another.

Finally, there are also impulse purchases in the store that were not planned at all. In Dutch supermarkets the in-store decision rate is as follows (Nauta, 2003):

- Specifically planned (both product and brand planned, and bought according to plan): 20.9 per cent.
- Generally planned (product planned, brand chosen in-store): 22.9 per cent.
- Substitute product or brand (product or brand planned, but the customer decided to buy an alternative in-store): 4.6 per cent.
- Unplanned, impulse (decided entirely in-store): 51.7 per cent.

In other words, some element of around 80 per cent of all purchases in Dutch supermarkets is decided upon in-store. In Belgium, the United Kingdom and Denmark the level is between 70 and 80 per cent. In Germany and Italy it is lower: about 40 and 50 per cent respectively. However, in all these countries the share of purchases that can be influenced by in-store communications is enormous. If retailers apply new technologies, like for example narrowcasting and self-service kiosks, this influence will probably only get bigger. Store design and visual merchandising then complement each other.

Consumers can choose between multiple stores for almost every product they need. In some sectors there is over-capacity, so a retail brand has to attract attention from among a host of other stores. A retailer can clearly differentiate itself from its competitors through a striking store design with a unique look and feel. The store design should reflect and enhance the brand identity. A differentiating store design can create emotions and sensory experiences, because well-designed stores have their own, distinctive personality. An appealing store design can give the retail brand a face. That is why store design and visual merchandising are extremely important touch-points for a retailer in building a strong brand. They are often the most effective media for retaining customers, and additionally, they can lead to increased sales.

Online retailers cannot control the environment and atmosphere in which consumers are shopping. Consumers sit at home and decide for themselves how they shop. In principle, offline retailers are able to control the shopping environment as they can create a total brand experience through their store design and visual merchandising. Delivering on the brand promise is the moment of truth in the store. If it communicates consistent brand values and delivers a strong brand promise, the store environment can support the retail brand.

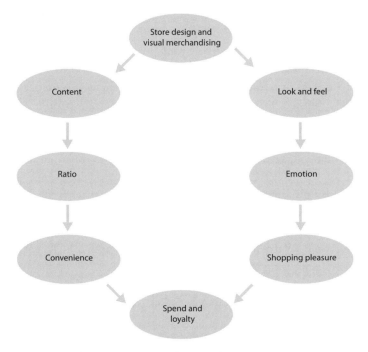

Figure 11.1 Functions of store design and visual merchandising

Store design and visual merchandising can fulfil both rational and emotional wants. The emotional function is mostly about making shopping more fun. The look and feel of the store design and visual merchandising influence the customer's perception. A pleasant look and feel can lead to a positive emotional response, making shopping more pleasurable. The rational function is mainly about the content of store design and visual merchandising, which makes shopping easier for the consumer.

The look and feel of a store's design and visual merchandising is about colours, shapes, materials, scents, sound, lighting and other sensory experiences. Together, these elements evoke positive or negative emotions in consumers. In turn, these emotions have a big influence on their buying behaviour. In one store consumers feel at ease; in another they do not. However, store design and visual merchandising also have a rational function. Together they have to create a shopping environment in which customers can shop quickly and easily. A clear layout, clear visual merchandising and clear and easily understood in-store communications make shopping easier and save time. Consumers want to be able to find products easily, and these products need to be clearly marked. Furthermore, there should be salespeople available when necessary, and there should not be any queues at the checkout. If a product does not meet expectations, it should be possible to exchange it without any hassle. If all these needs are met, the consumer will likely return.

Store design and visual merchandising, together with merchandise and employees, form the in-store brand experience. For example, Home Depot, the world's biggest do-it-yourself retail chain, discovered from research (Nardelli, 2004) that the most important factors in its customers' shopping experiences in its stores are:

- easy shopping, signage, store layout, cleanliness, product presentation: 38 per cent;
- product range, availability, quality, price: 22 per cent;
- store associates: 13 per cent;
- speed of checkout: 10 per cent.

Store design, visual merchandising and employees should be extensions of the retail brand. They give the retail brand a face and a voice. That is what makes store design, visual merchandising and employees strategic weapons, as it were; what makes the positioning and brand personality visible and tangible. Store design has to be more than a neutral background for products. Together with visual merchandising it is an essential part of the total brand identity. The store design, visual merchandising and employees form the brand environment, and can communicate just as strongly as advertising or direct marketing. The consumer needs to be persuaded to buy something via store design and visual merchandising, and the employees then have to close the deal. Alternatively, the store layout and product presentation have to be so clear that consumers can easily make their choice without any help from the sales staff. For example, men who are looking for jeans often give up searching after a couple of minutes if they cannot find the desired model or correct size.

It is not only retail brands in the higher price segment that have to pay attention to their store design and visual merchandising. Low-price brands also use these tools to communicate their desired positioning and brand personality. Stacking it high combined with a high merchandise density communicates low prices. That creates a totally different image from a luxurious clothing store where only a few pieces of clothing are hanging here and there. After all, it is not only prices that determine the consumer's price perception. The shopping environment in which the merchandise is presented is often just as important. An empty, brightly lit store mostly communicates low prices. In contrast, an expensively decorated store will create a high price image.

There can be a specific problem in designing a store when a retailer also operates vendor shops or concessions. Manufacturers will want to show their own identity as much as possible in their concessions. However, this can be at the expense of the overall store image and the retail brand's appeal. If the retail brand is not strong enough, concessionaires will impose their own brand design with little regard for the overall store design. But if every shop-in-the-shop has its own identity, the result can be a disorderly store. That is why it is wise for retailers that work with vendor shops to determine clear guidelines for their concessionaires on the design of their concession. For example, in department stores it is obvious that various cosmetics brands have to meet certain guidelines in the design of their counters. Every cosmetic brand has its own identity within certain limits. However, it is also clear that all these brands are part of the overall cosmetics department, and the department store as a whole.

The same problem arises when designing a shopping centre. On one hand all stores in the shopping centre should have the opportunity to communicate their own identity. On the other hand, the shopping centre also needs to communicate a certain overall appeal. After all, the shopping centre has to differentiate itself from other shopping centres. That is why most shopping centres have rules for what the retailers are and are not allowed to do when designing their stores. The Amsterdam Airport Centre goes particularly far in this. The individual stores hardly show their own identity, in contrast to for example the terminals at London Heathrow, where all the stores have the opportunity to create their own look and feel.

11.2 Multi-sensory communication

The challenge of in-store communications is to find the right balance between rationality (saving time) and emotion (shopping fun). That balance can differ for individual store formats. A department store like Bloomingdale's works more with emotions than Wal-Mart or Target. For the last two, store design and visual merchandising have a mainly functional aspect. But even with this type of store, emotions play a role in the buying process. This is also the case for brands defined by price, where the consumer is not only led by rational considerations. Positive emotions lead to more shopping fun, a longer stay in the store, higher spending and higher store loyalty.

These emotions are brought about through the five senses: sight, touch, sound, smell and taste. In a store customers can see, hear, touch, smell and taste the products. Those opportunities are more limited on a website. A website visit is mainly a visual experience, while a store has a multi-sensory environment. A store cannot compete with a website over the range or amount of information provided, however. But an effective store design and visual merchandising can trigger all the consumer's senses. Shopping is a multi-sensory experience, so a retail brand should be a sensory experience. Sensory associations can result in a strong emotional engagement and can therefore provide a retail brand with a lead over the competition. They can create a unique look and feel for the retail brand. Multi-sensory communication can even be the key differentiating factor between retail brands. After all, all the impulses of the five senses make up the brand experience.

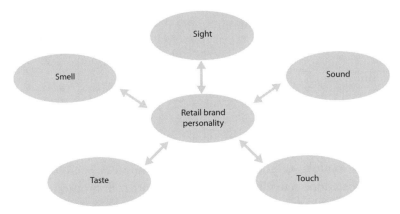

Figure 11.2 Multi-sensory communication

A few years ago Pier 1, a retail company in the United States that offers casual home furnishings, launched an advertising campaign with store graphics, direct mail and magazine and television advertisements based on its positioning statement 'Get in touch with your senses'. The campaign evolved from research revealing that its customers valued the sensory shopping experience at Pier 1. Campaign images evoked the sights, smells, sounds, textures and colours that envelop Pier 1 shoppers, especially the striking and specific smell of exotic flowers and spices. This smell makes Pier 1 clearly stand out from the competition.

EatZi's is a food store where all the senses are stimulated. This Texan retail brand is a combination of a supermarket and a restaurant. At EatZi's customers can get complete chef-developed, ready-to-heat meals, fresh produce, or the ingredients they need for their favourite recipes. Alternatively its chefs will cook for them while they shop. EatZi's is each customer's very own 'personal chef'. What makes EatZi's different is that its staff are passionate about food, and it shows. Its customers are a part of the energy created when the chefs prepare their food right in front of them, and they love shopping to a backdrop of classical music and the mouth-watering aromas of garlic, rosemary and fresh-baked bread wafting through the air. Everywhere in the store cooks are preparing meals. There's a real pizza oven, an impressive salad bar and lots of other departments, all with offerings that look just as tasty. At various locations the customer can enjoy a small taste of a dish ('this is just a sample, not a free lunch'). A lot of attention is paid to the interior and the stores does not economize on salespeople. That is why EatZi's is a store people can visit to really enjoy themselves.

In this store customers see products and various visual communications, they hear background music and other sounds, they smell the product aromas, they can touch all kinds of products and in many cases they can also taste or try them. All these touch-points influence the store image. That is also why stimulating all senses in a coordinated way is of utmost importance to every retail brand. However, in most stores there is no or hardly any focus on senses other than sight. More than 90 per cent of all in-store communication is still only visual. Other sensory impulses are neglected. The result of this is visual pollution in many stores, because too many visual impulses are asking for attention.

Although many consumers are visually oriented, offline retailers are missing out on opportunities to take an advantage over their online competitors. After all, not all five senses can be stimulated in e-commerce, while an offline retailer has many opportunities to communicate its brand positioning and personality through all the five senses. The stronger the sensory impulses are, the stronger the retail brand's competitive position will be. In that case, the prices charged are less important. For example, Starbucks with its multi-sensory experience of aromas, colours, materials and music, can afford to ask US$3.00 or more for a cup of coffee. 'Every Starbucks store is carefully designed to enhance the quality of everything the customers see, touch, hear, smell or taste,' writes CEO Howard Schultz. 'All the sensory signals have to appeal to the same high standards. The artwork, the music, the aromas, the surfaces all have to send the same subliminal message as the flavour of the coffee: everything here is best-of-class.' Starbucks is more than just a cup of coffee; it is a multi-sensory experience.

Store design and visual merchandising mostly appeal to the eye through light, shapes, colours, graphics, typefaces and movements. A store with round shapes and soft colours makes a more feminine impression than a store with rectangular shapes and harsh colours. The harsh colour combinations red/yellow, red/white and blue/yellow mainly communicate 'cheap'. That is why low-price and high-value retail brands often use these colour combinations. These kind of brands also have bright, white lighting and simple, straight-line layouts. Moreover, in visual merchandising the conscious decision is made to use voluminous product presentations, with the motto 'stack it high, sell it cheap'. After all, voluminous presentations communicate a low-price positioning, just as do high merchandise density and products that are still in bulk boxes.

Shape can be a very important visual element. For example, the golden arches of McDonald's can be recognized from afar everywhere in the world. While shapes come in an infinite variety, there are four key dimensions that should be considered in planning the style attributes of a retail brand: angularity, symmetry, proportion and size (Schmitt and Simonson, 1997: 88–92). Tinkering with these four dimensions can have a dramatic impact on customers' perceptions. Angular and rounded forms each carry a different set of associations. Angularity is associated with sturdiness, dynamism and masculinity. Roundness evokes harmony, softness and femininity. Similar to this distinction is that of the straight form versus the curved form. Straight shapes are often perceived as masculine, sharp, abrupt and choppy, while curved shapes are perceived as feminine, soft and continuous. For example, do-it-yourself stores with their mostly masculine customer base all have angular and straight forms. In contrast, department stores have a much more feminine appeal, created through rounded and curved forms.

Symmetry can create balance in a store and provide order and an overview. Finding your way might seem easier in a symmetric store, but symmetry actually does the opposite: it symbolizes confusion. In-store navigation becomes more difficult, because consumers find it more difficult to orientate themselves. A store that is completely symmetrical soon tends to be dull. This dullness can be overcome though by deviating from symmetry in some areas. Then there is still something to be discovered by the consumer.

This discovery aspect is not as important to stores that focus on replenishment shopping. In these types of store the customer wants to shop as efficiently as possible. The store then only needs some specific displays with stopping power in key locations around the store to prevent customers from walking through the store in a completely routine manner and only making their planned purchases. In contrast, for stores that focus on discovery shopping, building surprise moments into the store design is important, to give consumers the feeling that there is indeed something to be discovered.

Proportion is another major variable influencing the way people perceive a store. A long, narrow store is less inviting, because consumers gets the impression that there is hardly any room to access everything easily. A shallow store looks more accessible, because consumers immediately get an overview of the entire store when entering. Short angular shapes can seem more timid and meek. With round shapes however, proportion and symmetry are often blended, since perfectly circular shapes are also naturally symmetrical. Thus circular shapes appear less powerful than oblong shapes, but they create perceptions of harmony, resonating with softness and perfection.

The perceived brand personality is also connected with the size of the store. Large, tall or wide stores are perceived as powerful and strong, while small, short or thin stores appear more delicate and weak. Category killers like Home Depot, Staples and Bed, Bath & Beyond impress customers just their with enormous surface areas, wide aisles and voluminous presentations. However, the disadvantage of these kinds of huge store is that they can appear less pleasant and too mass-market focused.

The Selfridges building in Birmingham is like no other building (www.danda.be). The fluidity of its curvaceous form, recalling the fall of fabric or the soft lines of a body, strikes a contrast with conventional, angular buildings nearby. The Selfridges building curves three-dimensionally. Its design makes no distinction between walls and roof, and there are no abrupt angles to break the organic, flowing lines. Rising from the ground, the facade gently billows outwards before being drawn in at a kind of waistline. It then curves out again and over, in one continuous movement.

The exterior is enveloped in a skin made up of 15,000 aluminium discs, creating a fine, lustrous grain like the scales of a snake or the sequins on a Paco Rabanne dress. This surface remains constant across the whole building, reinforcing the unity of the structure and giving it the quality of a vast, sensuous architectural sculpture. Although this is a large building it gives an impression of weightlessness and can appear almost animate and breathing. A fluid, fleeting space also characterizes the interior. All four floors were developed by different designers, each with its own characteristic look. But on all floors, in different variations, the round forms that are so characteristic of the exterior are reprised. All fixtures, lighting and escalators have the same striking round form. Selfridges has developed an unique brand personality, partly because of this store design.

Colours can influence the mood and the behaviour of customers. The desired brand personality needs to be expressed in the store's colour mix. Many retailers feel that the colours of store design need to be as neutral as possible. They are convinced that in a neutral environment the merchandise can be shown to full advantage, because neutral colours will not clash with the colourful merchandise. This is why many stores choose white, beige, grey or similar colours for their store design. However, the result is that the store design does not really have its own identity. Expensive boutiques are all white, and cheaper stores choose neutral, unobtrusive variants of white. However, slowly a visible shift is taking place, because retailers are starting to realize that the colours in a store can be one of the means to communicate a specific brand personality. For example, the blue and yellow of Ikea underlines its Swedish origin, and all the associations that come with that. By choosing the right colours, and consequently using them in all out-of-store and in-store communications, a retail brand can build up an entirely unique visual identity.

Different colours evoke different associations. In western cultures some of these associations are:

- red: exciting, powerful, desirable, dynamic, aggressive;
- pink: sexy, feminine, caring, romantic, soft;
- orange: warm, cheerful, playful, wholesome, energetic, optimistic;
- yellow: joyful, warm, inspiring, happy, lively, affectionate;

- purple: luxurious, dignified, royal, wise;
- blue: peaceful, calm, cool, masculine, clean, trustful;
- green: fresh, natural, young, healthy;
- brown: solid, steady, dependable, conservative;
- grey: businesslike, tight, exclusive, serious;
- black: detached, sophisticated, elegant, mysterious;
- white: pure, clean, perfect, simple, innocent.

Colour can contribute strongly to communicating the desired positioning and personality. It can become a recognizable, unique element of the store. The green that The Body Shop used to have in its stores expressed its involvement with environmental concerns. After all, green stands for freshness and nature. For its new, more contemporary store design The Body Shop chose sand and other earthly colours. These colours also symbolize its involvement with humanity and the environment. In contrast, Dolce & Gabbana mainly uses the colour black in the design of its stores. In combination with chromium and lots of mirrors, this gives its stores a very glamorous look.

Red is the colour we pay the most attention to. Moreover, red is a colour that communicates aggressiveness. That is why red is often used by retail brands that choose a lowest-price or high-value positioning. Aldi, Target, Wal-Mart, Carrefour and Office Depot all use red in their store design and/or visual merchandising.

A combination of colours can also communicate a certain message. For example, price brands often use the combinations red/yellow, blue/yellow and red/white. These strongly contrasting colour combinations give the store an aggressive appeal. For example, Media Markt uses red/white in its stores and advertising, and Lidl chose blue/yellow. The rather different mix of red and black gives the Sephora perfume stores a luxurious appeal that adds an extra dimension to their merchandise.

When jewellery is presented in a robin's-egg-blue box, it takes on an added lustre because the recipient knows this box is from Tiffany, the New York jeweller whose name has been synonymous with luxury, exclusivity and authenticity since 1837. How much would a second-hand version of one of a store's packages sell for at auction? Some brands manage to impart magic and integrity through their packaging alone. Authentic Tiffany boxes and pouches have become marketable items, fetching up to US$40 on auction sites. The larger the box, the higher the cost. Large boxes hold big items.

Tiffany's delicate blue forms the basis of the store's colour scheme; it is the colour of the catalogues, it is used in advertisements, and of course on Tiffany shopping bags too. No matter how much money consumers offer Tiffany, they cannot buy just a box from them. The ironclad rule of the company is that boxes (or pouches) leave the store only I f they contain an item that has been purchased there (Lindstrom, 2005: 46).

11.2.2 SOUND

Shopping is not just a visual experience, it is a multi-sensory one. A retail brand's look and feel can also be communicated via a unique sound identity. Nordstrom department stores are not only known for their positioning on service: the live piano music played in every Nordstrom store also contributes to distinguishing them from the competition. TopShop in London is also known for its own music style. In this 'biggest fashion store of the world' a DJ plays a recognizable music selection. Good music can evoke the right atmosphere in a store. It is even possible to play different music on each floor. Associating the retail brand with a particular kind of music can strengthen the brand personality, and it can also influence sales.

Older shoppers shop longer and purchase more when background music is playing, while younger shoppers respond similarly to foreground music. When a wine store played French music, wines from that region outsold German wines by five to one. When it played German music, German labels outsold French wines by two to one. The maximum price diners were prepared to spend in a restaurant with no music rose nearly 15 per cent when easy listening music was played, and more than 27 per cent when jazz was introduced (Simons, 2005).

Sound evokes emotions. Music can be used to strengthen the emotional part of the brand and to give the store a nice ambience. But sound can also be used to attract more attention to specific products or to reach specific target groups. For example, Athlete's Foot chooses a music genre based on the type of customer at each of its stores.

The Bellagio Hotel and Casino experienced first-hand the power of sound. It took special note of the buzz of slot machines and the shower of coins falling into the winner's tray. These are great sounds to the winner's ear, but supposedly disheartening to his or her neighbour, who is still pulling that handle and getting nothing but the whirr of a losing combination. For a while the hotel replaced its noisy slot machines with 'cashless' ones, but to its dismay, it found its slot machine revenue falling noticeably. It seems that a machine is not a slot machine unless it whirrs and jingles, and this applies to losers and winners alike. In no time at all, the original machines were restored to service (Lindstrom, 2005: 73).

In most stores the sound system is only used for announcing promotions and broadcasting obligatory, 'nothing going on' music that is only used to break the silence. However, that means the store is passing by the opportunity to strengthen its brand personality through music. Differentiating music can, sometimes unwittingly, leave a permanent impression. If the music in the store and television commercial is consistent with the music on the website and the music people hear when calling the call centre, all these sensory impulses will strengthen each other. In a store, just like in a television commercial, music can create an atmosphere that suits the products and gives them something extra. Music can enhance the brand personality. The classical music in the Victoria's Secret stores enhances their prestigious, elegant, feminine personality and adds value to their merchandise. But the wrong choice of music can harm the total brand experience. The music must fit with the brand, and if it does so, it can be a very strong vehicle to strengthen that brand. A charming, feminine brand personality asks for different music than a rugged, no-nonsense personality.

Starbucks is a retail brand that evidently not only understands its target group, but also listens to what they are saying. Confident that it consistently delivered high-quality product, it looked to add another dimension to drinking a cup of coffee. Initially the shops felt like a friend's lounge, with comfortable sofas and internet hotspots: they were somewhere to shelter out of the rain for as long as people liked. Music was gently added to the mix. It was not just the favourite music of the individual shop manager, but specific music chosen to enhance the atmosphere, with acoustic architecture supporting the experience, so that it was never too loud or soft. The sound strategy was designed as an acoustic experience that would reinforce the very essence of

Starbucks values and branding. How often have we heard 'I wish that I could package that atmosphere and take it home?' Starbucks did just that, on a CD. Just like its coffee, the CD added value with its high-quality content and its unique availability to Starbucks customers (Ebenkamp, 2004).

11.2.3 TOUCH

Touch forms an important part of the brand and shopping experience, whether it is the feel of products, the materials that are used for the design or the temperature in the store. The feel and texture of the materials in the store can give the store a masculine or feminine look, and the temperature is also very important in creating the right shopping environment. Shopping time will be short if it is too cold or too warm in the store. Materials used for the floor, fixtures and other design elements can also have a big influence on the retail brand's look and feel. That influence will for the most part be unwitting. Consumers do not consciously observe which materials are used for the ceiling, walls and floor. But using soft materials like fabric and wood provides the store with a more friendly, warmer and more natural look than do hard materials like marble, glass and metal. Even the pace at which a customer shops can be influenced by the materials used. The consumer will walk faster on a smooth floor than on a somewhat rougher floor.

The extent to which customers can touch products also influences the appeal of a store. If customers can grasp or feel products, this can contribute to the shopping pleasure. A store – for example a jewellery store – in which all products are behind glass and the customer needs to enlist a salesperson in order to take a close look at a product, is soon considered to be distant and expensive. The ability to touch the product increases the chance that the product will be bought. Customers in a bookstore always want to look through books before buying them. Even if the book only contains text, they still want to look at it. Consumers like to fill up their own candy bag in a candy shop, and trying out cosmetic products adds an extra dimension to a visit to a perfumery.

Britain's Asda supermarket chain, which is a subsidiary of Wal-Mart, cottoned on to the economic advantages of touch. It removed the wrappers from several brands of toilet paper so that shoppers could feel and compare textures. This resulted in soaring sales for its private brand, and an extra 50 per cent store space was allocated to this product (Lindstrom, 2005: 87).

Self-service began several decades ago. The customer took over part of the salespeople's activities. That resulted in lower costs and prices, and is why self-service was introduced mainly by store formats that wanted to position on price. However, in the last few years it has become apparent that self-service is also being chosen for other reasons. By giving customers the ability to touch products, self-service becomes a means to offer them more shopping pleasure. The salad bar in a supermarket or restaurant does not derive its appeal from low price: customers enjoy selecting the ingredients themselves. And it becomes even more fun if, as at Build-a-Bear Workshop, the consumer is involved in making the product.

11.2.4 SMELL

Increasingly stores are using smell to differentiate themselves from the competition. Coffee shops, candle stores, perfumeries, bakeries and lots of other stores are characterized by the smell of their products, but this smell does not always differentiate them from other stores in the same sector. Smell is the most associative sense. It evokes lots of emotions more quickly and more intensely than any of the other senses. Smell can ensure that consumers develop positive associations to certain products; it can encourage them to stay longer in the store. Moreover, by using a specific smell a retail brand can achieve a stronger, more differentiating brand personality.

The smell has to be a precise match with the brand. For example, the natural beauty retail brand L'Occitane en Provence positions itself not only by its unique merchandise, but also by the smell of lavender and other Mediterranean fragrances in its stores. Together with the warm yellow-painted stores, these fragrances give the stores the look and feel of a sunny, Mediterranean, carefree way of living. That is why L'Occitane en Provence has a brand personality that is clearly different from other natural beauty retailers like The Body Shop, Bath & Body Works and Origins.

Many consumers cannot resist the temptation if they walk past freshly baked bread in a supermarket. Smell is called the most important human sense. For example, smell immediately evokes associations with events from the past. However, emotions evoked by smell are still insufficiently recognized in retail. Smell is often the automatic result of the presence of products. However, some stores are starting to use both real and artificial smells to influence the shopping behaviour of their customers (Raffray, 2003: 21–22). For example, Mothercare has pumped a bubblegum aroma into its toy section, the smell of baby powder into the bath section and aromatherapy scents into the maternity section. Woolworth's introduced the smell of mulled wine and Christmas dinner into a handful of stores. Thornton's pipes a chocolate smell into its stores, as the actual chocolate has to be refrigerated to keep it hygienic. The travel agency Lunn Poly projects coconut smells to evoke memories of tropical holidays. The designer of its flagship store was briefed to 'make the customers feel they have arrived'.

The American Victoria's Secret chain has been using smell in in-store communications for a long time. The smell of its specially composed perfumes is spread in its lingerie stores. This perfume is also for sale, so both at home and in-store the customer is confronted with the specific smell of Victoria's Secret potpourri. Long after a customer has left the store, she is still reminded of the brand.

The Sony Style flagship stores are scented with notes of mandarin orange and vanilla to differentiate them. The company is also exploring a way to make the New York store's Madison Avenue windows radiate the scent, so passers-by might be lured inside to sniff out a laptop or new digital camera.

In an American clothing store a test was run to determine how scent affected customers by gender. In the women's department a subtle smell of vanilla was diffused, and in the men's rose maroc (a spicy, honey-like fragrance that had tested well with guys). The results were astonishing. The receipts almost doubled on the days when scent was used. However, if the scents were reversed, using vanilla in the men's section and rose maroc for the women's, customers spent less than average (Tischler, 2005: 56).

11.2.5 TASTE
The combination of shopping and eating and drinking also enhances the emotional experience of shopping. Shopping is more relaxed, and customers who eat or drink something in a department store tend

to shop on average for longer than customers who do not. Spending increases as a result of shopping longer. That is why most department stores have multiple in-store restaurant concepts.

In the Dutch Vroom & Dreesmann department stores, the restaurant has become the most profitable department. Albert Heijn supermarkets have a coffee corner in every store, at which customers can have a free cup of coffee, and Barnes & Nobles bookstores have a complete coffee shop. The natural relationship between reading a book and drinking coffee is then used to further strengthen the brand identity. Coffee shops have now become an indispensable part of the Barnes & Noble brand.

Taste can also be stimulated in a different way: demonstrations of new or unknown products can make grocery shopping more attractive. For example, in many Japanese supermarkets demonstrations take place in multiple locations. They often use very simple equipment, but a pleasant atmosphere is still created. Customers can taste samples everywhere.

Suga Candy Kitchen in Melbourne and Sticky in Sydney take the candy experience to the next level by turning rock candy into a personalized, name-embedded feast for the eyes and stomach (Kelly Spinks, springwise.com). Candy is hand-made on the premises (a serious case of retail theatre), with crowds forming in front of the shop windows. The experience continues inside the store: customers can try out the various sweets, or participate in candy-making contests, enticing enthusiasts not only to become part of the experience, but to co-create it. Special events (birthdays, weddings and the like) are also catered for: customers can choose their own colours, flavours and message. Corporate clients, which include Kylie Minogue and Ralph Lauren, can purchase a 10 kg bag of customized rock candy for A$30. Capitalizing on the powerful combination of entertainment, high quality and niche focus, Suga Candy now has six shops in urban Melbourne areas, while Sticky has two shops in Sydney. The owners of Suga Candy have already expanded into chocolate: Melbourne-based Koko Black, featuring Belgian chocolatiers doing their thing in full view.

The personality of a retail brand can be translated in many different ways into style attributes like colours, shapes, materials, sounds, smells and other sensory expressions. With that, every retail brand can develop a unique look and feel. However, with every look and feel, four perceptual dimensions can always be distinguished (Schmitt and Simonson, 1997: 296).

Complexity: minimalism versus ornamentalism

Minimalism strives for simplicity of structure and form, viewing decoration as unnecessary excess. Ornamentalism on the other hand loves complexity, variety of motifs and multiple meanings. Ornamentalist fabrics and interior designs characterize the Versace brand stores, and hedonistic retail brands with their cheerful personality will also choose an ornamentalist store design. On the contrary, the fashion stores of Giorgio Armani have a rather minimalist look, just like Muji and other stores that want to position themselves as a no-nonsense back-to-basics brands.

Representation: realism versus abstraction

A store design can be viewed as realist if its form makes conscious use of associations to objects in the real world, and abstract if it does not. A particular form of realism is naturalism. In retail environments soothing sounds and music are often used to evoke natural associations such as water or wind. Unpolished woods, unbleached cotton, rough papers and natural, recyclable materials are essential for an environmentally friendly, thoughtful 'green' style. All these elements, in conjunction with soothing New Age music, subtle fragrances and soft light-brown colours, are found in the product line and retail outlets of Origins, the 'green' brand from cosmetics company Estée Lauder.

Perceived movement: dynamic versus static

A store design can have a dynamic or a more static appearance. For an innovative, trendy speed brand or a brand targeting a young customer base, it is essential to have a dynamic look. A store design that suggests movement can then help. The same goes for sports stores, for example. These stores also want to be perceived as fast and dynamic.

Potency: loud/strong versus soft/weak

The degree of potency refers to whether an identity comes across as strong, aggressive and loud, or as weak, subdued and quiet. The approach of low-price, high-value and bargain brands is often on the aggressive and loud side of the spectrum. With this kind of retail brand the store is usually full of copy like 'biggest sale ever' and 'now or never'. In contrast, premium brands with a sophisticated personality will use a softer approach.

11.3 Store design: a communication tool

In some ways, the store design of a retail brand is comparable with the packaging of a manufacturer brand. It is, as it were, the packaging of the merchandise offer of the retail company. The objectives a retailer can achieve with its store design are therefore also comparable with the objectives a manufacturer has for its packaging. The most important objectives of store design are to communicate the positioning and personality, add value to the merchandise and achieve efficiency and effectiveness.

11.3.1 COMMUNICATING POSITIONING AND PERSONALITY

The store design is a form of communication, so it should be aligned with the retail brand. Every design tells the customer a story. In the store the customer can see, feel, hear, smell and sometimes also taste the retail brand. Positioning and brand personality in particular can be expressed well through the store design. A low-price brand with a no-nonsense personality, like an efficiency brand, will choose a simple, functional design. After all, a no-frills design conveys low prices and efficiency. In contrast, a design brand with a glamorous or sophisticated personality will go for a store in which aesthetics dominate, and an ideological brand with a wholesome personality will try to translate its core values into the materials of the store design.

This store design must confirm and strengthen the known values of the retail brand. The shapes, colours, materials and all other design elements must evoke the right brand associations. The store should make a real brand statement. For example, a well-organized store communicates a personality of competence. Other stores try to add value to the shopping experience by providing ideas and suggestions, creating a store that looks like the environment in which the products are going to be used in. For example, Ikea shows many products in room settings. In every case, the store design and visual merchandising have to be surprising each time, so that the customer is always stimulated and given an impulse to buy. In that way a lead over the competition can be maintained.

In order to surprise the customer every time, store design and visual merchandising have to be as flexible as possible. In practice this will lead to less architecture, more flexible fixtures and more temporary sets instead of fixed, permanent elements. Retail companies can learn a lot from the entertainment industry in this area. For example, the sets for musicals are changed multiple times a night, and the movie industry also knows how to handle set changes well.

In some cases the look and feel of the store design is one of the few ways to create a difference from other stores. For example, Shell, Esso, BP and other oil companies all supply the same gas. The only difference is in the design of the gas station and the adjoining shop. The same goes for banks; the design of branches is often the only recognizable difference. But in practice, the store designs of gas stations and banks barely have their own identity. Because their positioning attributes are often the same as well, convenience of location and matter of habit often determine store choice. There is hardly any emotional bond with the retail brand.

Wal-Mart, Sam's, Costco and Home Depot all have several factors in common. These superstores cater to bargain hunters, to large families and to a wide range of incomes for an ultra-wide range of products and services. The store design should evoke for customers the unfinished, rough, aggressive, economical brand personality. Achieving this requires the use of strong materials, large spaces, organized aisles, visible stock, bright lights, large trolleys, minimalist styles and cost-saving family-oriented themes. However, not all superstores need this kind of store design. Barnes & Noble bookstores have designs that create an overall customer impression of being in a friendly, relaxing, pleasant, good-looking, modern, library-like and artistic environment. They create this impression with carpeting, wooden display shelves, polished metal ornamentation, green and brown organic colours, classic wooden chairs matching the wooden displays and complemented with large, sturdy modern tables; plush, relaxing living-room-like armchairs; and the inclusion of Starbucks cafés. The theme of this brand personality is that you have entered a relaxing library, and the styles resonate with this to create an impression that makes people stay. The longer people stay, the greater their likelihood of purchase (Schmitt and Simonson, 1997: 296).

When entering a store, target consumers should immediately get the impression that this store is for them, because a store never gets a second chance to make a first impression. But besides store design, visual merchandising and employees, the location and the store's customer base play an important role in communicating the desired brand loyalty. A store in London's Convent Garden will have a different appeal from a store in a less affluent area, and a store that attracts a very specific customer base will most probably repel other customers.

11.3.2 ADDING VALUE TO MERCHANDISE

The store design must ensure that the merchandise is shown to full advantage, and it should not overshadow the products. Products should rather benefit from the extra dimension it gives them. The merchandise is the hero and the store is the stage. In a Disney store everything is done to make shopping as fun as possible. Miss Sixty samples 1970s glamour in its New York store to create a world of human proportions. It has the alternately chilly and sensuous, worldly but shallow glamour of the 1970s. It has the appeal of a vain woman when experienced from afar: cool, seductive, yet slightly melodramatic and icy. On closer examination, it proves to be conscious of its own irony and vanity, and not at all reluctant to camp it up. Indeed the store there is a larger-than-life boudoir for young-at-heart women and the little girls they once were. Children dress up in their mothers' clothes (Moreno, 2003: 124).

11.3.3 CREATING EFFICIENCY AND EFFECTIVENESS

No matter how striking and differentiating the design is, if it cannot be shopped in efficiently and pleasantly it will fail. Clarity, excitement and interaction are important for the total shopping experience, but the retailer wants a store design that not only communicates the brand positioning and personality well, but also achieves the desired financial result. The available store space has to be used efficiently and effectively. Sales and gross margin per square metre should be as high as possible. The customer needs to be directed to the best products, and needs to be able to see as much as possible of the store. At the same time design and maintenance costs, and wages need to be kept as low as possible.

So an assessment of a store's design and visual merchandising does not only involve difficult-to-measure attributes like brand personality and added values: its contribution can also be determined in a quantitative way. For example, a large store remodelling will usually have to result in a 10 to 15 per cent profit increase to cover the costs.

The new Apple flagship stores in London, New York and San Francisco reflect the company's thinking on how to translate its brand identity from its software and hardware products to the user experience of the retail environment (Garret, 2004). There is a lot about the Apple store experience that can be applied to the design of many types of stores.

Create an experience, not an artefact

Coaxing visitors up to the second floor of a store is a challenge most retailers have long since given up on. The Apple store takes up the challenge with a bold statement, making the centrepiece of the store a staircase – a really cool staircase. It is difficult to resist the temptation to set foot on that first solid glass step. Once customers reach that point, they can catch a glimpse of the demo theatre at the top of the stairs. And the next thing they know, they have been swept up to the top level before they have even finished (or started) looking around the first floor. This attention to the customer's line of sight is carried throughout the whole space. It feels more like walking into a hands-on museum than walking into a store. Sure, Apple wants to sell products, but its first priority is to make people want the products, and that desire has to begin with their experience of the products in the store.

Honour the context

Instead of being organized according to product type (printers over here, cameras over there), the first floor of the store is organized by the context in which people use the products. With digital cameras, photo printers and Apple's iPhoto software set up together, customers can envisage using these products in their own life. By acknowledging this context in the design of the store, Apple encourages its customers to dream about possibilities.

Prioritize messages

The typical store is a cacophony of messages: packages, signs and promotional material are crammed into customers' field of vision, all jostling and jockeying to catch their attention. The visually spacious Apple store is strikingly different. With rare exceptions, product packages are kept below eye level and relatively few products are on display. Instead of having to find a place for every message, Apple focuses on the handful of messages that count.

Institute consistency

The Apple personality comes through every time the customer encounters the brand, whether on television, in print or outdoor advertising, or through interacting with one of Apple's products. The Apple stores are no different, and Apple is able to project that personality across all these channels by maintaining rigorous consistency of design. With all the brushed metallic surfaces on both the exterior and the interior of the store, people can't help but feel as if they are walking inside a product that came off the same assembly line as a Powerbook or an iPod.

Design for change

Where rapid change needs to be accommodated, the Apple store has mechanisms to support this. The front window displays are rigged using simple flat panels mounted on tracks and cables. This system allows the displays to be changed regularly, grabbing the attention of passers-by.

Do not forget the human element

A store is not just made up of shelves and tables and lights. The people who staff the store form an integral part of the overall experience. The Apple store employees do not look like run-of-the-mill retail workers.

Instead of nametags, they have business cards. And they all carry iPods on their belts, creating the impression that they do not just work for Apple; they live the lifestyle Apple is selling to customers. Apple's retail workers are brand emissaries.

11.3.4 TOUCH-POINTS OF STORE DESIGN

A store design has many touch-points that together give the retail brand a look and feel. The most important elements of store design are the exterior, the interior, the lighting, the layout and the fixtures. Together, all these touch-points form a consistent whole. Each of the design elements then has a specific function:

- exterior: attracting customers;
- interior: communicating the brand personality;
- lighting: dramatizing the merchandise;
- layout: navigating through the store;
- fixtures: showing the merchandise.

The tone and style of these five touch-points determine the brand personality of the store. Together, they can give a store a unique look and feel that makes the brand personality recognizable to the customer. As there are a lot of touch-points, retailers have to set priorities and pay attention to those that will deliver the desired brand message best.

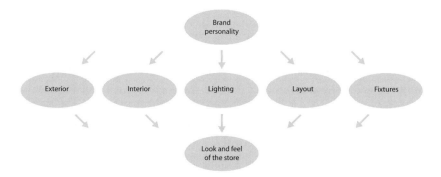

Figure 11.3. Touch-points of store design

Exterior

The most important function of the store exterior is to attract customers. The appearance of the building strongly influences the brand perception. The consumer will form an opinion on the retail brand's positioning and personality based on the exterior, and on this basis alone some customers will decide to pass the store, while others will be enticed to enter. Through its exterior a store has to attract attention, differentiate itself from the competition and draw the customer into the store. That is why the exterior has to quickly and effectively communicate what the store stands for. Department stores in particular have always differentiated themselves through their striking buildings. In many inner cities they are themselves well-recognized landmarks. Selfridges and Harrods in London, Lafayette in Paris, De Bijenkorf in Amsterdam and Bloomingdales in New York use their striking architecture as a permanent advertising billboard.

The store exterior should immediately communicate the brand promise. A retail brand that positions itself on range will use window displays if possible to greet the consumer with its unique merchandise offer. Category killers, which do not normally have window displays, communicate their brand name in very large letters, because in many cases that in itself communicates that the range is enormous. Brand names like Toys'R'Us, Sports Authority and PC World are examples of this.

The exteriors of stores for retail brands that use price as their differentiating attribute need to create a basic look with large price signals. In contrast, retail brands that mainly want to position themselves on convenience should emphasize their opening hours, parking facilities and other convenience aspects. Retail brands that want to offer the consumer a unique store experience will want this experience to start with the store exterior. For example, if they choose a very surprising design for the store exterior, this will make consumers curious about what is offered inside.

Eddie Bauer, a well-known American fashion retail brand, and Indiana University conducted tests to determine whether electronic signage, in the form of plasma screens in store windows, impacted consumer behaviour and store sales. Traffic devices were installed to count consumers walking past the Eddie Bauer stores in the study.

Interviews were also conducted to determine recall. Traffic jumped 23 per cent in those stores using digital signage, compared with the Eddie Bauer stores that did not use the digital signage. In addition, 23 per cent of surveyed customers recalled seeing the digital signage in the store window and nearly 10 per cent recalled the specific product advertised. Of the shoppers who remembered the product, 46 per cent said they would consider buying it. Although these results are encouraging, it is the impact on sales that is important. For Eddie Bauer, sales increased by 56 per cent after a nine-week period, prompting further investment (Coleman, 2000: B10).

The store exterior should communicate not only the brand positioning, but also the brand's human characteristics. In other words, the store exterior has about the same effect as someone's looks. On first impression people immediately form an opinion about a new acquaintance's character. That is the same for a store exterior. The first impression consumers get of the store immediately gives them a positive or negative feeling. The look and feel of the exterior should give consumers the feeling that the store will suit them very well. That emotion is mostly determined by design elements. A big, not very transparent building can appear massive and even somewhat threatening. In contrast, a spacious entrance can give consumers the feeling that they are really welcome.

The colours and materials chosen can play an important role as well. Smooth materials and black and grey can give a store exterior a distant look. For example, banks use marble to communicate their solidity. On the contrary, trendy clothing stores often have a shopfront of stainless steel or other modern materials, and supermarkets mainly choose a functional shopfront. So, it is important when designing the exterior that not only is positioning is taken into account, so is brand personality. The exterior's look and feel have to link up with that completely.

From a distance, the outside signage is the consumer's first contact with the store. The brand name and sign give a first impression of the store's brand identity. Signs have been used since ancient Greek and Roman times. Competition and the need for differentiation forced merchants and artisans to provide their store or workshop with a sign.

Because most people could not read, illustrations showed what kind of company it was. For example, a shoemaker had a sign with a boot, and a butcher a sign with a ham on it. Apart from that, a sign is only a modest way to make the shopfront stand out.

Some designer fashion stores in New York have impressive double-height frontages. Not only the size, but also the shape can make the shopfront stand out. Good examples of this are the Ron Jon surf stores in the United States. This company, which opened its first store in 1961, has now become the leading surf paradise of the world, with stores in New Jersey, Florida and California. All these stores have very striking exteriors. For example, the stores in Orange, California and in Fort Lauderdale, Florida have a huge wave with a couple of surfers on it attached to the front, and on the outside of the store in Long Beach Island in New Jersey hangs the world's biggest surfboard. Because of this enormous surfboard, 8 m long and more than 100 kg in weight, customers immediately knows they are entering a Ron Jon Surf Shop: a store that has everything for them to taste a little bit of the beach and surf lifestyle.

A retail company can also differentiate itself from the competition through its store windows. Store windows can entertain as well as entice. Department stores like De Bijenkorf, Lafayette, Harvey Nichols and Harrods are famous for their window displays. In December many people come just to admire the Christmas window displays. On the contrary, a no-nonsense department store like Hema has no store windows at all. From the outside the customer should already be able to see what Hema has to offer: a clear, well-organized and practical store, without superfluous design features. Luxurious windows do not go with that.

Particularly in high-traffic locations, store windows can draw customers and communicate a clear brand promise. The windows then form a transition between the exterior and the interior of the store. If there are only a few exclusive products in the store window, it will be clear to consumers, even without having seen any price tags, that it is an expensive, exclusive store. In the case of a low-price brand, store windows are mainly used to communicate the price message with big posters. There will be no products in them at all.

Interior

The image evoked on the outside has to be enhanced on the inside. Once the consumer is inside, the interior has to take over the communication function and communicate the same message about the brand promise as the exterior. The look and feel of the interior design should then appropriately communicate the desired brand personality. But the interior should not only communicate; it has to sell as well. If the interior design gets customers in the right mood, they will be more inclined to buy something. The first impression when entering often determines the entire brand perception. Therefore the first few seconds after customers have entered the store are the most important, as this is when they form their opinion about the entire store. The area at the entrance should immediately make the right impression on customers. A store never gets a second chance to make a first impression.

At Borders and Barnes & Noble, the superstores for books, the bestsellers are presented close to the entrance. Moreover, special offers for newly issued books and magazines placed at the entrance give the store an up-to-date, inviting ambience. Signage then makes it clear to customers where the various departments are. However, the best products should not be too close to the entrance. Products that are only a few metres from the entrance are often not seen clearly, because consumers need a little time and space to get used to the store. The front of the store is a kind of decompression area.

The ceiling, floor and walls all influence the look and feel of a store, even though consumers might not consciously observe them. A smooth wooden floor for example communicates different brand associations than a luxurious carpet. The walls can also be used as selling vehicles. For example, Bed Bath & Beyond uses the walls to present products on, right up to the ceiling. Therefore, consumers are confronted everywhere with the enormous range. Through visual merchandising the store's authority as a category killer is enhanced, and this presentation also acts as a directory, so consumers can quickly find their way around the store.

The ceiling should not draw attention from the merchandise, though, and needs to be as flexible as possible. The flagship fashion store of TopShop in Birmingham (UK) is a good example of this. It has been fitted with a special ceiling-grid system that allows graphics to be hung from a track at any point between the ceiling panels (Lyster, 2003: 18). The hanging mechanism allows TopShop staff to divide the space with graphics to create concessions or to alter the internal customer flow.

Lighting

The importance of good lighting is often still underestimated. However, lighting is incredibly important to any retail environment. General lighting, lighting to emphasize and coloured lighting can all give the store and the merchandise something extra and make them look more appealing. Lighting can bring drama into the store. It should not only light the store and products, but should also provide the desired atmosphere. It should be used to create relief and surprise. Lighting can be a real communication tool.

A retail brand that positions itself on price should choose bright, white lighting that is equally strong everywhere. White lighting gives the store a somewhat chilly and cheap look. Bright means cheap. On the contrary, an exclusive fashion store will have a much more cosy lighting scheme, where just as in a theatre, all kinds of lighting are used. In particular displays and products that deserve extra attention will be lit with spotlights. The variation of light and dark creates excitement in the store. This excitement directs the customer through the store. Some areas in the store will then get more attention than others. In a store's lighting plan it should be indicated where general, overall illumination is needed and where lighting emphasis should be used. These specific lighting plans can make stores look a lot more individual.

Layout

The most important function of the layout is the navigation through the store. To obtain optimal navigation, a few factors need to be taken into account when deciding on the layout.

First impressions

The product categories with which the consumer is confronted when first entering the store have an enormous influence on the total impression the store makes. The first sensory appeals will mostly determine the overall brand perception. For example, supermarkets present their fruit and vegetable department at the front of the store, because the colours and presentation possibilities of this department offer lots of opportunities to strengthen their quality image. In department stores the most recent or fashionable items are presented at the entrance. This strategy is one of those used by the Gap, Banana Republic, Victoria's Secret and other fashion stores. Placing a strong display at the entrance makes the transition from outside to inside easier.

Traffic flow

A good retail design is easy to navigate and leads customers to all the important product categories, without giving customers the idea they are being pushed in certain directions. Clear signage can help navigation and circulation. That is especially important in stores that position themselves on convenience. In each store a balance needs to be found between manipulating the traffic flow, and the needs and wants of the customer. So in determining the layout it is important to locate the focus points. These focus points are the areas in the store that receive extra attention in order to draw customers in.

In department stores and other large stores retailers often use the main aisles to guide customers through the store. However, in large stores the main aisles should not be long, straight passageways. Long, straight aisles come across as boring, and customers will not want to make the effort to walk all the way to the end. In order to draw customers towards the back of the store, aisles need to remain exciting, and there needs to be something at the end of each aisle section that draws the customer along.

There should be strong focus points everywhere in the store. For example, many stores use large, lit visuals or various dominant displays. The departments themselves should not be too deep, because then the customer will not be prepared to visit the entire department. In a store with multiple floors, an escalator at a striking point is an important means to obtaining strong vertical circulation. However, when it comes to the layout of a store, the customer's buying behaviour has to be taken into account: which product categories does the customer expect, and where?

Sales

The product category locations can have a big influence on sales. Family groupings of complementary product categories and the routing of the store then play an important role. Impulse groups like candy and magazines are mostly bought in supermarkets when located at checkouts where customers usually stand in line for a while. It is wise to present complementary products together. That is why department stores present socks with shoes and ties with shirts. And of course smell needs to be taken into account as well: it is best not to locate detergents across from the fresh bread department.

Efficiency

Store employees have to be able to work easily and efficiently. From that perspective, products that need to be replenished often and heavy, voluminous products need to be located as close to the warehouse as possible. This saves time and effort, and prevents the customer from being confronted with shelf-fillers everywhere in the store.

Operations

For technical and other operational reasons it can be wise to place product categories at certain locations. A working bakery is usually located at the side of a supermarket because it calls for lots of equipment. It can disturb the store design too much if located in the middle. Products subject to theft are presented close to or behind the checkout. Checkouts are usually located at the exit, so that employees can keep an eye on customers who are leaving the store. And at a bank the cash machine is located in such a way that money can be deposited and collected safely.

Easy shopping

Aisles should be wide enough to offer the customer a pleasant shopping experience. If aisles are too narrow, customers will avoid aisles where other customers are shopping. Moreover, wide aisles increase the visibility of products. In particular retail brands that position themselves on convenience should pay a lot of attention to these kinds of aspect.

Besides the factors mentioned, in practice the size and shape of the store and any possible restrictive building regulations will also have to be taken into account. A layout for a long, deep store is more difficult than for a wide store. And in some stores safety, environmental or other restrictive regulations can create extra problems. Therefore, sometimes there are big differences in layouts even within one store format. Nevertheless, a few basic layouts can be distinguished.

Grid pattern layout
This layout has straight aisles and long rows of parallel fixtures, and is very common in supermarkets, drugstores and stores that position themselves on low prices, high value or convenience. The straight aisles and parallel fixtures give the store a no-nonsense, but rather dull look and feel. The available sales area is used as efficiently as possible.

Free-flow layout
In this layout the fixtures are arranged in more irregular patterns, so the customer has more freedom to move around and browse. Fashion stores, department stores and stores that are positioned on range and experience use this kind of layout. The available space is used less intensively than with a grid pattern layout, and the look and feel of the stores is often more exciting and inspiring.

Racetrack layout
This type of layout can be found particularly at category killers and department stores. The customer is directed to all departments from a main aisle. The departments themselves then possibly have a free-flow or grid pattern layout. If the main aisle gives customers no alternative choice of direction, this might irritate them. Customers who are in a hurry will not appreciate it if they are forced to pass by all the departments.

So when choosing a layout the desires of both the consumer and the retailer have to be taken into account. Shopping has to be made easy and pleasant for consumers, and sales and profit should be as high as possible for the retailer. Customers should pass as many product categories as possible, particularly the most profitable products. A good balance needs to be found between manipulation of the traffic flow and the convenience of customers. But the following starting points definitely need to be taken into account.

- Most customers prefer shopping to the right, probably because most are right-handed. As a result the right-hand side of the aisle will receive most attention.
- Most customers prefer outside aisles. In general, the aisles on the inside of the store will be visited less.
- Customers prefer a wide aisle to a narrow one, and try to avoid corners.
- Customers follow a certain buying rhythm. They will shop faster when they are approaching the checkout. They do not like to turn round.
- Customers like to see something exciting at the end of the aisle: for example, a strong display or a nice, interesting product presentation. Such a focus point is an extra stimulant to walk into the aisle.
- Customers like a long aisle to be broken by a cross-aisle or a surprising display. That makes shopping less dull.
- Waiting times, obstacles and queues at the checkout cause lots of annoyance for the customer.

Selfridges has a World of Food concept in its flagship Birmingham store. Located adjacent to the homewares and cookshop departments, the food hall is also positioned to leverage related purchases, so woks and Asian homewares are sold alongside the appropriate food products. This offer is enhanced by the theatre of cooking, set against a background display of ingredients. Four World Food islands, integral to the concept, are located in the centre of the space, with core product categories around the perimeter. Each World Food island represents a different food region, and each has been designed complete with an open kitchen, seating and serving areas so that customers can purchase food to take away, sit and eat at the counters, or purchase the relevant ingredients for home cooking. Perimeter departments are treated as individual food shops to retain their own identities and to build on the atmosphere. The design focuses on photography, with portraits of people who produce food. The individual characters portrayed represent the main food hall areas. Implemented on large format displays, the images act as a pivotal graphic feature for each food area (Faithfull, 2003: 18–19).

Fixtures and equipment

Fixtures and equipment in the store have the primary goal of presenting the merchandise as well as possible. But they can also contribute to communicating the desired brand identity and especially the brand personality, which can be made tangible through them. The black gondolas on which the English store Harvey Nichols presents its food products give the department a very high-quality, luxurious look. It is a really indulgent department.

Many retail companies incorrectly choose designs for gondolas and other store furniture that are as neutral as possible. The thought is that the products will then stand out more. However, these stores miss opportunities, because retail companies can build up an entirely unique look and feel with the style and colour of their fixtures. For example, the American Office Depot painted all its fixtures in striking red, and that created an aggressive-looking store design which clearly distinguished the store from the competition. Costco, Makro and Metro partly use their high warehouse-style fixtures to evoke an aggressive no-nonsense store image. Aldi and Lidl also use as few fixtures as possible to create a no-nonsense store image. Almost all the products are still in their bulk boxes.

Even if fixtures have a neutral colour, they still very much influence the total store image. For example, fixtures that are all of equal height create a dull image. To create a more interesting store atmosphere, the heights of the equipment should be varied. A variation in height creates excitement in the store, and emphasis can be given to specific parts of the range.

11.3.5 ROLLING OUT A NEW DESIGN

Rolling out a new store design requires large investments, which are in general written off within five to seven years. From an economic perspective, this term of five to seven years can be considered wise. However, from a marketing perspective seven years is way too long. After all, the lifecycle of store formats is becoming shorter and shorter. To communicate the desired message, brands need to be able to adapt their shopping environment, and in particular brands differentiated by speed or design will need to do this quite frequently. So it is important to make store design as flexible as possible. It should be possible to give the store a more up-to-date look by replacing a few parts of the overall design package.

Rolling out a new store design can be very complicated and very expensive for a chain with hundreds or maybe even thousands of stores. However, if all the stores do not have the same design, this can be disturbing to the customer's brand perception. It can create confusion for customers who visit multiple stores of the same chain. With such issues in mind, many retailers have chosen more graphical approaches to their store interiors, or examined ways in which makeovers can be achieved on a budget. Among the measures that can be taken are (Faithfull, 2003: 18–19):

- Taking the key elements from a new design and introducing only those across the store portfolio.
- Looking at how people use the store. Maybe performance could be improved simply by changing the layout.
- Researching a new store design before full implementation. Half of the changes probably account for 90 per cent of performance improvements.
- Using graphics to freshen up a store without introducing new fixtures and fittings. They can also be updated regularly.
- Considering whether a store is underperforming simply because signs are lacking where people intuitively look for them.
- Considering reworking fixtures, using informative and emotional graphics.
- Searching for innovation. For example, remote-controlled spotlights now come at a price not far above the cost of fixed ones. These enable store staff to redirect the focus when merchandise is moved.
- Investing where customers notice: the tills, the changing rooms and basics such as easy navigation.
- Involving shopfitters early and asking for ideas on alternative materials.
- Warehousing preconstructed units and shipping them to new stores when they are needed, providing economies of scale and guaranteed availability.

In these ways, a retail brand can ensure that the store can always have an up-to-date store design without having to rebuild everything. Despite some differences in design, all stores in a group will still have a more or less similar look and feel.

11.4 The power of visual merchandising

Visual merchandising takes place at the point of purchase. Immediately preceding a purchase decision, visual merchandising can be the most powerful, most effective communication tool. Consumers have more access to product information and inspiration in the store than anywhere else. A retail brand can react to that opportunity with its method of presentations, displays, graphics and signage.

11.4.1 THE IMPORTANCE OF VISUAL MERCHANDISING

A store is more than a distribution centre where all products are stored. Stores in both the higher price segment and the basic, lower-priced segment need visual merchandising. In all these types of stores products need to be brought to the customer's attention. Moreover, emphases need to be made within each store's range. After all, not all products are of equal importance to the retailer. Visual merchandising is used to make the store more than just a distribution centre. In addition, a very important benefit of good visual merchandising is that it communicates the brand promise. Together with store design, visual merchandising clarifies what the brand stands for. Product presentations, displays, and graphics and signage determine for the most part the look and feel of the store.

Visual merchandising injects life into the store as well, dramatizing the retail brand and the merchandise offer. It is the art of illusion and a silent salesperson. Products need to stand out and be presented as appealing, clear and dominant as possible so consumers will want to buy them. Consumers need to be tempted. Browsers need to become buyers. With effective visual merchandising the conversion rate can be increased. But retailers miss opportunities here, because many stores are dull and very predictable.

It is not only short-term profit that is important. Visual merchandising also needs to communicate the brand's positioning and personality. Visual merchandising should navigate, inform, inspire and activate customers. If this is done well, then brand loyalty will become stronger and short-term and long-term sales will also be influenced.

Giving life to a retail brand and the merchandise is now of more importance than ever.

Differentiation

Because of the enormous competition and sector blurring, the ranges of retail brands are starting to look more alike. In particular retail brands that only sell manufacturer brands are confronted with this problem. Unique visual merchandising can ensure that a retail brand differentiates itself from the competition.

Effectiveness

As far as obtaining sales is concerned, visual merchandising is in general more effective than other out-of-store and in-store marketing communication tools. That is important, given that now every retail brand has to focus on costs, efficiency and effectiveness more than ever. A display usually results in a higher profit than an (expensive) advertisement could achieve. After all, with visual merchandising a store can communicate with customers at the best possible moment: when they are already in the store. Visual merchandising can help the retailer to acquire more sales by showing consumers products that are not on their shopping lists. In some types of store the majority of sales are impulse purchases. Visual merchandising then plays a big role. Speed brands in particular need to organize their visual merchandising in such a way that they continually evoke a new image, not only with their range but also with their presentation.

Customers expect stores to react quickly to trends and changes in the market. It is easier to adapt visual merchandising than store design. Effective visual merchandising can influence the customer's buying behaviour. Visual merchandising can stimulate desire and persuade customers to buy a product.

Ikea was one of the first stores to use actual room sets in its visual merchandising. Dozens of realistic room settings provide consumers with ideas on interior design. Range brands and experience brands in particular have to pay a lot of attention to giving ideas to their customers. In order to persuade the customer, a product presentation needs to come across as dominant. In stores like Media Markt in Europe and Best Buy in the United States, televisions are presented against the back wall, so customers are confronted with the enormous range on offer in this product category as soon as they enter the store.

Replacing sales employees

In retail, wages make up about half the total costs. That is why retailers try to lower the wage bill where possible, for example, by introducing self-service features. However, the fewer sales employees there are in the store to assist customers, the more important it will be to pay a lot of attention to visual merchandising. Visual merchandising needs to inform and inspire customers, because even when there are sales employees present, customers often want to orientate themselves before asking for assistance. They do not always appreciate the intervention of salespeople at this point. Through visual merchandising a store can still influence consumers' buying behaviour. In this case visual merchandising replaces the sales employee. Through visual merchandising selected products can stand out more and, in addition, more information can be provided about product features and benefits.

Complementing sales employees

Visual merchandising can partially replace sales employees, but it can also complement them. Particularly at busy moments the sales employees cannot advise every customer, but product presentation and all the other supporting in-store communication features can partially take over the role of the sales employees. With good visual merchandising a store can communicate with customers even when the sales staff are busy elsewhere. Graphics and signage can communicate product quality and benefits. That is why visual merchandising can lead to lower costs. Sales employees can spend their time more efficiently, because visual merchandising is a kind of silent salesperson.

For example, some liquor stores have a wine information system, which uses number codes to give customers a simple classification for the types of wine. Fashion stores use visual merchandising to enable customers to experiment with mixing clothes and accessories without any help from the sales staff. However, information needs to be kept short and sharp in the store, because customers will not take the time to read extensive notes and instructions. More extensive information can best be given in a catalogue or on the website.

Clarity

In most stores there is an unprecedented abundance of products. Choosing has become more difficult than ever. Customers run the risk of not seeing the wood for the trees. Maybe the product is there, but the customer cannot find it. Visual merchandising can be used to arrange the merchandise more clearly. The store can be arranged in a way that is logical for the customer. Products that complement each other can be presented together, and department signs, aisle signs and other signage can help customers locate products more easily. The way in which the store is arranged and the merchandise is presented should not leave customers with unanswered questions. In particular, clarity is needed for stores that want to position themselves as efficiency brands. After all, these stores owe their existence to making shopping as easy as possible.

Most of the money spent on commercials, advertisements, brochures and other out-of-store communication will be wasted if there is no follow-up in the store. However, in the store hundreds or even thousands of products will be asking for attention. In an average supermarket there are at least 15,000 products, and an average visit to a supermarket lasts no more than 30 to 40 minutes. So in a fraction of a second a product needs to try to draw the customer's attention. It will only be successful if there is a clear hierarchy of all visual merchandising on the overall store, departmental, category and individual product levels. If everything calls for attention in the same way, it is likely nothing will stand out. With visual merchandising less is sometimes more.

In their in-store communications, retail companies use a lot of pricing cues to try to convince people to buy their products or services (Anderson, 2003). The most straightforward of these pricing cues is the 'sale' sign. It usually appears somewhere near the discounted item, trumpeting a bargain for customers. However, customers are not easily fooled. They have learnt that even Oriental rug dealers eventually run out of 'special holidays' and occasions to celebrate with a sale. They are quick to adjust their attitudes toward sale signs if they perceive evidence of overuse, which reduces the credibility of discount claims and makes these pricing cues far less effective. The more sale signs are used in the category, the less effective those signs are at increasing demand. Retailers face a trade-off: placing sale signs on multiple items can increase demand for those items, but it can also reduce overall demand. Total category sales are highest when some, but not all, items in the category have sale signs. Past a certain point, the use of additional sale signs will cause total category sales to fall.

Another common pricing cue is using a 9 at the end of a price to denote a bargain. Consumers react favourably when they see prices that end in 9. For instance, when an American women's clothing catalogue raised the price of one of its dresses from $34 to $39, sales jumped up. But when the price was raised from $34 to $44, there was no change in demand. Some retailers reserve prices that end in 9 for their discounted items. For instance, Ralph Lauren generally uses 00-cent endings on regularly priced merchandise and 99-cent endings on discounted items.

11.4.2 METHODS OF PRESENTATION

The presentation of the merchandise has a big influence on sales and the retail brand's appeal. Presentation can vary from the most simple box presentation for a low-price brand to the most aesthetically pleasing visual merchandising for a design brand, but visual merchandising should always be customer-oriented. The products must be shown in a way that relates them to the shopper's needs, preferences and aspirations. Through visual merchandising the customer should be able to get a good idea of the merchandise proposition of the store, so the family grouping and presentation of the merchandise should be done in a logical way. The presentation should also be done in such a way that the brand positioning and personality are shown to their full advantage.

Ranges can be divided up in different ways. The way the merchandise is arranged leads the method of presentation, which could differ between departments or product categories. The final choice depends mainly on the positioning of the retail brand. The methods used most for product presentation are discussed below.

Presentation by colour

Presentation by colour is mainly used by speed brands in fashion. The clear presentation of new fashion colours gives the retail brand the opportunity to emphasize its relevance to the times, so at most fashion stores the clothing is presented by colour. Benetton uses its United Colours theme not only in its advertising, but also very literally in its stores. By playing around with the colours of the clothing in the store, Benetton creates a clear distinction from the competition. Liquor stores also often present part of their range by colour: in the wine department the white, red and rosé wines are displayed separately.

Presentation by end use

Another method that is often used is presenting together products that are used simultaneously. This presentation technique is mainly used by product-mix brands. Crate & Barrel with its high-style, reasonably priced products for household and home decoration is known for its excellent visual merchandising and theme displays. For example all the products needed for a pasta meal are presented together, from a pasta-making machine and a pasta pan to special pasta plates and wine glasses. Italian cookbooks and a bowl for Parmesan cheese are of course also included. Crate & Barrel presents its products to help the customer's eye focus on shape, form, colour and function. Its homewares and furniture are creatively presented in a crisp, clean, architectural setting designed to make customers feel at home, so they can visualize how the goods might be put to use in their own homes. Crate & Barrel paces the customer's experience in its stores with a surprise at every turn. An unexpected take on things will catch the customer's eye; a spontaneous setting will invite him or her to touch. A thoughtful pairing of objects will make customers think, what if?

Presentation by brand

Some consumers are looking for a specific brand, so it can be useful to present all kinds of product from one brand together. Retail companies that want to position themselves as brand-mix brands will always present their goods in this way. Department stores are especially well known for fashion and cosmetics brands with shop-in-the-shop concessions. In these vendor shops the manufacturer often takes care of all the fixtures and visual merchandising, and the manufacturers often employ the sales personnel as well. Selfridges and Harvey Nichols have divided almost their entire department stores into branded concessions. At Sephora, brands are presented in alphabetical order.

Presentation by style

In this case, products with a similar style are presented together. For example, in a bookstore there are separate departments for, amongst other things, travel books, cookbooks and study books. In furniture stores furniture in classical, modern and romantic styles is usually presented separately. Most wine merchants divide their stores according to country of origin; however, in London there are wine stores that categorize their products by taste profile. In fashion stores a distinction is usually made between casual clothing and more formal clothing. In particular retail brands that focus on multiple lifestyles will choose to present by style.

Presentation by size

In shoe stores shoes are generally presented by style: the customer first chooses the desired model, then asks a sales employee if the right size is available. However, low-priced and efficient shoe stores often choose to group by size. The presentation will then come across as being more in-bulk and cheaper. Moreover, it will be easier for customers to shop because they can immediately see if the desired shoe is in stock in the right size. Children's clothing is almost always presented by size because parents then know exactly where to look for their kids' sizes.

Presentation by target group

Retail brands that focus on multiple target groups often choose this type of presentation. Many department stores have a special department for teens besides their more traditional departments. In such a department clothing, accessories, music and lots of other products are sold, all in a distinctively designed environment that differs from the rest of the store. For example, Lafayette in Paris opened a teens department in the basement with an atmosphere that deviates strongly from the rest of the store.

Presentation by price

Many stores offer the customer a choice between good, better and best products. Stores with a large private brand range will generally pay extra attention to these goods in their visual merchandising. In supermarkets, these brands are presented at eye level. The more expensive national brands will be presented above them, and the cheaper brands will be found on the lower shelves.

Whichever method of presentation the retailer chooses, product dominance is essential in all cases. The products themselves are the most important means of communication, leaving the other ways subordinate to them.

11.4.3 DISPLAYS

Displays are an important aid in visual merchandising. They can be used to give special emphasis to certain stock items, and to give customers specific ideas about product usage. In practice, there are two kinds of displays: selling displays and ambience displays. With a selling display customers can pick up the products, because the stock is part of the display. So the most important function of the display is to tempt the consumer to immediately buy the product. In particular, supermarkets, drugstores and other stores selling convenience products use this type of display. In the case of an ambience display only a few products are shown, usually in combination with special fixtures and props. Customer cannot touch the display itself, but the stock for sale is situated close by. The function of an ambience display is mainly to identify a department and give the consumer an idea of what it is offering.

A good display draws attention to a certain product, because products are literally and figuratively taken from the shelves. Dozens of products can receive extra attention via a display. If this is done successfully, a display will lead to higher sales. In addition, a striking display can ensure that weak areas in the store are strengthened. An attractive display will draw the consumer to certain areas in the store.

A display can also strengthen the retail brand in the long term. The style of the display contributes to expressing the desired personality, and the products chosen for presentation say something about the retail brand's positioning. Big, mass displays with aggressively priced promotions strengthen a low-price brand's price image. Displays with the latest products will give a speed brand an up-to-date image, and those that give customers design or usage ideas increase the shopping pleasure for an experience brand.

Effect of displays

The eventual sales effect of a display partly depends on several factors.

Type of product

Well-known products and brands sell more quickly and easily from a display than unknown brands. Moreover, it helps if products are sensitive to impulse purchasing. For example, candy and seasonal products usually sell very well if they are presented on a display stand.

Price reductions

Of course the attractiveness of a promotion is connected to the size of the discount. Whether a display will lead to a purchase also depends on the price elasticity of the product. A display of cartons of salt, for example, will most likely not lead to extra purchases, even if it is beautifully presented and marked down enormously. After all, the price elasticity of salt is very low. A markdown will not tempt consumers to buy extra.

Type of display

The look and feel of a display do not only influence the perception of brand personality: the shape, appearance, size and colours of the display will also influence the attention paid to it. In addition, there should always be sufficient stock on or next to the display, and readily available relevant product information.

Location

Displays work best in high-traffic locations. Many customers walk by these locations, therefore the attention level is already high. In a supermarket, these are the outside aisles. Almost all customers visit these aisles.

Marketing communication support

If the promotion on display is also supported by advertising or direct marketing communications, the chances of higher sales will be increased. In the store, customers are reminded by the display of the special promotion they saw at home.

Market

Factors like season and competition can also have an important influence on eventual sales. If there is no demand for a product on the market, it will be difficult for an individual store to create that demand.

11.4.4 GRAPHICS AND SIGNAGE

Images last longer than words. With the help of graphics like oversized photographs or illustrations, a store can add an extra dimension to the merchandise. Today's graphics are almost synonymous with lifestyle, therefore lifestyle graphics are appearing in window displays, interior displays, on fascias over stocked merchandise and even integrated with the merchandise on wall displays. The graphics show people living a particular kind of life: cycling on an autumn day, strolling through a park in April, enjoying a prom date, a family picnic, a power lunch in a smart restaurant, or a romantic candlelight dinner. The lifestyle photo enlargements often appear either as framed or unframed background panels, or in light boxes illuminated from behind. Many of the graphics in speciality stores like the Gap and Eddie Bauer are actually oversized enlargements of their ads that appear in the fashion magazines, or are stills from their television commercials or reproductions from their current catalogue or store mailing. If customers have seen the picture before, on television, in an ad or in a catalogue, the visual impact and association with the retail brand will be even greater (Pegler, 2001: 238).

Signage can help consumers navigate the range of products found in the store. Without in-store communications customers would find shopping more difficult. It would be harder to find the right products, and they could miss information they need to make the right purchase decision. Graphics combined with some signage can be an effective instrument in communicating the desired positioning message. But messages should not be wordy, because extensive messages will not be read in the store. Communications should be short and powerful.

In the store consumers are mainly product-oriented and are looking for relevant information. All other impulses will barely be taken notice of. Only very striking, big changes in graphics and signage will be consciously perceived by consumers. In-store communications should be not only short and powerful, but also concise and clear. Therefore not too many things should be communicated simultaneously. There should be a coherent overall information hierarchy, and the store should not be cluttered with displays and other in-store materials from suppliers. These displays and in-store materials can usually be found in competitors' stores as well, and resulting danger is that the retail brand's own identity could become somewhat lost.

With graphics and signage a distinction can be made between three communication levels.

Thematic communication

Thematic graphics and signage have the primary goal of communicating a brand's positioning and personality. In the case of price brands, mostly price claims like 'cheaper nowhere else' and 'lowest price guaranteed' will be communicated. For example, Trader Joe's, a supermarket chain in the United States, has a big sign with the following words in all supermarkets:

How we keep prices so low: We buy direct from our suppliers, in large amounts. We bargain hard and manage our costs carefully; we do not pay exorbitant amounts to create a fancy store; we are not open 24 hours a day; we do not conduct couponing wars or fancy promotions. And we do not borrow money. We pay in cash, and on time, so our suppliers like to do business with us.

The choice of an aggressive design for this thematic message strengthens the positioning statement even further.

Service brands generally emphasize the services with which they differentiate themselves from the competition. Range brands will mainly use thematic communication to emphasize the uniqueness of their merchandise. For example, Lush communicates the following in its cosmetics stores:

We believe in hand-made preparing our fresh products, printing our own labels and preparing our own aromas. We believe in the right to make mistakes, losing everything and starting all over again. We also believe that words like 'fresh' and 'organic' have a real meaning that goes further than advertising.

The handwritten copy on black chalk boards once again emphasizes the artisanal character of Lush.

With experience brands, thematic communication mainly has to create the right atmosphere. The look and feel of signage and graphics are perhaps more important for these types of brands than the actual content of the communication. For example, in the Build-a-Bear Workshop stores there are signs with the following 'Bearisms':

Bear in mind: always be kind. Be the bearer of good news. Take time to taste the honey. Remember your very first teddy. Ask not what your bear can do for you, but what you can do for your bear. Nothing beats a bear hug. Life is always sweeter with a taste of honey. Don't judge a bee by its buzz.

Actual functional information is not given, but this kind of signage does contribute to giving life to the brand. Because this thematic decoration is always about communicating the brand's positioning and/or personality, it stays in the store for a longer period of time.

Selling communications

Graphics and signage focused on selling are more short-term focused and are therefore also changed more frequently. The frequency of change mainly depends on the frequency of purchase. The higher the frequency of visits, the higher the frequency of change will have to be. By regularly changing graphics, the store can keep evoking an up-to-date, surprising image, because it can continue to offer the consumer a new experience at low cost. This is of course not so possible with the more fixed, expensive store designs.

Selling signs should inform customers what kind of product it is and why they should buy it now. Price is of course an important element, but it is not only about price. A good selling sign will always give customers another reason to buy the product. For example that could be the topicality, quality or uniqueness of the product. This type of in-store communication should tempt the customer to make an impulse purchase.

Service communications

In-store communications can help consumers to quickly find their way in the store. In addition, service communications can inform customers what kind of services the store offers, and provide practical information like where the restrooms are and where the exits can be found. That is why service communications are usually designed in conformity with the company's house style. If executed in the right way, these service communications can be an important part of the brand environment.

11.5 Employees: living the brand

Employees are the link between the customer and the retail brand. Online retailers miss this human interaction, but for offline retailers, employees are maybe even the most important communication tool. Employees should reflect and reinforce the brand in their behaviour. They are almost the brand themselves. The millions spent on advertising, direct marketing communications, store design and visual merchandising will be wasted if a customer has a bad experience with an employee. Strong retail brands therefore spend time, money and energy making sure that external and internal branding connect well. Employees who understand what the retail brand stands for and also believe in that can become true brand champions, because every contact with an employee is a moment of truth. In many cases employees are the top priority in building customer loyalty. Just like other service providers, retailers are therefore more vulnerable than manufacturers. After all, in the retail environment many more employees are in contact with the customer than with a manufacturer, so more things have the potential to go wrong.

Employees can make the difference in retail. Good employees are more difficult to imitate than range, price, convenience or store experience. But employees are also the biggest cost factor in retail. However, this should not result in less attention being paid to the internal branding. After all, employees are not only a cost factor, they are also responsible for a large part of the revenue. For example, at Ikea a quarter of the revenue can definitely be attributed to the quality of its human resources policies (Martens, 2005: 21).

Employees also have a large influence on brand perception in stores where the emphasis is on self-service. They are the human face of the retail brand, and also need to continue to prove the brand promise every day in these types of store. The employees deliver the brand. The brand positioning and the brand personality are eventually proven and confirmed by the employees in the store. Service improvements can almost always be attributed to personnel-provided activities as well.

> We never set out to build a brand. Our goal was to build a great company, one that stood for something, one that valued the authenticity of its product and the passion of its people. When I looked back, I realized we had fashioned a brand in a way no textbook could ever have prescribed. We built the Starbucks brand first with our people, not with our consumers; the opposite approach from that of the crackers and cereals companies.

This statement by Howard Schultz, chairman of Starbucks, explains very well how important employees are in building a strong retail brand. Employees can really be a competitive differentiator.

When building a brand, retailers often tend to look at their advertising and other types of out-of-store communication. However, all other marketing investments are worthless if something goes wrong in the contact between customer and employee. Employees must live the brand. They should bring the retail brand to life, and their personal values should match the corporate values, the brand values and the personality of the retail brand. If employees are themselves enthusiastic about what the brand stands for, they will sooner act according to the brand's values.

The human touch can determine the winners and the losers in retail, and can make the difference with online retailers. Committed employees lead to customer satisfaction and retail brand loyalty. A strong retail brand is one where the employees really live the brand values. It comes down to four key aspects.

Awareness

Living the brand of course starts with clear communication from the management about the values of the retail brand. The brand promise should be communicated not only externally, but also internally to the employees. Every employee engaged in activities that directly or indirectly affect the customer experience should know exactly what the positioning and personality of the retail brand are. Only if this is done can the employees act according to it. External branding should be translated into internal branding. The vision, mission and corporate and brand values should be no secret to the employees. Employees should know what these mean in order to conduct themselves appropriately. Through every contact with the customer a consistent message should be given about the retail brand.

Understanding

Employees should understand why and how the retail brand is relevant to customers. Every employee should also understand how important his or her own behaviour is in delivering the brand promise. If all employees know and understand what the retail brand stands for, this will determine their decisions. The training needed for this will have to be brand-specific. After all, during this training it should become clear how the retail brand differentiates itself from other brands.

Acceptance

All employees should be committed to the brand, so it is essential that they not only know and understand, but also really believe in the brand values. When hiring employees, attention should be paid to the competencies applicants have and therefore the likelihood that they will behave in the right way. The right attitude is often more important than the right skills. Skills can be trained, but attitude has more to do with the applicant's personality.

Pret A Manger, the fast-growing UK sandwich chain, takes a very special approach in hiring new employees. Prospective employees are asked to work in a store for a day. At the end of the day the store's employees are asked to vote on whether the person should be hired or not. Only 5 per cent of the people who apply for jobs at Pret A Manger are accepted. The reason for this unusual recruitment method is that, according to Andrew Rolfe, the former CEO, the company believes that one of the biggest responsibilities of management is to look after the corporate DNA (Smith, 2003: 202–3).

Behaviour

If employees really understand the brand promise and are highly committed to it, they will deliver the brand. Their behaviour will meet customer expectations. They will live the brand identity in their day-to-day interactions. At the warehouse club Costco the clerks take note of the products customers purchase as they pass through the checkout lines. The clerks sometimes ask customers where they found the product in the store. With their curiosity, they are subtly emphasizing how rapidly the merchandise changes at Costco. The clerks also comment on the great price of certain products: not the staple items, such as peanut butter, but the unusual higher-end items. It reinforces part of the unspoken Costco message: 'We've got such great value goods that you need to buy them now. If you don't, the merchandise probably will not be there when you return' (Barlow and Stewart, 2004: 60).

Successful retail brands invest in their employees to make sure that they understand which promise the brand is making to the consumer. Internal branding is at least as important to a retailer as external branding. If everyone in the company shares the corporate culture and values, this can drive the store performance. Committed, loyal employees will create satisfied customers; and the reverse is also true. Consumers who decide to no longer buy at a certain store often do not do so because of a disappointing product. The reason is usually employee indifference to their requirements. Only a small portion will complain about this to the retailer. The majority of the disappointed customers will not complain, but will simply go to another store. After all, there are plenty of stores to choose from.

Employees who know and live the brand have enabled REI to become America's most intriguing retailer of outdoor apparel and gear. All employees are either involved in the outdoors or aspire to be involved in the outdoors. At each store, managers go out of their way to recruit and retain employees who are true outdoors enthusiasts and who end up 'selling' REI. They do so on the basis of their authentic experience in and enthusiasm for outdoor activities, their deep knowledge of the equipment that REI sells, and their ability to size up and influence members and other customers in the store. The best comments that REI gets back from customers are about their interaction with the employees. They are the best at developing relationships and trust, and that builds the loyalty customers have for REI. Internally, employees are expected to live the brand. Employees go out and take long bike rides at lunchtime, go running or do outdoor yoga just to make sure they get out and enjoy themselves. REI employees really live their outdoor lifestyles and understand them. They are not there just to make a sale but to help customers learn about the outdoors, and get out and enjoy it as much as they can (Buss, 2005).

The commitment and loyalty of employees in retail will mainly be obtained through brand ideas that need a number of attributes (Ind, 2001: 192–95).

Imaginative

To create meaning in our working lives, we need to believe in the value of what we do. For most people brand statements that stress ideas connected with cost or profitability will not be ultimately engaging. This does not deny the power of monetary reward, but it does indicate that brand ideas need an emotional appeal to our larger goals as human beings. For this reason, the most significant brands have strongly emotive elements. The brand should touch the lives of the people that work for the organization, and have a set of values that stir their imaginations.

Authentic

Consumers want to see behind companies and to understand what they are really like. There are no hiding places. Whatever the language used, employees and other audiences are too knowing to be fooled for long. Authenticity means saying what you do and doing what you say, in a language and a manner that is credible.

Courageous

Brands have increasing difficulty in differentiating themselves. The only way they can create a realizable competitive advantage is by having a distinctive point of view. However, stepping outside the norms is highly risky. There is safety in being part of the pack. Courage means confronting the anxiety that goes with difficult choices and then committing to the ideas that ensue. To build a courageous brand, the brand idea itself has to contain a tension. If the values simply reinforce what the organization does well, there is little incentive for experimentation. However, if the values stretch and pull the organization, a sense of dynamism emerges.

Empowering

Empowerment is important because it uses the full intellectual power of the organization to solve problems. The real challenge here is to change a manager's mindset, from an approach that focuses on selling an idea to others in the organization, and to a more organic method. Once the seed of an idea has been planted, it grows through the involvement and enthusiasm of others.

The brand positioning and brand personality of the store determine the attitude and behaviour of the employees. The brand positioning mainly influences the nature of the activities. Employees of a low-price brand will mainly be replenishing shelves and working at the checkouts. There is no room for more extensive contact with customers. In contrast, employees of other retail brands may have a more extensive function.

The personality of the retail brand has an influence on employees' appearance and the way in which they do their work. An employee of a retail brand with a feminine, sexy personality will need to have a different appearance from an employee of a retail brand with a masculine, athletic personality. The appearance of both employees is completely different, while the type of work can be the same.

Figure 11.4 Influence of brand positioning and personality on employees.

11.5.1 ROLE OF EMPLOYEES

Personal selling remains very important especially for complicated, expensive or infrequently purchased products. For these types of products customers need extra information and support. Salespeople can then have a big influence on the customer's buying behaviour.

A cellular phone contract is just such a purchase. The Carphone Warehouse, the largest independent retailer of mobile communications in Europe, with more than 1,300 stores in 10 countries, has several times been voted the UK's best retailer. Charles Dunstone set up the company in 1989 with £6,000 in capital. The retail brand started out with a simple proposition: offering 'simple, impartial advice' to consumers wishing to navigate the minefield of cellular phone contracts. The company now offers value-added services and competes against British Telecom, among others. Its new brand proposition, 'for a better mobile life', reflects this shift. However, what has not changed is its focus on differentiating the brand on the basis of the customer experience. The vision and core values first introduced by Dunstone remain unchanged, and the company continues to be driven by total dedication to customer satisfaction. Fundamental to the brand is the performance of its people. At the Carphone Warehouse everything the employees do is based on the company's 'five fundamental rules'. These five simple operating principles are:

- If we don't look after the customer, someone else will.
- Nothing is gained by winning an argument but losing a customer.
- Always deliver what we promise. If in doubt, underpromise and overdeliver.
- Always treat customers as we ourselves would like to be treated.
- The reputation of the whole company is in the hands of each individual.

The rules speak for themselves and need little embellishment. However, it is worth stressing that the rules are applied not only in Carphone Warehouse stores, but in its call centres and support functions too, to ensure that it provides the best possible customer experience. The principles are unusual in that they focus people on behaviours rather than high-level values like 'trustworthy, valued or responsive'. The way in which the Carphone Warehouse applies them also sets it apart. For example, it invests four times the industry average in training. New employees must undergo two weeks of intensive training and a rigorous assessment before they are allowed in front of a customer. The message here is that successful brands focus less on brand image and more on brand action (Smith, 2003: 102–3).

So the employees' role can depend on the nature of the products. Personal selling can play a bigger role with difficult products than with simple products. However, the nature of the contact between customer and employee is mainly determined by the retail brand's positioning. Even pretty complicated products like computers and sound equipment can in principle be sold almost entirely through self-service. The role of the employee and the expectations the customer has from the employee are strongly determined by the retail brand's positioning.

No employees spend all their time dealing with customers: non-customer-related tasks are part of the job of every store employee. However, a distinction can be made between employees who have a lot of interaction with customers, and those that have a little. Depending on the nature of the interaction, the following employee types can be distinguished in retail.

Replenishers

The most important function of replenishers or shelf-stackers is to replenish the store's display stock. Customer interaction is limited to pointing out the location of a certain product to customers. These employees will not try to initiate customer contact. Especially with low-price brands and bargain brands there is little interaction between customer and employee.

Checkout employees and bagging employees

Both types of employees have some interaction with customers. However, that interaction is limited. When an employee is ringing up and bagging groceries there is little or no time for an elaborate conversation with the customer. Nevertheless, this interaction with employees can still have a big influence on the brand perception. The store's last impression can damage someone's previous positive experiences. Long checkout queues cause irritation.

Salespeople

There are many different types of salesperson, from the employee in the fish department of a supermarket to the salesperson at a car dealership. Customers often prefer to be left alone in a store, but if necessary, a salesperson needs to be available. Only then can there be active selling. That is why this type of store employee continues to spend more time on passive selling: taking care of the visual merchandising. The merchandise needs to be presented in such a way that customers can make their own choice.

Advisers

By no means every retail company employs advisers. There will be no or hardly any advisers in a low-price or bargain brand store. In order to keep costs low, as much as possible is left to the customer. There is no employee available for customers to appeal to for product information and to answer other questions. The customers need to gather any necessary information themselves, perhaps from the retail brand's website. However, retail brands that are focused on range or service will have employees who play a primarily advisory role. For range or expertise brands the employees mainly need product knowledge to be able to advise customers. Service brands, however, call for a more thorough knowledge of the customer. After all, if employees know the individual customer's needs and wants in detail, they will be able to offer the right service.

Personal shoppers

A retail brand that wants to profile itself through excellent service may use personal shoppers. Personal shoppers or style advisers can make shopping much easier because they know their customers very well. They know their needs and wants, and what they do and do not like. The personal shopper walks through the store with the customer, and from the many thousands of products he or she selects those that meet that customer's needs. When new merchandise arrives, he or she knows straight away if there is something in the selection that will appeal to a specific customer, and if the customer does not have time to come to the store, the personal shopper will go to the customer's home or office with the goods.

Performers

Particularly for entertainment brands in retail, this employee is a kind of performer, playing an important role in the retail theatre. He or she is an actor who performs on the store stage. For example, in Disney stores this role contributes to entertaining customers.

Sephora has four types of salespeople. The function of these employees is recognizable from their outfits. There are stylishly dressed advisers walking around in the store, who help customers make the right purchase decision. Customers who want a makeover can have that done by a kind of performer. These performers demonstrate the newest cosmetics products in the middle of the store. Because cosmetics manufacturers usually employ the performers, their outfits are clearly different from Sephora's advisers. Replenishers wear yet another different, functional outfit. To customers it is clear straightaway that these employees do not have an advisory role. Finally, the fourth category of employees at Sephora are the people at the checkouts, who are also dressed very stylishly. So the last customer interaction confirms the glamorous brand personality of Sephora as well.

Office Depot is one of the success stories of the American retail industry. Established in 1986, Office Depot reached a turnover of US$10 billion in 13 years, a milestone that was not even accomplished by Wal-Mart in such a short period of time. During this turbulent growth period, Office Depot spent hardly any time thinking about the company culture or values. As Office Depot grew larger and more complex, its management leadership needed changes. In 2000 David Fuente stepped aside, and Bruce Nelson was appointed chief executive officer. Nelson's charge was challenging: to guide Office Depot at an exciting and defining time in the company's evolution. Nelson immediately undertook several new management initiatives geared to making Office Depot a more compelling place to work, shop and invest. After extensive internal workshops, among other things, the following core company values were formulated: respect for the individual, fanatical customer service, and excellence in execution. In these core values both beliefs and rules of conduct were formulated, and the strategic vision of Office Depot was strongly reflected. This vision simply was: 'the best place to work, shop, and invest'. So employees are most important in this vision.

So-called stretch goals were developed by Office Depot for each of the elements of the vision (Heskett, 2003: 120–21): (1) become one of the top 100 companies to work for in two years; (2) become the fastest growing company in each of its business segments (retail, commercial, catalogue and internet, and international); and (3) provide outstanding returns to its investors.

To reinforce the vision and goals, a scorecard was developed reflecting each dimension of each of the three values. Managers at all levels of the organization were encouraged to convene their employees to develop similar measures most appropriate for their area of responsibility. For example, the measures extended down into the stores for the retail business. They were developed for each of the company's 24 US distribution centres and each of its call centres for direct sales from the catalogue and the internet.

Among the more important decisions made by Office Depot's management team were those concerning the rollout of its ideas. The management decided to involve all 48,000 employees in a process designed to communicate the values, vision and strategy to everyone, and to challenge them to think about what needed to be changed if these were to be achieved, what would be needed to do it, and how it would have to be done. Each was asked to think about barriers to change that would have to be eliminated, and what he or she would have to do differently.

By the end of 2001, only 18 months after taking over, Bruce Nelson and his colleagues could point to significant accomplishments. Poorly performing stores had been closed. New international retail, commercial, and internet services had been initiated. The company's growth had enabled it to avoid layoffs in the wake of a deepening recession and the terrorist attacks on the United States. Measures of customer and employee satisfaction and loyalty had shot up. The company's shares had risen by 160 per cent during the year.

11.5.2 JUDGEMENT BY CUSTOMERS

Because brand performance and brand perception strongly depend on the employees' activities, it is important to regularly determine what the target customer group thinks about the employees. In practice, the customer's judgement is usually based on the following factors.

Availability

The availability of employees is important to every retail brand. At the moment the customer needs an employee, someone needs to be there. People are less patient than they used to be, so queues at checkouts should not be too long.

Appearance

The appearance of the employee needs to be appropriate. Outfits can communicate a lot about the positioning and personality of the retail brand. They can give the sales employee authority. The white coat of a pharmacist adds to his or her credibility as a medical expert. In addition, wearing an outfit can help salespeople to be more readily recognizable to customers. Especially in stores where employees no longer stand behind a sales counter, this can make shopping easier for the customer.

Friendliness

Whatever the positioning and personality of the retail brand, every customer wants salespeople to be friendly. In price brand stores, customers do not expect any professional knowledge from the employees. Consumers understand that low prices are at the expense of the expertise of the salespeople. However, friendliness is an absolute must for every employee. However, employees will only smile at customers if they have a reason to smile. Therefore employees need to feel appreciated and need to enjoy their work. If they enjoy their work, the customer will also enjoy shopping.

Expertise

Salespeople and advisers need to have all the necessary knowledge to be able to really help customers. Employees who have the required knowledge and experience show more confidence and authority. For that reason, Home Depot and other do-it-yourself companies tend to employ older people who can communicate that they have done every do-it-yourself job themselves. At the entrance of Decathlon sport stores there are pictures of employees mentioning their favourite sports, how long they have been practising that sport, and which prizes, if any, they have won. For Decathlon this is an excellent way to communicate the employees' expertise. This expertise is enhanced even more through things like customers being confronted with a bicycle repair department when they enter the store.

Eagerness

Especially in the case of service brands, the employee needs to be prepared to make that extra effort. An employee can tell a customer where to find a certain product, but he or she can also walk with the customer to the right aisle and show that he or she is really eager to help.

The importance of each of these five factors can differ from moment to moment, between products and between retail brands. With the purchase of a staple commodity, the availability of people at the checkouts is probably most important to customers. In the case of a more complicated product, customers may want to call on the employee's expertise. The customer's expectation level can differ from one retail brand to another. The expectations with which a customer walks into a department store or a specialist store are totally different from those on a visit to a low-price store. Customers know they cannot make the same demands on an employee in a low-price store as they can on an employee in a premium price store. Customers who buy wine in supermarkets know from the start that the available salespeople will most likely not know a lot about wine. They will therefore not mind if they do not get a good answer to a question. However, if the same customers go to a specialist wine store, they will expect expert advice and are likely to be very disappointed if they do not receive it.

In particular, retail brands that pay a lot of attention to low prices in their positioning have to emphasize availability and friendliness when training their employees. Retail brands that offer additional benefits to the customer have to coach their employees in expertise and eagerness as well.

11.5.3 COMPANY CULTURE

Because employees are so important to the branding of a store, the big turnover in retail is a huge problem. The costs of this turnover are high. These include not only the direct costs of hiring new employees, but more indirect costs. New, inexperienced employees make more mistakes and sometimes deal with products the wrong way. Employees who stay longer with the company build up a relationship with customers and can give colleagues training and advice. The total costs of employee turnover run into billions of dollars in American supermarkets alone, so it is of the utmost importance to keep this turnover as low as possible.

Brand power and company culture, as well as pay and working conditions, are important reasons to continue to work for a company. The company culture is formed, among other things, by the company's history, mission, vision and corporate values, types of managers and employees, and the personality of its founder. This company culture needs to be closely connected to the brand personality. The way in which employees interact with each other needs to be in harmony with the way in which they interact with customers.

Wal-Mart's low employee turnover rate is partly because of the company's culture. This company's culture, propagated by 'nice' people, advocates competition and fun at all levels. Most of this activity, however, has a dual purpose: to foster involvement in the Wal-Mart 'family' and to boost sales. For example, headquarters executives regularly choose merchandise items that they will 'sponsor' for internal sales contests implemented in cooperation with store managers. This requires senior executives, who spend most of their time in stores, to maintain close contact with both customers and the store management in an effort to get their 'sponsored' items promoted and sold. Some might view this as wasted valuable time. As a result, however, Wal-Mart's senior management maintains an unusual sensitivity to merchandising and store operating problems while enjoying a business-fostering competition. This might explain Wal-Mart's unusually low turnover rates in both frontline and management ranks. Employees become caught up in the excitement generated by the constant activity created by the contests and other events, getting to know management better than in most general merchandising organizations (Heskett et al, 2003: 17).

In the case of Burger King, the company had to find a way to teach its brand values effectively to a young workforce that turns over completely twice a year. One major concern was the appearance of its workers, which the company believed was important to the dining experience. Burger King therefore developed image guidelines that lay out clear grooming rules. The guidelines offer illustrated examples of how employees can be stylish and comfortable and still meet the rules for hygiene and appearance. Warning about clean hands for example, the guidelines suggest that employees might want to get a manicure. Scented body lotion is preferable to cologne. The guidelines point out that hair must be kept out of the food but offers a variety of options, such as braiding, scrunching or using gel, to accomplish that (Reinan, 2003).

Customer service is The Container Store's core competency, so hiring people who are self-motivated and team-oriented with a passion for customer service is key. The Container Store places so much importance on service that every first-year, full-time salesperson receives more than 235 hours of training, in a retail industry where the average is about seven hours. And training continues throughout an employee's career. The Container Store has full-time employees who are dedicated to training all store employees on the features, advantages and benefits of each product, as well as specific training on how to best service and sell to customers. At The Container Store, service equals selling. The trainers are in the stores every day ensuring that store employees are knowledgeable and empowered enough to offer the excellent customer service that The Container Store is known for in the industry. The salespeople do not work on commission; instead, they are salaried or paid by the hour, with wages far above the industry norm. They often work in teams to find a complete solution for a customer, a method which allows them to spend as much time as necessary to help customers find exactly what they need.

Part 5
The future

12. SOME FORECASTS

The retail trade will change dramatically in the future. In the next few decades there will be more changes than there were in the past several centuries. Only those retail companies with strong and unique brand associations will survive. Price will be a critical success factor for almost all retail brands. Retail brands that cannot compete on price will definitely lose the battle. Other retail brands will have to differentiate themselves through other positioning attributes, and mostly through their personality. As for the positioning mix, it will mainly be high-value brands with a mix of low prices and added value that will be the winners. A unique personality will also become more important to all retail brands.

Home Depot, the category killer that until recently set up only in big boxes on the edge of town, recently opened home improvement stores with window displays right in Manhattan. In that same Manhattan, Comme des Garçons, an exclusive fashion brand, opened a store of which the poor-looking exterior does not give away that an expensive, luxury brand is sold inside. Large, well-known retail companies, like the Dutch VendexKBB and the German KarstadtQuelle for example, have big problems and are disappearing, downsizing, being split up or taken over by competitors. Newcomers like Ikea, Media Markt, H&M and Zara have turned whole sectors upside down and succeeded in building up dominant positions in a very short period of time. The enormous power of Wal-Mart is only getting bigger every year. And Dell continues to succeed, having become the biggest computer seller in the world through selling solely via the internet.

The dynamic in retail is huge. That is why it is difficult to predict the future. Retail brands that are successful today can be overtaken by a competitor tomorrow. Competition is getting tougher, and consumers can buy anything, anywhere and at any time. Many traditional store formats that do not meet these changing market circumstances will disappear. Others will take their place. So retail will change drastically over the coming years. Fifteen important trends are described below.

12.1 Only strong retail brands will survive

Companies with a strong brand identity have a future in retail. Consumers are overloaded with advertising and marketing messages, and can choose from many stores in every sector. Today consumers have more choice than ever before. Brands are used much more as orientation points, as they make it easier for consumers to choose. Therefore the brand will become one of the most valuable assets of a retail company. The store itself should become a brand, and creating a differentiating positioning, personality and communications will be the challenge for the coming years. The development of a retail brand will then no longer occur accidentally, but be part of a well-planned strategy.

The emphasis will then shift from functional to emotional aspects. Brand positioning is mainly about concrete attributes that the store offers the consumer. Every strong brand identity is based on a good positioning mix of range, price, convenience and store experience. Many stores already fail at this point, because they do not stand out from the competition. A retail brand does not have to be unique in its positioning, but it should be better, quicker and cheaper than the competition. Without such a positioning base a store is unlikely to be successful. It will be difficult for it to create a sustainable differentiation in the long term with only a functional approach towards the consumer. Functional positioning attributes are important, but can also be imitated relatively easily. That is why in the coming years, the emotional relationship with customers will become much more important in retail, as it is for manufacturer brands. Functional positioning attributes will more often be translated into emotional benefits, but even then it will be difficult to create a distinction. Consumers will then more often prefer retail brands whose personality fits with their own (desired) self-image.

The emotional component will also become more important in brand communications. Retail brands will further strengthen their brand equity with an entirely unique look and feel to their communications.

Positioning, personality and communications all have a number of dimensions. As far as brand positioning is concerned, range, price, convenience or store experience can be chosen as the differentiator. The same goes for brand personality, where the best mix will have to be chosen from various alternatives. With brand communications the retailer again has multiple tools available, in which the content and look and feel can be implemented very differently. In principle, all these dimensions can be mixed together, because all three circles of the retail brand circle turn around each other, as it were. However, the challenge is to mix the three ingredients of the retail brand circle in such a way that a consistent, clear and differentiating brand identity is developed.

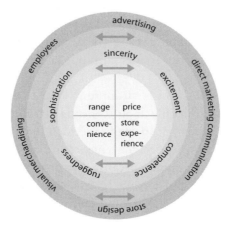

Figure 12.1 Retail brand circle

Retail companies that succeed in creating a differentiating brand positioning, personality and communications, and turning these three brand identity components into a fully integrated whole, are the brand champions of the future. With these retail brands their positioning and personality will be in line with each other, and their communications will be a perfect reflection of this positioning and personality.

Aldi and Zara are good examples of retail brands with a differentiating and integrated brand identity. These brands have strong synergy across brand positioning, personality and communication, in which the components mutually strengthen each other. (See Table 12.1.)

Brand identity	Zara	Aldi
Brand positioning	Fashionable, very quickly changing range at low prices. Only private brands.	Small stock of private brands. Everyday low food prices. Sharp promotions on general Merchandise.
Brand personality	Fashionable, trendy, surprising, young.	No-nonsense, down-to-earth, aggressive, masculine.
Brand communications	Stores often in characteristic premises in high-traffic locations. Shop windows with alluring and strong fashion appeal. Frequently changing store design. Hardly any advertising.	Simple premises in less expensive locations. Simple store designs. Basic visual merchandising. Aggressive, functional advertising.

Table 12.1 The brand identities of Zara and Aldi

Zara offers consumers fast fashion at low prices. The range changes every couple of weeks. It only sells its own collections, and manufactures a large part of the range in its own factories. The clothing has high-fashion appeal, but nevertheless prices are very attractive. Zara clearly differentiates itself from other fashion stores with this mix of range and price. Zara is succeeding in continuing to assemble a differentiating range, but it has also succeeded in developing a completely unique brand personality. Its positioning on fast fashion with an haute-couture-like character is consistent with the trendy, young, fashionable and surprising brand personality. This personality can clearly be seen in all the stores. In line with its unique, differentiating collections and fashionable brand personality, Zara prefers locations with clearly unique characteristics. For example, in Antwerp Zara is located in a majestic old bank building. The shop windows have strong fashion appeal in order to emphasize how trendy and surprising the brand personality is. Without coming across as luxurious, it still communicates a very up-to-date fashion image. And because Zara is always located in high-traffic locations and the shop windows and the stores themselves continue to communicate a different fashion image all the time, the chain hardly needs to use any advertising. Customers come to the store anyway.

Like Zara, Aldi only sells private brands, but in contrast to Zara it has a range that barely changes. Only in the non-food sector does it regularly have one-off merchandise. The range is very limited compared with other supermarkets, but the prices are among the lowest in the market. Aldi's positioning is mainly based on low prices, and is consistent with the no-nonsense, down-to-earth, masculine personality of the brand. This brand personality can be recognized in everything Aldi does. For example, in its advertising Aldi communicates straightforward ('Aldi informs') products and prices. The advertising is functional and has an aggressive appeal, and is a perfect reflection of the store. The store also has a very sober look, which emphasizes the low prices once again.

12.2 A further power shift from manufacturers to retailers

Stores are becoming strong brands, and marketing is becoming professional. Unique mind positions and loyal customer bases are being built up with the help of differentiating brand identities. Private brands then play a very important role. Because stores become brands themselves, it is easier for them to introduce a private brand and become less dependent on manufacturer brands. Moreover, in many cases, these manufacturer brands are mutually exchangeable. Only the very strong, top two or three manufacturer brands in each sector have built up such a position in consumers' minds that retailers cannot do without them. In all other cases retailers have a lot of freedom in choosing the manufacturers they want to do business with.

Manufacturers will then be played off against each other to achieve terms that are as favourable as possible. That is why in most sectors the power will shift even more from the manufacturer to the retailer. A larger proportion of the total margin earned by both parties will go to the retailer. Retailers will improve their profitability at the expense of manufacturers, and will therefore gradually decrease their arrears in profitability. In the battle of the brands between retailers and manufacturers, retail brands will more often end up as winners. After all, retail brands have more opportunities to interact with their customers.

12.3 Each retail sector will be dominated by two or three megabrands

Many retail markets are stagnating. In order to still be able to grow, retailers will need to take market share from other companies. That is why the competitive battle will become fiercer, and only the strongest retail brands will survive. The big retail brands will continue to get bigger. In each market there will be room for only a few brands. Both nationally and internationally every sector in the future will be dominated by only two or three mega retail brands. In some countries many retail sectors are already dominated by a few of these megabrands. In the United States Barnes & Noble, Borders and Amazon dominate the book market, Home Depot and Lowe the home improvement market, and Best Buy and Circuit City the electronics market. A similar situation is apparent in lots of other countries.

In total, a maximum of 100 global retail brands will dominate the world market. Retail brands that do not belong to the top three in their sector will lack the required market dominance and will therefore face difficult times. The position of weak, colourless retail brands will be taken by innovative players. And if they are successful, these newcomers will quickly expand in order to challenge the current players, through franchising and other strategies.

Alongside global retail brands there will continue to be room, both nationally and internationally, for niche players. However they will need to be market leaders in their specific niche. Market leadership, and especially mental market leadership, is more important than the size of the company. After all, market leaders can build up a strong position in consumers' minds. Manufacturers will go through a similar process. Once more two or three megabrands, nationally and internationally, will dominate each individual market, and there will also be smaller players that focus on niche markets. So, alongside a small number of powerful retail brands there will be a small number of powerful manufacturer brands. Together they will fight a battle of the brands.

12.4 Internationalization with one global store format

In the future, internationalization in retail will mainly occur with one store format that will differ little if at all from country to country. In fashion, replicators like Zara and H&M prove that a retail brand with one store format can be successful in a large number of countries. At the most, a couple of adjustments in the range are needed for each different country. After all, fashion trends continue to spread fast over multiple countries via the internet, music stations and popular television programmes. Global communication channels make global branding easier.

In the home decorating market Ikea operates everywhere with one global format. Electronics retailer Media Markt and discounter Aldi are other examples of retail brands that do not, or scarcely, change their store format in different countries. These examples will be copied increasingly by online retail brands, like for example Amazon, which is almost automatically global in its marketing approach.

International retail brands will benefit more from economies of scale and will further strengthen their market position. In the first instance it will mainly be low-price and high-value brands that will internationalize with one store format. After all, these retail brands have a strong focus on costs. But differently positioned international retail brands will also begin to streamline their store format and will not, or will barely, change it from country to country. Everywhere in the world the consumer will come across familiar retail brands.

12.5 Newcomers will change the rules

A retail brand continually needs to innovate in order to maintain a sustainable advantage over the competition. After all, the lifecycle of store formats is becoming shorter and shorter. Existing retail formats will age quickly. Retail brands that are highly successful suffer most from imitation. That is why continuous innovation is essential for sustained growth. Retail brands that do not take a critical look at their store format every year and adjust it to the changing market will get into trouble. They will suddenly be confronted with the need for drastic change, when it is already too late. This change of course is likely to be necessary because a new retail brand has quickly changed the rules of the game.

However, experience teaches us that it is almost impossible for established retail brands to drastically change their format. Big breakthroughs will come from newcomers to the retail sector.

In recent years retail was confronted with lots of disruptions. This will not be any different in the future. Disruptions will even occur more often. Successful innovations will change the rules of retail. Within a few decades Ikea gave the home decorating sector a totally different look, and Aldi did the same with the food industry. Other newcomers will do this in other sectors. Established retail companies that are not prepared for this and do not react on these innovations will lose the battle with the competition.

12.6 Polarization between functional and emotional shopping

The retail market will become increasingly polarized between functional and emotional shopping. On one side of the market, retail brands will focus on functional and solution-driven shopping of (replenishment) commodities like food, household products, drugs and basic textiles. On the other side retail brands will operate that sell expressive merchandise with strong emotional appeal, like fashion, domestic accessories and perfumes. Functional stores will mainly choose price, range and/or convenience as their positioning attributes. In contrast, emotional stores will mainly position themselves on range and store experience. Retail brands in between, that do not make a clear choice between functional and emotional shopping, will disappear.

In the case of functional shopping, consumers will want to spend as little time, money and effort as possible. After all, this is about routine purchases of products and services that are needed daily: temptation and inspiration are of minor importance in this case. Purchasing decisions are mainly made rationally and hassle-free shopping is most important. The requirements the consumer then sets for the retail brand will become much higher.

There will also be room for a small number of retailers that offer the service of doing customers' shopping for them at a premium price. After all, time will be even more scarce and some consumers will be prepared to pay extra for retailers that can save them even more time. But most consumers would rather spend their money on other products and services than on replenishment commodities. Retail brands in this market segment will therefore have to pay a lot of attention to their costs to maintain their customer base. That is why functional stores are being forced to change their location, simplify their store design, decrease their range, reduce their number of suppliers, lower their prices, simplify their visual merchandising, streamline their store operations and fully integrate offline and online. These are all measures to keep costs as low as possible, and at the same time make shopping as easy as possible for the consumer.

New technologies will play a big role. Functional stores and their online colleagues will increasingly develop into kinds of distribution centre, in which all attention goes to optimizing the flow of products. Store design and visual merchandising will mostly be efficiency-oriented. Navigation in the store will need to be as easy as possible, and employees will have little of no interaction with customers. Because the buying process is so rational, online retail brands in this sector will be able to grow rapidly.

Because functional stores will increasingly develop more and more into no-frills distribution centres, the differences between functional stores and stores that focus on emotional shopping will become bigger. Emotional retail brands focus on self-expression and discovery shopping, and mainly pay attention to their range and store experience. The range needs to fit with the (desired) self-identity of customers, and to continually surprise them.

Because store experience is very important for emotional shopping, a lot of attention will be paid to store design, visual merchandising and employees. Together with the merchandise these items need to make shopping a memorable experience. These emotional stores will therefore look nothing like functional stores. To the consumer, a visit to an emotional store is about more than just buying products. These types of retail brands focus on emotional needs for status, adventure, beauty or comfort. Consumers will use these brands to display their status or to feel good. These needs are satisfied by a unique and extensive range, but also by a surprising store design, inspiring visual merchandising and motivated employees. In most cases these stores will be speciality stores.

12.7 Disappearance of medium-priced retail brands

There will not only be a clear dichotomy between functional and emotional retail brands: a strong polarization over price will also occur. Price will continue to be an important driver in retail in the coming years. Consumers want to save money in some stores in order to be able to afford premium prices in other stores. This will cause a clear dichotomy in retail: low-price and high-value mass retail brands on one side of the market, and premium-priced niche retail brands on the other side.

Low-price and especially high-value mass brands will grow rapidly. After all, for most consumers it is not about the lowest price; it is about the highest value. Some consumers are forced to buy at cheaper stores because of their low income. However, most consumers not only want to pay less, but also have high demands about other aspects. They will want the most value for their money. That means low, but not necessarily the lowest prices. Consumers do not only look at prices when making their choice of store, but also at attributes like range, convenience and store experience.

In contrast to these low-price and high-value brands, premium niche brands will position themselves as deriving their appeal from their exclusivity and very high prices. The difference between these luxury premium retailers and the low-price/high-value retailers will become bigger than it is now. While low-price/high-value stores will emphasize their range and price, premium stores will pay attention to range, service and often to store experience as well. Premium brands offer unique products, that you are not going to see everywhere in the city. But retail brands that offer very high, exclusive service, which everyone knows only the wealthy can afford, belong to this store category as well. Store experience receives a lot of attention in all these premium stores. The store always appears well taken care of and the employees make sure that the customer enjoys himself. This kind of conspicuous consumption is of course taking place in a much smaller number of stores, unlike with low-price and high-value brands. Premium brands almost always focus on niches. However, the number of premium-priced stores will likely increase in the next few years. The more the likeness of products and stores increases and the service levels drop, the more consumers will be willing to pay that premium price for something that is really exclusive. After all, exclusive stores, products and services are a subtle way of communicating ones own personality and of distinguishing oneself from other people. But with the increasing democratization of luxury, premium brands will continuously have to innovate to make sure that they stay ahead of the crowd.

For years, the middle segment was the largest part of the market, but that is going to change. Just like with the functional and emotional retail brands, the middle segment will also disappear. Retail brands that are stuck in the middle will loose territory at a quick rate. These medium-priced retail brands will get squeezed between the low-price and high-value brands on one side of the market and the premium brands on the other. To the consumer they do not have a clear offer. If price is an important criterion for store choice, low-price and high-value retail brands offer a strong proposition. And if the consumers really want something unique, price will hardly play a role and they will go to a premium-price store.

12.8 The splitting-up of retail into four extremes

The differences between stores will become larger. Mid-priced stores and stores that do not make a clear choice between functional and emotional shopping will disappear. The disappearance of these mid-market stores will lead to a split of the retail market into four extremes:

efficient routine, small pleasures, affordable dreams and luxurious experiences. After all, functional shopping can occur both at low price and high value and at premium prices, and the same goes for emotional shopping. Stores that are stuck in the undifferentiated middle will not survive in the future.

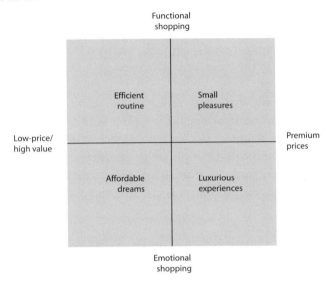

Figure 12.2 Four extremes in retail

12.8.1 EFFICIENT ROUTINE

Retail brands in this market segment will grow strongly during the coming years. Efficient routine brands position themselves on a mix of low prices and convenience. They make routine shopping as cheap, efficient and easy as possible for the consumer. Characteristics like no-nonsense, masculine and reliable make up their brand personality. Traditional convenience stores are expensive, but successful retail brands in this segment are not only convenient, they are cheap as well. They create savings that consumers can spend elsewhere. Their range consists mostly of replenishment commodities, like food, drugs, household products and basic textiles. Everything is sold under one roof, at everyday low prices.

The choice is not bigger than is strictly necessary. After all, more choice leads to more confusion for customers and higher costs for the retailer. There are promotions with one-off merchandise only. The products can be found easily, partly because the number of variants of each product is limited. Paying at the checkouts is fast, and store design and visual merchandising are very simple and strongly process-oriented. The store environment contains less temptation and is businesslike. These stores are more distribution centres than traditional stores. Merchandise and customers need to be able to move as efficiently as possible to and through the store. Merchandise receives all the attention in the store, and design and presentation elements are of less importance.

Employees have little interaction with customers. Their main responsibilities are replenishing the store and working at the checkouts. Efficiency for the customer and the retailer comes first. as only then can costs and prices stay low. Examples of these efficient routine stores are Aldi and Wal-Mart, and also stores like Staples, which tries to make the replenishment of office products as efficient and cheap as possible.

12.8.2 SMALL PLEASURES

Retail brands can make daily, functional shopping something special as well. Consumers are willing to pay premium prices for products and services that really matter to them. Retail brands in this market segment, just like efficient routine stores, sell food, drugs, household products and basic textiles. However, they differentiate themselves from efficient routine stores by their positioning on range and/or service. They do not sell the regular commodities, but the small pleasures of life. The quality is better, or product variations are offered that are not being sold in efficient routine stores. Because of the exclusivity, the retail brand can ask a premium price for these specialities.

These stores also take over the work of the customer. For example, food products are sold ready to cook or ready to eat. Other products are completely tailor-made to the customer's wishes. And if customers wish it, the order is delivered to their home at an agreed time. Demonstrations are given everywhere in the store, and the store design and visual merchandising emphasize the quality and specialness of the merchandise, without losing sight of efficiency. After all, time remains a critical factor in the purchase of these types of products.

Employees in the store are occupied not only with products, but also with customers. Customer intimacy is very important, and customers receive individual treatment. Characteristics like original, wholesome, charming and caring are most important in these stores' brand personality.

Consumers with a lot of money but little time will choose to leave as much as possible to the retailer in the case of functional shopping. In addition, they are looking for specialties instead of regular products. Then it is no problem that a premium price will have to be paid. Starbucks, Dean & Deluca and lots of other food specialists are proving that daily. They turn regular products into something luxurious, and sell that at a premium price.

The organic supermarkets of Whole Foods are also a good example of a retail brand in the small pleasures segment. At first sight these supermarkets look like other conventional supermarkets. However, what differentiates them from the competition is the enormous range of organic food, ready-to-eat food and other food specialities. It does not matter that prices are higher than at other supermarkets.

The Rituals home and body cosmetics stores turn everyday events into something special, and enrich people's lives. Because of these added values, the premium prices of all these retail brands are no obstruction to a strong expansion. But in total, this segment will remain smaller than the segment of the efficient routine stores. Most of these retail brands will focus on niches. After all, not everyone can afford to pay premium prices.

12.8.3 AFFORDABLE DREAMS

With their positioning on range and price, retail brands in this market segment focus on a large consumer group. With their low prices these stores make dreams come true for everyone. They position themselves through great products and great prices. These are products with strong emotional appeal, like for example clothing and home decorations. Consumers like to buy these products, because they fit their desired identity or give them a good feeling, so almost every consumer is interested in these kinds of dream product.

However, the dreams need to be affordable, and that is where stores in this market segment put their focus. It concerns not prestige brands but massive brands. The emphasis in the store is on the merchandise.

Store design and visual merchandising meet the minimum requirements set for emotional shopping. The store environment only adds a limited luxurious value to the merchandise, and employees provide limited added value as well. Self-service is used as much as possible in order to keep prices low.

Examples of stores in this segment are H&M, Zara, the Gap and Ikea. All these retail brands sell attractive products at very low prices. They popularize design and democratize luxury, because they charge prices that most people can afford. The clothing line that was specially designed for H&M by Karl Lagerfeld is a perfect example of this. The proposition of these affordable dreams stores is so strong that it can be assumed that this segment will grow strongly in the next few years and will become very large. Vertically integrated mass fashion retail brands are particularly likely to conquer the market, as they will dress the masses.

12.8.4 LUXURIOUS EXPERIENCES

Buying expensive, luxury products gives consumers emotional benefits, like belonging to a very small group of the happy few who can afford these premium prices. Visiting a luxurious experiences store is a symbol of achievement. The utility of the products is often less than their symbolic meaning.

This segment of stores selling emotional products at premium prices will remain small. After all, the target group consists of the top end of the income pyramid. However, luxurious experiences stores are the ultimate shopper's paradise. Their merchandise is on everyone's (secret) wish list. The higher the price of the luxury and prestige brands, the bigger the appeal.

Stores in this market segment mainly position themselves on their stock and store experience. Characteristics like exciting, imaginative, innovative and glamorous make up their brand personality. The luxurious, aesthetic store design and visual merchandising give the products yet more surplus value. The shopping environment is enhancing, surprising and inspiring. It is a multi-sensory experience, because all senses are stimulated. The merchandise and shopping environment strengthen each other, and employees do everything they can to give customers the feeling that they are kings. A visit to this type of store is a real, memorable experience. It is not only a symbol of achievement, but also a kind of personal reward.

Examples are the Nordstrom department store, Tiffany's for jewellery, Victoria's Secret for lingerie, American Girl Place for dolls and Sephora for perfumes and cosmetics. Online retail brands lack the atmosphere and the multi-sensory experience to be able to offer a strong proposition in this case. Customers for them are only drawn by the low prices they can ask for well-known brands.

The middle of the market will disappear. Retailers that do not clearly choose one of these four market segments, but are positioned somewhere in the middle of the market, will lose out. To the consumer, these stores will have no recognizable, differentiating brand identity. The four market segments will increasingly grow apart. Most victims will be in the middle of the market. Retailers that clearly choose one of these segments will then have to differentiate themselves from one another within a given market segment. Through their own mix of positioning attributes, differentiating personality and unique brand communication, they will have to build up a unique brand identity. Until then a store will not become a brand; a brand with loyal customers.

12.9 Speed, an important driver for retail success

The speed at which retail brands can respond to changing consumer demand will have a big influence on their success. The pace of change is accelerating, because products and store formats quickly succeed each other. Consumers are sooner done with retail brands, and store loyalty disappears if a better alternative appears on the market. That is why store formats that do not continuously renew themselves will inevitably get into trouble. Consumers continually want to be surprised in a store. Dullness is not appreciated.

Stores that focus on functional shopping will also have to adjust to changes in the market all the time. A range that never changes loses its appeal; this is also the case for functional low-price or high-value brands. Consumers want to be inspired by new products and other presentations during a store visit. This need will only become stronger in the future. That is why retail brands that are able to quickly follow the market because of strong operational excellence, and those that continue to launch new merchandise onto the market, will be able to obtain a competitive advantage. Vertically integrated retailers, that design, manufacture and market their own private brand, can react quicker than their unintegrated competitors.

In the fashion sector, Zara, the Gap, Victoria's Secret and H&M have already shown that they can quickly build up a strong market position in this way. But speed will become a more important factor in other sectors as well. This is true not only in the non-food sectors, but also in food. Ranges will change faster in supermarkets. Lots of short-lived food trends and hypes will develop, and there will be more promotions of one-off merchandise. Moreover, store design and visual merchandising will change faster to continue to inspire consumers. Speed will even become the most important driver for success for lots of retail brands.

12.10 Brand personality is more important than brand positioning

The traditional way of creating a competitive differentiation is not always enough any more. It is getting more difficult for retail brands to achieve a sustainable competitive advantage through a differentiating functional positioning mix alone. Often the enormous competition forces retailers to quickly copy other retail brands. That is why the uniformity in retail is getting greater and greater.

According to the Americas Research Group, three-quarters of consumers in the United States say stores within a given retail sector have similar appearances and product mixes. Most stores offer the same merchandise at the same prices, and there are hardly any differences in store design and visual merchandising either. Commoditization seems to be the trend in retail. A retail brand that succeeds in successfully creating a distinction in its range, price, convenience or store experience is soon copied by competitors.

In order to still create a distinction from the competition, retail brands will have to take other roads. Retail brands are therefore becoming more comparable with products and services. Just like products and services, retail brands will increasingly try to find new ways to differentiate and create a unique brand personality. A strong brand identity will still be based on functional positioning attributes, but that will no longer be enough. Retail brands will have to win the competitive battle by differentiating on brand personality. This emotional brand personality will transcend the functional positioning. It is much more difficult for the competition to imitate a brand personality. That is why product-focused retail brands will increasingly be replaced by personality-focused retail brands. Via their personality, retail brands will connect emotionally with customers. And these emotions will have more and more influence on store choice decisions.

12.11 The merchandise mix will be more target group or end-user oriented

In most speciality stores there is still a traditional range. Only a limited number of product categories are offered. Clothing stores only sell clothing, the range of shoe stores contains not much more than shoes and opticians limit themselves to glasses and contact lenses. Product relationship is still the most important criterion if the range is extended. In the future, target group or end-use specialization will increasingly replace these kinds of product specializations. In assembling the range, customer orientation will become more important than product relationship. With a certain target group or end-use as the starting point, retail brands will implement their range. Traditional sector limits will then be crossed. New store formats with completely new merchandise mixes will develop. For example, clothing stores will extend their range with shoes, accessories, cosmetics and perhaps even glasses. That will turn clothing stores into real fashion stores that sell everything that has to do with the customers appearance. Stores at stations and at gas stations will tune their range even more to consumers who are on the move. Domestic caterers will not only offer ready-to-eat meals, but will also offer domestic services for example. And baby and children's clothing stores will perhaps also open up day-nurseries and arrange for baby-sitters at night. Because of these other types of specialisation, specialist stores will increasingly develop into a new generation of department stores.

12.12 Ongoing problems for department stores

Everywhere in the world, traditional department stores are in trouble. These problems have to do with their format. There are only a few exceptions that, after serious reorganization, are doing well. But most department stores have still not succeeded in finding a fundamental solution to their format problem. The format of department stores no longer has the appeal of the last 150 years. Department stores are lacking the unique merchandise they used to have, because now every department of a department store competes with specialist stores and category killers, which usually have a wider range. In addition, more and more well-known fashion designers are opening their own stores, which are often bigger than their shop-in-the-shops in the department stores. Department stores not only lose a big part of their appeal through their range, however. They are also often losing out to the competition over price. Department stores are often more expensive than low-price and high-value retail brands because of their high cost levels and limited scale. And the higher prices are not compensated for by a unique store experience. As a result of cost cutting, big events occur only sporadically and generally lack the allure of a few decades ago.

For all these reasons, consumers have less reason to visit department stores. They are often difficult to visit anyway because department stores are often located in hard-to-reach downtown areas. In addition, shopping itself is not always easy in a department store, with its many different departments. Sometimes products are hard to find, and paying for them can sometimes also be difficult because each department or floor has its own checkout.

So as a store format, department stores have lost a big part of their competitive power. That is why their market share is likely to decline even further over the coming years.

To survive department stores will have to be unique brands again. Only drastic format changes will be able to stop this decline. For example, department stores can develop into a kind of shopping centre with brand stores that each have an autonomous appeal and can compete with (super)speciality stores. The mix of these brand stores, coupled with an inspiring shopping environment, can provide the department store with its own identity again. Downtown and often also in a shopping centre, a mix of stores more or less develops by itself, but in a department store the brand and product mix can be controlled completely. All departments can then be entirely tuned to each other, so that a logical and consistent whole is developed for the customer. However, such drastic changes will take years and it could be too late for some department stores.

12.13 Multi-channel retailing will grow dramatically

It is consumers who determine how and when they shop. Consumers like stores to be open until late in the evening and on Sundays. We are living in a 24-hour society. A large proportion of all online shopping takes place in the evening and at night. In the future, retail brands will have to be reachable always and everywhere. Stores, catalogues and websites will need to be fully integrated to serve the customer well. The three communication and selling channels will complement and overlap each other. Brand positioning, personality and ways of communicating through these channels will have to fit perfectly. Retailers will have to learn to deal with the specific opportunities and limitations of each channel. The internet and catalogues are convenient for customers, but they lack the ambience of a shopping environment.

Many one-channel retailers will disappear because they do not offer enough convenience and simply do not meet the customer's needs. Online retailers will open bricks-and-mortar stores in order to have more brand exposure and communicate more trust, and offline retail brands will have to succeed in making their internet activities profitable. The websites of functional retail brands will mainly develop into sales channels. After all, ordering online is not restricted by to time and can be done from any location. For retail brands that focus mainly on emotional shopping, the internet function will be more focused on providing information and inspiration. In most cases, consumers will want to see products with strong emotional appeal before buying them either in the store or via the internet. With all the information they have gathered from the internet, customers will often have more product knowledge than employees.

12.14 More flexibility in store design and visual presentation

The lifecycle of stores and department concepts is getting shorter and shorter. The success formats of today can be the failures of tomorrow. That is why continuous innovation is extremely important. A store that has not been changed in years soon looks outdated. Consumers can choose from lots of stores, and that is why they place higher demands on their favourite stores. At each visit they want confirmation that they have made the right decision. If they are disappointed, they will not hesitate to choose another store, because store loyalty only exists when there is no better alternative.

Retailers will have to judge their long-term investments more critically, because the investments will need to be earned back in a shorter period of time. Leases for premises will last no more than a few years. After all, shopping patterns can change drastically within a few years. The arrival of a new mall or a strong category killer can suddenly make a good location worthless. More flexible, temporary equipment will be used for store design and visual merchandising. Walls will be replaced by sets that can be changed quickly, like stage sets in a theatre. Aisle fixtures will be less rigid. This way it will be easier for the store to adjust to changes in market circumstances. After all, remodelling will have to be done more often and at lower cost.

Speed and design brands, which continually have to launch new collections and new concepts, will particularly have a strong need to change their shopping environment regularly and emphasize their positioning and personality in this way. Supermarkets will have a different presentation in the morning than in the evening. This already occurs in restaurants, where tables are set differently for breakfast than for dinner. As soon as this is possible operationally, supermarkets will follow this example as well.

12.15 Further growth of private brands

There is still plenty of room for further growth of private brands around the world, because this growth no longer depends only on economic factors. The range is the basis of each retail format. However, it is difficult for a retail brand to obtain a lasting differentiation from the competition with only manufacturer brands. With a private brand this is possible.

Private brands are no longer the exclusive domain of supermarkets. Ikea, Home Depot, the Gap, H&M, Hema and Wal-Mart are also very successful with their private brands. With these brands they offer consumers not only functional benefits, but also increasingly emotional benefits. Private brands have gained acceptance and credibility with consumers. In the eyes of consumers they are now often just as good as manufacturer brands.

In addition, retail margins on well-known manufacturer brands will be under more pressure over the coming years. Consumers no longer simply accept that a retailer might charge a higher price for these brands than its competitor. Both developments will lead to further growth for private brands, and this trend will be enhanced because manufacturers will have less budget for product innovations. After all, retailers will try to compensate for the lower margins on manufacturer brands by negotiating lower wholesale prices. Even large manufacturers will not be able to (partly) avoid meeting this demand. Therefore the difference between private and manufacturer brands will become smaller. Lower-tier manufacturer brands will suffer from this in particular. Second and third-tier manufacturer brands will therefore lose out a lot.

Manufacturers will become retailers, and retailers will more often take over part of the role of manufacturers. The computer manufacturer Apple is opening up its own stores everywhere in the world to secure distribution for its range, and Nike now has a large number of its own stores as well. In order to sell its Nespresso coffee, Nestlé has an internet operation: and by doing so, it avoids the power of the retailer. This strategy will often be followed by other manufacturers in the future.

Zara and Benetton are completely integrated companies. Clothing sold in their stores is mostly manufactured in their own factories. This forward integration, in which manufacturers open up their own stores, is noticeable in lots of retail sectors. It is a trend that will become even stronger in the future. Manufacturers that integrate forward can avoid being negatively affected by the growing power of retailers. Moreover, they can sometimes obtain economies of scale, and they can increase the speed at which they can react to the market. This last advantage in particular will have an increasingly strategic importance over the next few years.

In contrast to this strong forward integration is the weaker trend of backward integration. Retailers will not suddenly open up their own factories, because they are afraid of losing their flexibility. However, because private brands are becoming strategically more important and retailers are also confronted with the need to react quickly to the market, retailers will most likely want to have more control over production. Long-lasting, exclusive deals between retailers and manufacturers will occur more often, because it will be more difficult to find manufacturers that can deliver differentiating merchandise at a low price. Good contacts and contracts with manufacturers who can deliver on this will then be essential.

The future will determine which of these trends will carry on into the next few years. Some trends will diminish; others will gain power, and trends that cannot be perceived yet will suddenly appear. However, one thing is for sure. Retail will change more in the coming decades than it did in the past few centuries. Only retailers that really succeed in branding their store will survive in this dramatically changing environment.

REFERENCES

Company information, unless mentioned otherwise, comes from the websites of the companies concerned.

Aaker, David (1996) *Building Strong Brands,* New York, Free Press

Accenture (2001) *The Daunting Dilemma of Trade Promotions,* Chicago

Accenture (2003) *The Daunting Dilemma of Trade Promotions,* Chicago

Ander, Willard N and Stern, Neil Z (2004) *Winning at Retail,* Wiley, Hoboken, NJ

Anderson, Eric (2003) Minding your price cues, *Harvard Business Review,* 30 September, pp 98–100

Aufriter, Nora A, Elzinga, David and Gordon, Jonathan W (2003) Better branding, *McKinsey Quarterly,* 4

Barlow, Janelle and Stewart, Paul (2004) *Branded Customer Service,* Berret-Koehler, San Francisco

Berry, Leonard L (1999) Creating customer excitement with superior service, *Arthur Andersen Retailing Issues Letter,* November

Boston Consulting Group (2001) Keeping the promise: how big brands can win online, New York

Bras, E (2004) RIN Holistic Shopper Study, paper for Conference, What's going on in retailing, Rotterdam, 14 April

Buss, Dale (2005) REI – working out, www.brandchannel.com, 7 November (accessed 20 June 2006)

Catoni, Luciano, Förisdal Larssen, Nora, Naylor, James and Zocchi, Andrea (2002) Travel tips for retailers, *McKinsey Quarterly,* 3

Chan Kim, W and Maubourge, René (1999) Creating new market space, *Harvard Business Review,* January–February, pp 83–86

Chernatony, L and McDonald, M H B (2003) *Creating Powerful Brands: The strategic route to success in consumer, industrial and service markets,* Butterworth Heinemann, Oxford

Coleman, Calmetta Y (2000) Eddie Bauer's windows add electronics, *Wall Street Journal,* 28 November, Eastern edition, p B10

Corstjens, Marcel, Johnson, Tim and Steele, Richard (2004) *Hey Retailers, If You're So Powerful, Why Aren't You More Profitable?,* Insead Working Paper

Court, David C, Leiter, Mark G and Loch, Mark A (1999)
Brand leverage, *McKinsey Quarterly*, 2, p 100

Crawford, Fred and Mathews, Ryan (2001) *The Myth of Excellence*,
New York, Crown Business

Dru, Jean-Marie (2002) *Beyond Disruption*, Wiley, New York

Ebenkamp, Becky (2004) Out of the box: songs in the key of flee,
Brandweek, 16 February

Faithfull, Mark (2003) In graphic detail, *Retail Week*, 7 March, pp 18–19

Floor, Ko (1996) Trade marketing, *Academic Service*, Schoonhoven, p 40

Frank, Robert J, George, Jeffrey P and Narasimhan, Laxman (2004)
When your competitor delivers more for less, *McKinsey Quarterly*, 1

Franz, Giep and van den Berg, Marieke (2002) *Strategisch management van
merken*, Kluwer, Deventer

Garret, Jesse James (2004) Six design lessons from the Apple store,
www.adaptivepath.com, 9 July (accessed 20 June 2006)

GDR Creative Intelligence (2004) Social climbers, *Retail World*,
October, p 25

Gobé, Marc (2002) *Citizen Brand*, Allworth Press, New York

Hancock, Liz (2002) The end of fashion, *Viewpoint* 11, Spring, p 45

Henderson, Terilyn A and Mihas, Elizabeth A (2000) Building retail
brands, *McKinsey Quarterly* 3, pp 110–17

Heskett, James L, Sasser, W Earl Jr and Schlesinger, Leonard A (2003)
The Value Profit Chain, Free Press, New York

Holzhauer, F F O (1992) Merkpolitiek als vorm van
productdifferentiatie, *PHLO-cursus Marketing in de agribusiness*,
Wageningen

Humby, Clive and Hunt, Terry (2003) *Scoring Points*, Kogan Page,
London

Ind, Nicholas (2001) *Living the Brand*, Kogan Page, London

Joachimsthaler, Erich and Aaker, David A (1999) Building brands
without mass media, *Harvard Business Review*, issue on Brand
Management, pp 13–14

Kalish, Ira (2004) *Assessing Retail Globalization*, Deloitte & Touche USA

LaBarre, Polly (2002) Sophisticated sell, *Fast Company*, 1 December,
pp 92–96

Lindstrom, Martin (2005) *Brand Sense*, Free Press, New York

Lyster, Samantha (2003a) Top shopping, *Retail Week*, 10 October, p 18

Lyster, Samantha (2003b) Sale away, *Retail Week*, 24 October, p 18

Martens, Albert (2005) Talk at *Elsevier Retail Congress*, July 2005, p 21

McKinsey & Co (2003) Competing in a value-driven world, February, p 3

Meijssen, J (2003) Aldi snijdt ieder uur in kosten, *Elsevier Retail*, September

Mikunda, Christian (2002) *Brand Lands, Hot Spots and Cool Spaces*, Frankfurt/Vienna, Wirtschaftsverlag Carl Ueberreuter

Moreno, Shonquis (2003) Young at heart, *Frame*, May–June, p 124

Nardelli, Bob (2004) Strategic overview, Home Depot Investor and Analyst Conference

Nauta, Bram (2003) *The Consumer is a Chameleon*, Popai, Netherlands

New Paper (2005) In new Moscow shop, you need more than $1.0 million to buy just one thing, 21 February

Pegler, Martin M (2001) *Visual Merchandising and Display*, Fairchild, New York

Pinto, David (2004) Carrefour connects to shoppers, *Mass Market Retailers*, 23 February

Raffray, Nathalie (2003) Walking the senses, *Retail Interiors*, October, pp 21–22

Reinan, John (2003) Companies spread the brand gospel among their employees, *Star Tribune*, 28 September

Retail Interiors (2003) House of food and pop, October

Retail Week (2003) Out of this world, 21 November, p 44

Retailforward (2003) Twenty trends for 2010: Retailing in an age of uncertainty, April

Rice, Berkeley (2005) In-store clinics: should you worry?, *Medical Economics,*16 September

Ryan, Nicky (2002) Vegas baby, *Retail Week*, 2 May, pp 14–15

Schmitt, Bernd and Simonson, Alex (1997) *Marketing Aesthetics*, Free Press, New York

Schonfeld & Associates (2003) *Advertising Ratios and Budgets*, Libertyvill, Ill, June

Schwartz, S H and Bilsky, W (1987) Toward a universal psychological structure of human values, *Journal of Personality and Social Psychology*, 53 (3), pp 550–62

Schoolcraft, Lisa R (2003) Dollar stores booming in Atlanta,
    Atlanta Business Chronicle, 17 October
Simons, Ruth Putting the metrics into music, *Songseekers*, August
Smith, Shaun (2003) Brand experience, in *Brands and Branding*,
    pp 102–03, Economist/Profile Books, London
Tischler, Linda (2005) Smells like brand spirit, *Fast Company*,
    August, p 56
Verbeke, W (1993) De flexibiliteit van de consument, talk for Schuitema
    Congress day, 10 November 1993, The Hague
Wood, Zoe (2003) In the house of brands, Retail Week, 11 April,
    pp 18–19

ACKNOWLEDGEMENTS

This book on branding a store is built on my 35 years of experience in retail, so this book simply would not have been written without all of the consulting clients for whom I have worked during the past years. All these clients have contributed directly or indirectly to the ideas in this book, and they still continue to teach me every day how to turn a store into a strong brand. Some retailers do this with accurately outlined strategies, others do it more with their intuition. But all these retailers are continually working on making their store even more appealing to their customers. How far they succeed in doing this becomes obvious every day when consumers decide where they are going to shop.

Special thanks go to Giep Franzen, John van Nuenen and Hans Preeker for their assistance in shaping and formulating the content of this book. Their professional and constructive comments on the first draft of the manuscript helped me to clarify my thoughts and to further optimize the book on a large number of points.

Marieke van de Pol helped me enormously in collecting books and articles that were interesting for my book. Many thanks for that.

I would also like to thank Jurgen Bernardy and TBWA, one of the leading advertising agencies in the world. This book would not have been published without their support. Their ideas about creativity and the need of disruption have been a source of inspiration for me.

Very special thanks go to my wife Ina and my daughter Bojoura. My daughter took care of the translation from Dutch into English, an enormous job because translating a book almost means writing a book a second time. But she did the translation with just as much pleasure as I had in writing the book, and was helped in this by Heidi Devcich of TBWA. My wife accompanied me with the same enthusiasm on all my store visits, both domestic and abroad. Because we both like shopping just as much as each other, we are a unusual couple.